A NATIONAL LEGACY

The publication of *A National Legacy* has been made possible by our generous donors:

Sue Anderson & the Tett Sisters
Thomas Arneson
Ronald Brown
Lynn Bury
James Boyce
Rosario Castro Macmillan
Valerie Cunningham
Elizabeth Garaas
Lynn A. Glesne
Nancy Gibson & Ron Sternal
John Goetz
Sally A. Hausken Trust
Carrol & Ethelle Henderson
Craig Henderson & Family
Eric Hill, Story Hill Farms, LLC
Hebe Shipp
Allison Campbell Jensen
Linda Johnsen
Rebecca L. Keenan, In Memoriam, Patrick Keenan
Gretchen Mehmel
David Netten
Charles Newhal
Nicholson Family Foundation
Richard & Nancy Nicholson Fund
Eugene Ollila, M.D. & Julie M. Ollila
Kent Peters
Paula Ramaley
Deborah Reynolds
Jeff Rule
Susan S. Schmidt, c/o M. & S. Schmidt
Beth Siverhaus
Linda L. Slagter
George W. Soule
Cleone Stewart
David E. Tudor & Pamela R. Tudor
Rico Vallejos
Kristin Von Seggern
Paige Winebarger

Crown Bank, Jeff Wessels
Department of Natural Resources, Kristin Hall
Minneapolis Audobon Society, Beverly M. Richman

A National Legacy: Fifty Years of Nongame Wildlife Conservation in Minnesota.

AFTON PRESS

Afton Press
Ian Graham Leask, Publisher
6800 France Avenue South, Suite 370
Edina, MN 55435
www.aftonpress.com

Distributed by the University of Minnesota Press
111 Third Avenue South, Suite 290
Minneapolis, MN 55401-2520
http://www.upress.umn.edu

First Edition 2025
Library of Congress Control Number: 2025945818
Printed in the United States of America
10 9 8 7 6 56 4 3 2 1
ISBN: 978-1-8904-3411-3
Book and cover design by Gary Lindberg
Cover photograph by Carrol L. Henderson

This project was made possible in part by the people of Minnesota through a grant funded by an appropriation to the Minnesota Historical Society from the Minnesota Arts and Cultural Heritage Fund. Any views, findings, opinions, conclusions, or recommendations expressed in this publication are those of the author and do not necessarily represent those of the State of Minnesota, the Minnesota Historical Society, or the Minnesota Historic Resources Advisory Committee.

A NATIONAL LEGACY

Fifty Years of Nongame Wildlife Conservation in Minnesota

Carrol L. Henderson

AFTON PRESS
Minneapolis

A National Legacy is dedicated to the memory of my parents, Curtis and Leona Henderson, in appreciation for instilling a deep appreciation for wildlife and natural resource stewardship in me as a child. I am also indebted to my grandparents, Martin and Emma Holland and John and Lena Thorsnes, for stimulating an interest in birds and all wildlife in me.

This book is also dedicated to my wife Ethelle. I met her while studying in graduate school with the Organization for Tropical Studies (OTS) at the University of Costa Rica in February 1969. I returned to Costa Rica in July of 1969 for additional OTS studies in tropical ecology. We were engaged that summer. My parents and I returned to Costa Rica the following December where Ethelle and I were married. She has been a wonderful source of love and inspiration throughout my professional career in the DNR, on our international ecotourism adventures, and in our family life over the past 56 years.

"Always do right. It will gratify some people and astonish the rest."

–Mark Twain

"May we leave many astonished people in our wake."

–Carrol L. Henderson

Also By Carrol L. Henderson

Birds of Costa Rica
Field Guide to the Wildlife of Costa Rica
Landscaping for Wildlife
Butterflies, Moths, and Other Invertebrates of Costa Rica
Landscaping for Wildlife and Water Quality
Traveler's Guide to Wildlife in Minnesota
Woodworking for Wildlife: Homes for Birds and Animals
Wild about Birds: The DNR Bird Feeding Guide
Workbook for a Career in Wildlife Management and Natural Resource Conservation
Feeding Wild Birds in America: Culture, Commerce, & Conservation
Oology and Ralph's Talking Eggs
Birds in Flight: The Art and Science of How Birds Fly

Table of Contents

Foreword

Marshall Johnson

Chief Conservation Officer, National Audubon Society

Marshall Johnson oversees science, policy, conservation, and chapter engagement. He leads the strategic direction for hemisphere-wide conservation work at the National Audubon Society to address climate change and biodiversity crises facing birds.

Marshall Johnson on a Midwestern prairie.
Photo courtesy of National Audubon Society

As the National Audubon Society's Chief Conservation Officer, I have been blessed to work alongside many amazing conservation, community, and business leaders, ever since one faithful morning where I found myself enthralled by the booming, dancing mating ritual of the Greater Prairie Chicken: my spark bird.

Upon arriving in Minnesota as a teenager, I quickly noted two endearing traits seemingly inherent to the state—the goodness of the people, and their passion for wildlife and the outdoors. Minnesota is a state defined by its natural beauty and iconic species such as the Common Loon, Northern Cardinal and Trumpeter Swan, to name but a few. Equally so, the people of the state embody a sense of care, innovation, excellence, diversity, and a desire to leave things better than they found them. These are almost a prerequisite for citizenship. Perhaps no leader embodies these traits as profoundly as Carrol L. Henderson.

One struggles to adequately describe the enormity of Carrol's contributions to wildlife conservation, wildlife awareness, and species recovery; and while Minnesota has been the canvas upon which Carrol's art of action has come to life, the impacts of his contributions have and will continue to be felt across the hemisphere.

His work is felt by North St. Louis County teenagers in Missouri who flock to the confluence of the Missouri and Mississippi Rivers each winter to glimpse thousands of Trumpeter Swans, riverine dignitaries, many of which make their way from the lakes of Minnesota, where their existence was once on the brink of extirpation.

Perhaps you are one of the many thousands more female biologists across state wildlife agencies who have been inspired by the example set by the extraordinary team of women hired by Carrol at a time when this was anything but the norm. It's hard to truly gauge the far-reaching impact of Carrol's leadership in this regard.

Given the significant role of Minnesota's state nongame program in the Department of Natural Resources, perhaps you are coming to this reading as someone who dutifully checks the box on your tax returns, opting to do your part for the state's nongame wildlife—if not, you should!

Dedicating one's life to the preservation of wildlife and wild places can be painstaking, grueling work, but for nearly fifty years Carrol has stood as the personification of a happy warrior, innovating, advocating, and building relationships on behalf of nature and her special critters. Across every page of *A National Legacy: Fifty Years of Nongame Wildlife Conservation in Minnesota*, his exuberance for life and the opportunities to make a difference each day ushers in a refreshing and welcome salve for readers from all walks of life, eager for optimism and real-world examples and tools for how to find and use your voice for nature and a better world.

As America's ninety-plus million birders, and anyone who loves and appreciates nature and its wild wonders, we only need to look to one another and to our neighbors for inspiration as we endeavor to recover the three billion birds lost since 1970. This book offers an inspirational, practical rubric as we follow a guided tour from the conservation legend himself, giving us the gift of his Why and How, pulling back the curtains, and inspiring us with a cadre of lessons hard earned and learned through the course of a remarkable career. Carrol has certainly fulfilled his obligation of leaving things better than he found them, and then some.

As you begin your journey with Carrol, I leave you with the wisdom of the Lorax: Unless someone like you cares a whole awful lot, nothing is going to get better. It's not. Carrol L. Henderson sure cared for nature and her song, a whole awful lot.

Chapter 1

My Farmland Beginnings in Iowa

I grew up on a farm in central Iowa in the 1950s. It was originally purchased by my grandfather in 1915. We raised beef cattle and hogs, along with a family milk cow, a few sheep, chickens, and a few pet rabbits and Muscovy ducks. I was the oldest of six, with three sisters and two brothers.

Going for a ride with my father, Curtis Henderson, on our F-20 Farmall in 1947.

Planting corn with my Grandpa, Martin Holland, and our team of draft horses, Dick and Queen, in 1951. Photos by Curtis and Leona Henderson

As a toddler, my dad would carry me around the farmstead as he did chores. When I was older, it was also my job to run cold meat sandwiches and coffee in a Mason jar out to the field for Grandpa's lunch while he planted corn.

As a teenager, my parents instilled a work ethic in me for additional family responsibilities. They taught me skills for animal husbandry, gardening, carpentry, and soil conservation. I frequently helped my dad and Grandpa Holland with carpentry work when we made improvements to our outbuildings and built additions to our house.

An aerial view of our farm in the late 1940s showing oat shocks in the field ready for harvesting. Photo by Curtis Handerson

My three sisters, Jean (left), Julie (front right), Linda (right), and little brother, Don, 1956. Photo: Curtis Henderson

The author watching over the Henderson chicken flock in 1951. Photo by Curtis Henderson

I developed a passionate curiosity about the natural world as I explored our land for bird nests and animal dens and looked for animal tracks along Minerva Creek, which flowed through our farm. I loved to explore the wild corners of our farm—brushy fencerows, pastures, and willows along the "crik."

My father, Curtis Henderson, was an exceptional farmer, mechanic, carpenter, and land conservation steward. The farm has been in our family since 1915. He taught me how to hunt pheasants, rabbits, and fox squirrels and how to trap muskrats, minks, and raccoons with the same traps he used as a young man during the 1920s and the 1930s. He taught me how to make a figure-four box trap to catch rabbits and how to catch cottontail rabbits by hand.

He grew up during the Great Depression and hunted small game to provide supplemental food for his parents. He also trapped muskrats, raccoons, and skunks to earn money from their furs. The pelt of a striped skunk in that era was worth $1.25, which was the same amount a grown man could earn from a full day of work in a factory or on a farm. I still have a wooden skunk fur stretcher that my dad made and used as a youth.

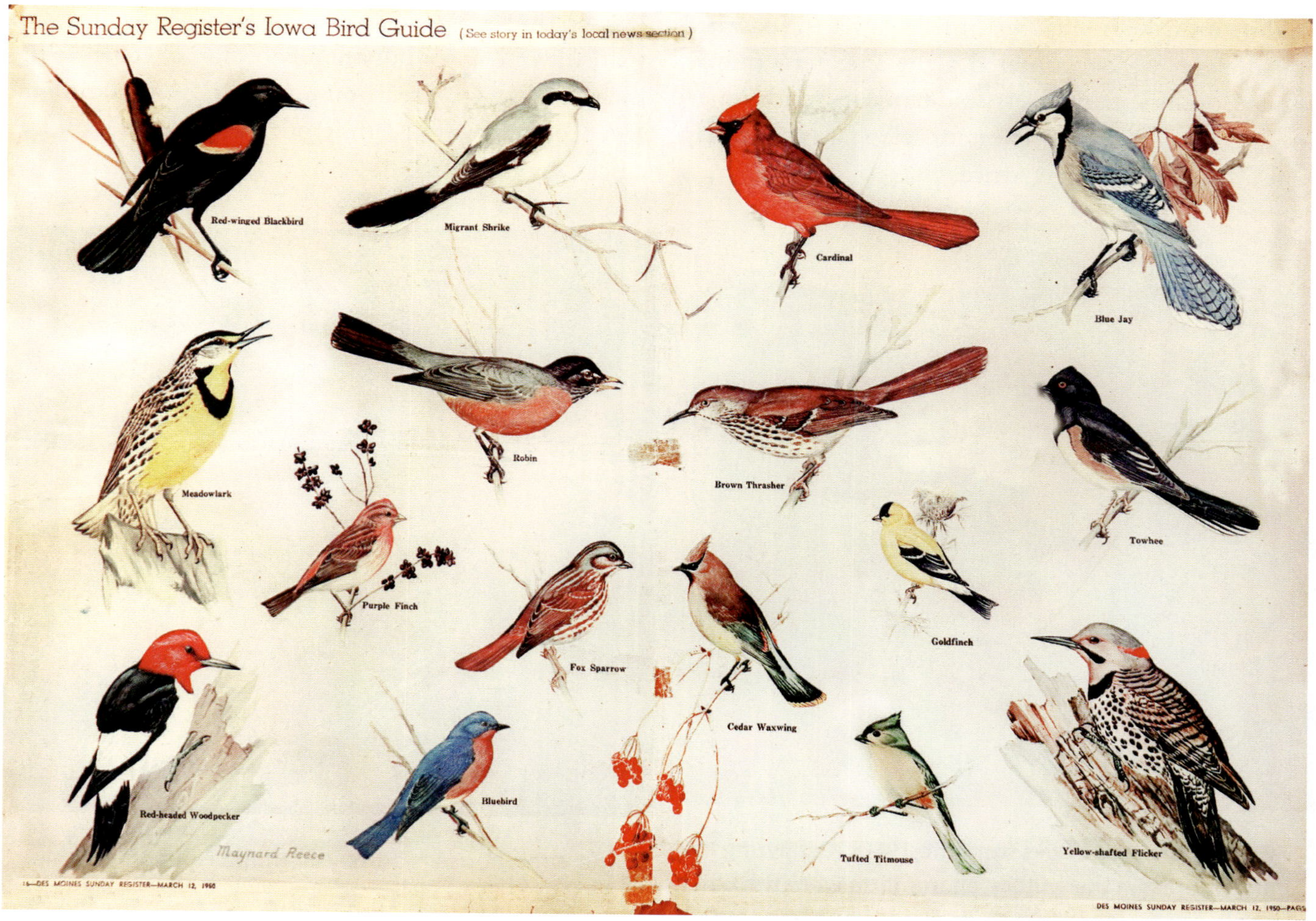
The Sunday Register's Iowa Bird Guide (See story in today's local news section)
Red-winged Blackbird
Migrant Shrike
Cardinal
Blue Jay
Meadowlark
Robin
Brown Thrasher
Towhee
Purple Finch
Fox Sparrow
Cedar Waxwing
Goldfinch
Red-headed Woodpecker
Bluebird
Tufted Titmouse
Yellow-shafted Flicker
Maynard Reece
16—DES MOINES SUNDAY REGISTER—MARCH 12, 1950
DES MOINES SUNDAY REGISTER—MARCH 12, 1950—PAGE

When I was nearly four years old, I saved this "songbird centerfold" by famous Iowa wildlife artist Maynard Reece from the "Des Moines Register Picture Magazine" on March 12, 1950. Brad Reece, son of Maynard Reece and the Reece family graciously gave me copyright permission to use this image.

Song sparrow
House wren
Ceder waxwing
bluebird
Redheaded woodpeck
Meadow lark

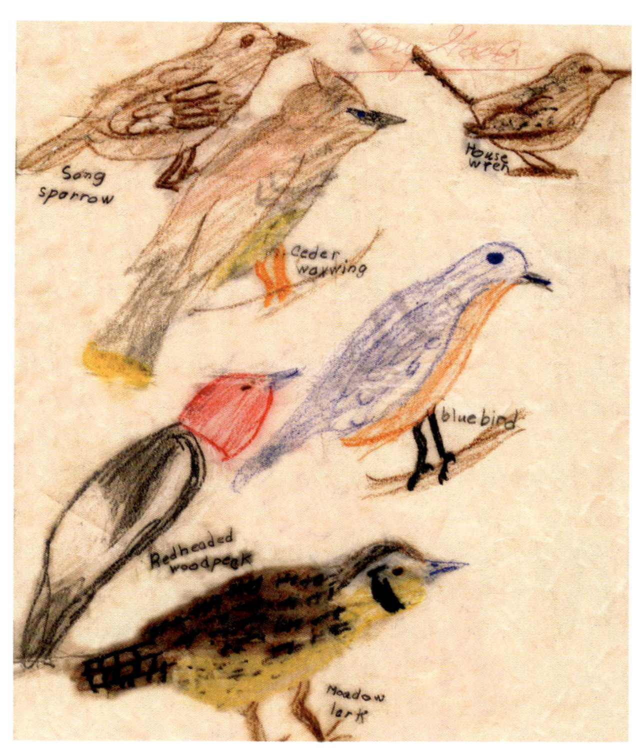

An early effort to draw a songbird poster.

My Nature Library

I had my own little wildlife library: *The Golden Guide for Birds* by Herbert Zim and Ira Gabrielson (I wore the cover off that book), *Water Birds* which was part of Walt Disney's True-Life Adventures (a gift from Grandpa and Grandma Holland in 1956), and the Red, Yellow, Green, and Blue Birds of America books. Grandpa and Grandma Thorsnes also had two wildlife books that I read nearly every time we visited them at their home in Story City as I stretched out on the carpet of their living room floor: *American Wildlife* and *Wild Life the World Over.*

One of my most coveted worn-out books was *Wild Animals of the World* by William Bridges. I received it from my parents for Christmas in 1953 at age seven. It stimulated my interest in wildlife throughout the world—wildlife I never dreamed I would see. Yet those dreams came true decades later while leading wildlife tours with my wife, Ethelle. Over the past several decades we encountered giant anteaters, pumas, jaguars, ocelots, giant otters, and tapirs in South America and cape buffaloes, cheetahs, elephants, leopards, lions, and rhinoceros in Africa.

My well-worn bird books from the 1950s. Catalyzing my early interest in the wildlife on our farm were the bird books my parents and grandparents bought for me.

When my grandfather, Martin Holland, was a young man he traveled from Iowa to northern Minnesota to earn money trapping timber wolves. He caught no wolves, so he had to work in a logging camp to earn enough money to get back to Iowa. In 1915, he bought our 132-acre family farm near Zearing. I now own half of that farm and have developed thirty-seven acres of that farmland into Conservation Reserve Program prairie pollinator plantings, wildlife food plots, and a six-acre marsh, financed through the federal Conservation Reserve Enhancement Program.

My "Portal" Wildlife Species: House Wrens and Killdeers

I once heard wildlife planner Ted Eubanks describe "portal" wildlife species. He explained that most avid wildlife conservationists recall a pivotal moment when a bird or animal encounter served as a portal into a lifetime of passion for wildlife. A close encounter with a flicker sparked Roger Tory Peterson's interest in birds. For legendary Minnesota birder Bob Janssen, it was a western meadowlark. My interest was sparked watching a busy family of house wrens raising their chicks in a wren house on our family farm and an encounter with a family of newly hatched killdeer chicks in our cornfield.

The wren house made by Grandpa Holland and me.

When I was about five years old, Grandpa Holland took me to the woodshop in his basement to build a birdhouse for house wrens. It was like magic watching the small pieces of wood coming together to form the little birdhouse. When he finished, Grandpa let me help paint it blue and white. Next time he came to our farm, he brought the wren house and hung it under the eve of our garage roof so we could watch it from our yard. When the wrens showed up, their bubbling, musical calls were a daily highlight as we watched the wrens bring twigs to build their nest. After the chicks hatched, we watched the parents feed them with insects. The wrens returned to that nest box for many years and provided much enjoyment. I still have that wren house as a treasured memory of time spent with my grandfather.

Killdeers in the Cornfield

When I was seven or eight, my father told me about a killdeer nest that he found while cultivating corn. When he spotted the nest beside a hill of newly sprouted seedlings, he lifted the cultivator and drove past the nest to avoid disturbing the eggs. Then he lowered the cultivator so he could continue across the field.

He took me to the nest. As we approached, a killdeer fluttered away. My dad explained it was doing a "broken wing" act. He said normally a predator would follow a bird that appeared injured so the nest would remain undisturbed. Ignoring the killdeer's ruse, we searched among the sprouting corn plants and were soon looking down on four speckled eggs, each pointed at one end. I was captivated by the speckled beauty of the eggs and the simplicity of the nest—a shallow depression in the soil.

After school I would run out to the cornfield to check the nest. About a week later, my persistence paid off. The nest contained eggshell fragments, and I was assaulted from above by the killdeer parents. They screamed their "killdeer—killdeer" calls at me and tried to lead me away with their broken-wing acts. There must have been lots of killdeers nesting in the area because I was assaulted by seven different killdeers circling, calling and trying to lead me away. The precocious chicks had left the nest after hatching. Knowing the chicks had to be nearby, I cautiously walked up and down the corn rows and soon discovered one of the cutest baby birds I have ever seen. The little killdeer was like a brown, black, and white cotton ball with big eyes and toothpick legs. I didn't want to keep the parents from their young, so I quickly left the field.

My drawing of a killdeer chick.

I Learned the Conservation Pledge

My passion for birds, hunting, trapping, and all nature matured through grade school. My sixth-grade teacher, Hazel Appenzeller, taught a six-week course in Natural Resource Conservation with a workbook produced by the Iowa Conservation Commission. One of our lessons was to memorize the original conservation pledge created by *Outdoor Life* magazine in the year I was born—1946. That simple pledge empowered my life.

"I give my pledge as an American to save and faithfully defend from waste the natural resources of my country—its soil and minerals, its forests, waters, and wildlife."

As a farm boy growing up in Iowa, I was fascinated by the furbearers on our farm: muskrats, raccoons, minks, red foxes, badgers, and even striped skunks and spotted skunks (we called them "civet cats" then). I eagerly read my *Fur, Fish & Game* magazines for information about farmland wildlife and furbearers. I bought books by Dr. Paul Errington of Iowa State University. He was considered the world expert on muskrats.

One time I set a trap to catch barn rats just inside the door of our hog feed house. The next morning a very upset civet cat was in the trap and sprayed my dad when he opened the door. Uffda! I had to pull up my barnyard trapline. Another time my trapping skills helped me redeem myself with my parents. Muskrats from our creek came through a quarter mile of tile line from the creek to our basement. Mother panicked when she discovered wet muskrat tracks leading from the drain in our basement across our basement floor. It was like an invasion of "giant rats!" She was so grateful that I came to the rescue for the basement where she stored our canned goods and managed the eggs from our chicken flock. I set traps in the basement to ease her trauma of encountering those muskrats. I caught several.

My early life was also enriched by ring-necked pheasants, western meadowlarks, bobolinks, red-headed woodpeckers, common flickers, common nighthawks, fox squirrels, Franklin's ground squirrels, cottontail rabbits, and white-tailed jackrabbits. I learned to identify birds, feathers, wild bird eggshell fragments, animal tracks, bird calls, and bird nests. I also developed an interest in in-

An annual highlight for our family was the opening of pheasant season on our farm. Pictured here is our 1972 morning's bag of game and our family of Henderson hunters from left to right: me, my German shorthair Macho, brother Don, uncle John Henry Thorsnes, brother Dave, and uncle Les Pearson. Photo by Curtis Henderson

sects and butterflies after enrolling in an entomology project in our local Lincoln Livewires 4-H club. I was an enthusiastic pheasant hunter. In the fall I trapped muskrats, raccoons, and minks and used the income to help buy 4-H calves. I subsequently used my 4-H calf income to help pay my tuition at Iowa State University which was a modest $115 per quarter when I started college in 1964.

While attending Nesco High School at Zearing, I also developed an interest in writing. I became editor of the high school newspaper and high school yearbook. I graduated as valedictorian in my class of forty-three in 1964.

Nature photography has played an important role in both my personal life and in my wildlife conservation career since the time my father gave me a vintage 35 mm. Argus rangefinder camera while I was in the air force in 1972. It was the perfect gift. I learned photography basics like manually calculating the proper exposure with a light meter setting and film speed (ASA). The camera was then adjusted for the correct shutter speed and f-stop. It was necessary to cock the camera to take the photo and then manually advance the film for each exposure. After returning to Keesler Air Force Base in Mississippi, I photographed monarch butterflies migrating through the Biloxi area with my Argus camera. I submitted some of those photos in a photography contest sponsored at Keesler Air Force Base, and I won several awards. I decided this could be a wonderful and rewarding hobby, and it became a significant part of my life and work.

My First Mentors

While attending Nesco High School I encountered the first "mentors" who played a significant role in my life and career. I don't recall any discussions about mentors while growing up. Mentors are friends, teachers, and leaders who provide inspiration and direction in our lives and careers.

George Knaphus was a World War II hero and rifleman in Company B of the 112th Infantry Division. Their company of 150 men defeated a German battalion of over a thousand soldiers in a pivotal battle in the Battle of the Bulge.

However, by the end of their early morning battle, about 120 men in their company were injured, dead, or missing. George received a bronze star for his service. An account of his experience was preserved on the 50th anniversary of the Battle of the Bulge on National Public Radio. It can be located by googling NPR archives and "George Knaphus, Battle of the Bulge."

Dr. George Knaphus, my inspirational high school science teacher when I was a sophomore, and his wife Marie, my high school Latin teacher. Photo provided by George and Marie's daughter Dawn Bovenmyer

George Knaphus was a joy to know. His cheerful perspective on life added so much to his teaching skills as my science teacher in high school. He convinced me to switch from engineering to a conservation-based curriculum at Iowa State. George had a remarkable passion for botany, science, and all nature, and he was also an avid hunter and marksman. His passion for teaching was infectious among his students. I decided to major in zoology with minors in botany and physics at Iowa State. His wife Marie taught me typing and Latin in high school. George and Marie provided me with a lifetime of important skills. My knowledge of Latin became a huge benefit for understanding the Latin names of the wild creatures I have worked with throughout my life.

George got his doctoral degree in botany at Iowa State University while I completed high school, and then he became my botany professor at Iowa State. When it was time to pick a college major and decide which college to attend, some teachers and counselors urged me to major in engineering because they didn't think my interest in becoming a wildlife biologist would pay very well. However, after deciding to attend Iowa State University, I was motivated by advice from my high school science teacher, George Knaphus. He was the first "mentor" in my life who guided me in the direction of a lifetime career in wildlife conservation.

Dr. Eugene P. Odum, founder of the University of Georgia Institute of Ecology and author of *Principles of Ecology*. Photo credit: University of Georgia, Marketing & Communications

After graduating from Iowa State in 1968, I felt if I wanted to be the best, I should study under the best—"the person who wrote the book." I enrolled at the University of Georgia to study under the professor who wrote the textbook *Principles of Ecology*, Dr. Eugene P. Odum. Dr. Odum became my second inspirational mentor. When I first arrived at the University of Georgia campus on a Sunday morning, I didn't know anyone, but I had Dr. Odum's phone number. I called him, and he graciously spent the rest of the day driving me around Athens, introducing me to the campus, and telling me about his activities underway in the Institute of Ecology. In 1987, Dr. Odum won the Crafoord Prize in Ecology from the Royal Swedish Academy of Science—the biologists' equivalent of the Nobel Prize.

I was inspired by his continuing dedication and enthusiasm during my studies with him. I enrolled at the University of Georgia to study ecology and wildlife management, but I felt I would also be more competitive as an aspiring wildlife biologist if I "cross-pollinated" my coursework. I had previously learned of a conservation communications graduate curriculum at the University of Wisconsin that had been developed by Dr. Clarence (Clay) Schoenfeld. I was tempted by that program, but I felt I would benefit from attending graduate school in another region of the country.

During my graduate studies, there was a divergence in philosophies between advocates for providing huntable populations of game, deer, ducks, grouse, and geese et cetera, and other biologists who were committed to protecting and managing ecologically healthy and biodiverse habitats for all wildlife. I decided to diversify my curriculum with a broader ecological spectrum of wildlife by studying ecology, forestry, and wildlife management and cross-pollinate my graduate studies with courses in feature writing, public speaking, and public relations. It was the right decision. In the 1940s, ecologist Aldo Leopold had written about preserving the ecological roles of lesser-known wildlife: "To keep every cog and wheel is the first precaution of intelligent tinkering."

My 3rd and 4th Mentors: Dr. James H. Jenkins and Dr. Daniel H. Janzen

Dr. James H. Jenkins was my most influential wildlife management professor in the School of Forest Resources at the University of Georgia. He was an inspiring and creative biologist who was a co-inventor of the hypodermic dart gun, which was developed for capturing white-tailed deer on the offshore islands of Georgia. The deer were transplanted to mainland Georgia where they had been locally extirpated. The hypodermic dart gun subsequently became an essential tool for wildlife biologists to capture and study wildlife around the world.

Dr. Jenkins was also renowned for his pioneering revelation of how Chinese atomic bomb tests in the Pacific in the 1960s released radioactive Cesium-137 into the atmosphere. This resulted in radioactive contamination in Georgia. The radiation encircled the globe and began showing up in Georgia wildlife like white-tailed deer, feral hogs, and fox squirrels. He discovered Cesium-137 was deposited from rainfall and concentrated in forest mushrooms. When the mushrooms were eaten by deer, feral hogs, and fox squirrels, it was passed on to humans when they ate the meat of those animals, including myself after I shot a wild hog.

Dr. James H. Jenkins, my inspirational wildlife professor from the University of Georgia.

One day Dr. Jenkins stopped me in the hall at the School of Forest Resources and asked if I would like to study in Costa Rica. I said "Sure." Then I went to my office to look up where Costa Rica was. Charles Darwin once wrote "Nothing can be more improving to a young naturalist than a journey to a distant country." He was right. I took two two-month courses from the Organization for Tropical Studies in 1969, one in tropical agriculture and land use and one in principles of tropical ecology. Those experiences changed my life.

I studied tropical ecology in Costa Rica under Dr. Daniel H. Janzen in the Organization for Tropical Studies program. A tropical entomologist, he was the fourth wonderful mentor who inspired me with his professional dedication, hard work, and enthusiasm for preserving tropical dry forests and the thousands of species they harbored. He discovered many new insect species. In 1984 he also received the biologist's equivalent of the Nobel Prize—the Crafoord Prize in Ecology—for his pioneering entomology studies in Costa Rica. Dr. Janzen continues his research and has been instrumental in raising millions of dollars to save tropical forests in Costa Rica through the nonprofit Guanacaste Dry Forest Conservation Fund.

Dr. Daniel H. Janzen, mentor, professor, ecologist, and lifetime inspiration who taught me tropical ecology in Costa Rica through participation in the Organization for Tropical Studies program in 1969.

The author in Costa Rica participating in a tropical ecology course in Costa Rica in 1969. He is holding an oropendola nest that had fallen from a tree.

My 340-page Master of Forest Resources paper, *Fish and Wildlife Resources of Costa Rica, with Notes on Human Influences*, reviewed the status of Costa Rica's wildlife resources and the human influences causing endangerment of the country's wildlife. I provided recommendations to the Costa Rican government for improving their laws protecting rare and endangered species. I am grateful that some of my recommendations were adopted.

After graduating from the University of Georgia in 1970, I became a captain in the United States Air Force as a Military Airlift Command communications maintenance officer while stationed in Mississippi and Oklahoma. I trained soldiers how to set up a mobile field communications center on a bare airfield to bring in an air force fighter squadron. I completed my air force service in 1973. During my service at Keesler Air Force Base in Biloxi, Mississippi, I taught evening classes in environmental conservation for the University of Southern Mississippi. While at Altus Air Force Base in Altus, Oklahoma, I taught evening courses in natural resource conservation for Altus Junior College.

My interests have since expanded to birding, nature photography, gardening for wildlife, and bird feeding over the past thirty years.

The author and his wife Ethelle have led sixty-nine birding tours throughout Latin America, Africa, and New Zealand since 1987. They are shown here in Ecuador in 2011.

Chapter 2

My Wildlife Conservation Career Begins with the Minnesota DNR

My career vision became reality in 1974. I was interviewed by Roger Holmes, Section of Game chief in the Minnesota Department of Natural Resources (DNR). I was hired to be assistant manager for the 27,000-acre Lac qui Parle Wildlife Refuge near Milan in western Minnesota. My duties included habitat management for deer, pheasants, and Canada geese, game surveys, hunter surveys, duck and goose banding, management of wood duck nest boxes, prescribed burning of native prairies, enforcement of game laws, and hunter education programs. I also documented the presence of nongame wildlife like Richardson's ground squirrels, burrowing owls, upland sandpipers, marbled godwits, sandhill cranes, and golden plovers. It was the kind of hands-on wildlife management I had always dreamed of.

The author with a Canada goose ready for banding.

But in summer 1976, my world as a wildlife manager at Lac qui Parle crumbled around me. At the age of thirty, I was stricken with Guillain-Barré syndrome. It is a disease of the immune system that is sometimes fatal. Within three days I could no longer walk. I was transferred from the hospital in Montevideo to the North Memorial Medical Center in Minneapolis. I began three months of occupational and physical therapy which included learning how to walk again.

I have always had a very positive outlook on life, but my patience, determination, cheerful attitude, and optimism were challenged. However, I believed then and still believe that attitude is everything. On the day that I got my diagnosis of Guillain-Barré, I made up my mind that I would get better. My sense of optimism in life was inspired by a story my dad told me when I was a child. A psychologist was studying two little boys. Billy was a pessimist and Bobby was an optimist. He took Billy into a room filled with many new toys and told him he would be back in an hour. He took Bobby, the optimist, into a room that was knee-deep in horse manure. He told Bobby he would be back in an hour to see how he was doing. An hour later he entered Billy's room and saw Billy sitting quietly amid all the toys. The psychologist asked Billy why he wasn't playing with the toys. Billy said he didn't know how to use them, and besides, he might get hurt. Then he entered Bobby's room. Bobby was down on his hands and knees, digging like a dog as fast as he could, and the "caca" was flying off the walls and in every direction. The psychologist exclaimed, "Bobby! Bobby! What in the world are you doing?" Bobby finally looked up and said, "Mister, with all this stuff in here, there just has to be a pony somewhere!" So, just remember, when life finds you knee-deep in horse "doodoo," keep looking for the pony.

I had to learn to walk again. My recovery required daily physical and occupational therapy that included lifting fishing sinkers, stacking paper cups, and trying to squeeze my fingerprints into Silly Putty™. My weight dropped from 145 pounds to 120 pounds. I was so weak at one point that I could only lift a pencil, so I began writing a story for the DNR *Conservation Volunteer* magazine with a pencil, and I drew pencil sketches of ducks and deer from my hospital bed.

I remained cheerful as the nurses attended me. I got the impression they appreciated cheerful patients rather than sullen or grumpy ones. I maintained the outlook that "A problem is just an opportunity that needs to be repackaged!" I was sick, but I was determined to get better. I was able to go home after three months.

My Selection as Minnesota's New DNR Nongame Wildlife Program Supervisor

While I was in the hospital, Roger Holmes, chief of the Minnesota DNR Section of Wildlife, had created a new Nongame Wildlife Program supervisor position in St. Paul, and I applied for the job. It was the first time that position had ever been offered in the DNR. I think the mixed skill-sets from my farm background, hunting experience, taxidermy skills, media skills, writing ability, speaking experience, and ecology-based education gave me the edge. I was hired in January of 1977.

Meanwhile, between 1974 and 1977 the DNR Section of Game had been changed to the Section of Wildlife. It was the beginning of a new era for the DNR when wildlife species not considered as huntable game would finally become a priority for conservation in Minnesota. That has been a long process, and it is still evolving.

My early experiences on the farm, in high school, at Iowa State University, University of Georgia, University of Costa Rica, United States Air Force, and my first three years of experience as a wildlife manager at Lac qui Parle provided the building blocks of experience for later success in my nongame wildlife conservation career. It was the beginning of a wonderful forty-one-year opportunity to shape the direction of stewardship and conservation for Minnesota's nongame wildlife and inspire thousands of Minnesotans to become personally involved in helping Minnesota wildlife.

My supervisor and chief of the Section of Wildlife, Roger Holmes, gave me total discretion to develop my program vision, species priorities, and choice of which projects to pursue. His management style was "management by exception." That meant I only needed to consult him when I was not sure which strategies

The author at his desk in charge of the Nongame Wildlife Program, 1977. I was like the proverbial kid in a candy store.

I needed to pursue for one of my projects or how to address legislative or supervisory issues.

I began developing a vision and a structured process for creating Minnesota's new Nongame Wildlife Program. I spent much of my first year traveling throughout Minnesota identifying my clientele and listening to them. That included interviews with state and federal wildlife biologists, wildlife managers, college and university wildlife professors, bird club members, and citizen science experts who shared with me what species and projects they thought should be priorities.

I applied my optimism, enthusiasm, education, and experience with writing, public speaking, media skills, and networking to build a fledgling program even though I was a supervisor in charge of a statewide program with no staff and a budget of only about $30,000 per year, half of which was my salary. My goal was to provide a comprehensive statewide conservation program for non-hunted species of wildlife to preserve biological diversity and provide the public with opportunities to enjoy the benefits provided by healthy and diverse wildlife populations. Over the next three years, I carried out twenty-five projects with a staff of one. I hired Diane Vosick, a graduate of Evergreen College in Washington, who had grown up in Minnesota. She enthusiastically worked for me through the federally funded Young Adult Conservation Corps (YACC) program.

My early projects focused on common loons, eastern bluebirds, sandhill cranes, great blue herons, bald eagles, and piping plovers. I gathered information from volunteer observers about dozens of nongame wildlife species by initiating mail surveys. I initiated and achieved my river otter restoration goal; I documented the impact of toxic lead ammo on bald eagles; and I protected the Lamprey Pass heron colony from development.

My "Four-H" Approach to Wildlife Conservation

When appointed Minnesota's first Nongame Wildlife Program supervisor, interestingly on Groundhog Day in February of 1977, I sought to create a comprehensive wildlife conservation program that extended well beyond the existing focus on game species. I created my own "Four-H model" for wildlife conservation: It was comprised of a focus on **Habitat**, a **Holistic** approach, **High-Profile** species, and **Hands-On** experiences for citizens to become personally involved in helping wildlife. My Four-H Concept for wildlife conservation had evolved nicely since I first learned the Conservation Pledge in sixth grade.

I recognized the need for identifying, protecting, and managing **Habitats** of primary significance to nongame wildlife like great blue herons, piping plovers, common terns, colonial waterbirds, prairie birds, lakeshore wildlife, and backyard wildlife. I was also aware that some people would be willing to develop, sell, or even donate their property to the DNR Nongame Wildlife Program for the benefit of nongame wildlife. Those areas could be designated as publicly-owned Wildlife Management Areas, Aquatic Management Areas, or Scientific and Natural Areas.

I recognized the need for identifying, researching, protecting, and managing little known nongame species that were important ecological components of natural communities. They needed to be included as part of a **Holistic** approach for comprehensive conservation efforts. These species had been largely ignored in past conservation efforts, including American white pelicans, river otters in southwest Minnesota, greater sandhill cranes, prairie songbirds, forest songbirds, nongame fishes, turtles, frogs, dragonflies, butterflies, moths, rattlesnakes, and bats, among others. This approach included the need for conducting both surveys and research to determine the status, distribution, and management needs for these little-known species and implementing management plans for the benefit of those species.

There was a third need for providing benefits to **High-Profile** wildlife species that were better known but neglected and threatened with extirpation or continuing declines. There was potential for bringing back species like the peregrine falcon, trumpeter swan, and bald eagle, but not being huntable game species, they lacked public funding or agency commitment for restoration. Working on high-profile species would also create the opportunity to get citizens motivated to help the broader range of lesser-known and lesser-appreciated nongame wildlife species and to fund our entire nongame wildlife conservation program.

Finally, there was a need for Minnesota citizens, conservation organizations, and public agencies to become personally involved in **Hands-On** efforts to help wildlife. Conservation should not just be the domain of public agencies to preserve and restore nongame wildlife. There is also a need for actions on behalf of eastern bluebirds, pur-

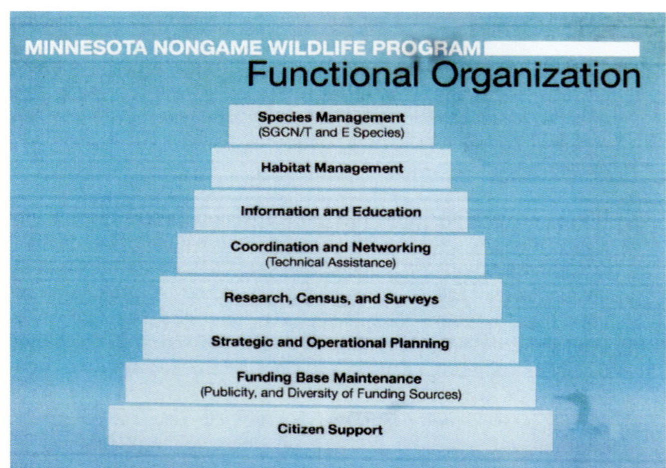

The organizational structure I developed for Minnesota's Nongame Wildlife Program.

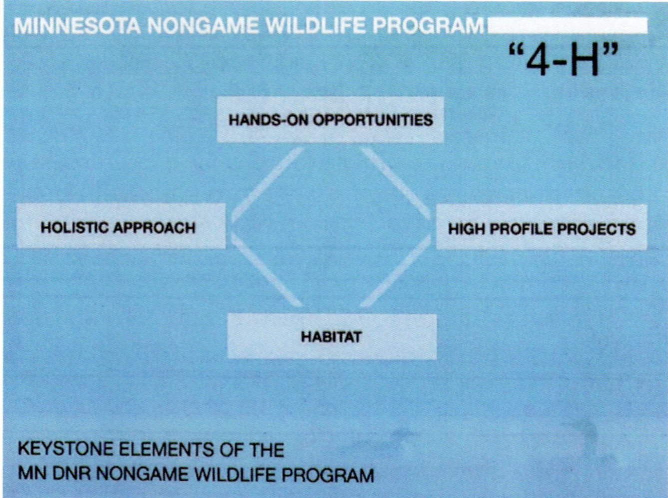

A diagram of my keystone "Four-H" strategy for developing a strategically balanced nongame wildlife program.

ple martins, wood ducks, eastern screech-owls, common loons, and even bumblebees that could benefit from construction and management of nesting boxes and nesting platforms and creating habitat for wildlife.

This included advocacy for wildlife habitat plantings, pollinator gardening in backyards, lakeshores, farms, and woodlots—and bird feeding to broaden the scope of wildlife benefits and abundance in backyards of homeowners. This hands-on approach included efforts to identify and involve many publics who were advocates for nature preservation of all wildlife—not just game species. However, many of these potential new publics had ignored the efforts of the DNR in the past because they thought the DNR was only concerned with promoting game management for hunters.

This long-term effort also needed to include advocacy and support for nature tourism and creation of birding trails by garden clubs, bird clubs, conservation clubs, nature photographers, woodworking enthusiasts, environmental educators, and local, statewide, and national media. We also needed support for nongame conservation efforts from other state agencies like the Office of Tourism and the Minnesota Pollution Control Agency. We needed to publish books and write popular wildlife conservation articles that were specific to Minnesota, and we needed long-term funding to support Minnesota's nongame wildlife conservation efforts.

There was also a Fifth H that subsequently evolved from my program philosophy—a **Historic Perspective**. Citizens need to know and appreciate what had happened to Minnesota's wildlife during the pioneer settlement era when game management included routinely killing eagles, hawks, peregrine falcons, owls, white pelicans, sandhill cranes, and other wildlife. We needed to undo those misperceptions and collateral damage to our nongame wildlife populations.

Some wildlife species were shot on sight because they ate fish (like pelicans), ate ducks (like peregrine falcons) and killed grouse (like northern goshawks). This perspective was made clear in the 1940 dissertation by the University of Minnesota's doctoral student Evadene Burris Swanson: *Use and Conservation of Minnesota Game, 1850-1900.* Evadene's dissertation highlighted the tragic effects of the persecution and exploitation of the state's wildlife from 1850 through 1900. Much of that ruthless exploitation continued through the 1930s, 1940s, and even into the 1950s. Evadene was the first of Minnesota's women who distinguished themselves in the field of wildlife conservation in Minnesota by earning her doctoral degree in wildlife in 1940. Dr. Swanson's dissertation was republished as a book by the Nongame Wildlife Program and is now available online at the Minnesota DNR website.

Conservation Education: An Important Component of a Successful Nongame Wildlife Program

The third important component of my new Nongame Wildlife Program model was conservation education. I designated my strategy for this effort as the Chocolate Chip Model. I considered conservation education to be a structured process that needed to include both education and public relations/media components. The process begins at the bottom of the chart and proceeds upward through six steps.

Step 1. Little or no awareness of the need or value or need for conservation education efforts of the species or natural resources at risk and needing resolution.

Step 2. Create awareness of the need for a conservation education effort.

Step 3. Create appreciation of the need for implementing this effort.

Step 4. Build an understanding of the benefits that can result for the natural resources or wildlife species at risk.

Step 5. This step involves a transition from understanding to concern for the species or resources involved.

Step 6. Take action to implement conservation education actions and media/public relations actions to resolve the problem or problems affecting the species or natural resources involved.

This is the process by which my staff and I developed conservation education projects like promoting the Nongame Wildlife Checkoff, Project WILD, Project WET, Digital Photography Bridge to Nature, and Southern Wings as well as developing support for land acquisition sites like the Lamprey Pass Wildlife Management Area. Conservation education is a far more important natural resource program component than usually believed.

Whenever wildlife management programs budgets are cut, educational components are usually the first to go because they do not compete well with the number of habitat acres saved or managed. However, this is how citizens, both adults and youths, can be educated and recruited to participate in and contribute to future conservation efforts.

I promoted citizen science, planning, research, surveys, educational programs, habitat management and preservation strategies undaunted by my shoestring budget and lack of staff. Then, in the middle of the night on April 1, 1980, the Minnesota legislature created a Nongame Wildlife Checkoff on the state's income tax forms! Citizens could make tax-deductible donations to help Minnesota's nongame wildlife.

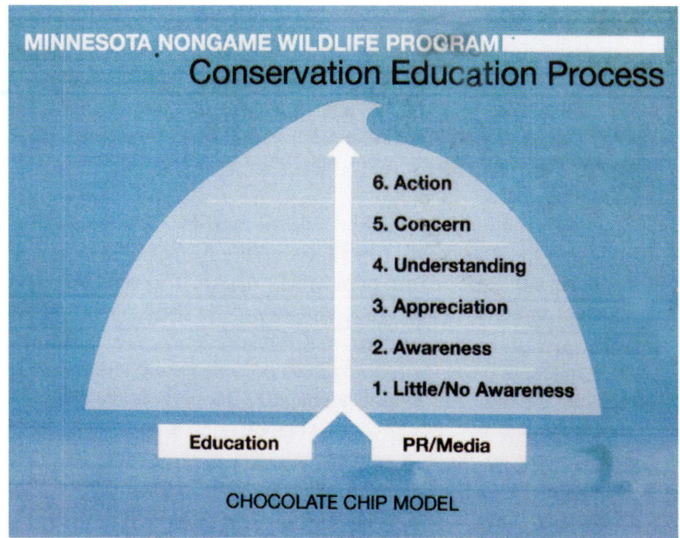

My Chocolate Chip strategy chart for developing our conservation education efforts.

Diane Vosick, my first employee in the Nongame Wildlife Program, played an integral role in helping with this remarkable development. After she worked for me for a year in the federal Young Adult Conservation Program, she deeply understood the importance of my dedication for helping Minnesota's nongame wildlife on a shoestring budget. She had subsequently taken a job working as an aide to state senator Collin Peterson who represented the Detroit Lakes area. Diane had convinced Senator Peterson about how much the DNR Nongame Wildlife Program desperately needed more funding to help Minnesota's nongame wildlife like bald eagles, loons, and other wildlife.

Senator Peterson heard two news reports on March 31, 1980, about a new voluntary tax checkoff option on their state income tax forms that had just been approved by the Colorado legislature for helping nongame wildlife. He thought it sounded like an idea that could be implemented in Minnesota, so he asked Diane to contact legislators in Colorado and have them send the wording of the new tax checkoff amendment right away because he was going into the Minnesota legislature's final tax conference committee meeting that night to finalize the state's income tax legislation. Diane chased down the nongame checkoff wording and got the proposal to Senator Peterson in time for him to take it to the meeting. He had the discretion to introduce this new proposal to the tax conference committee on the last night of the year's legislative session.

When he first introduced the checkoff amendment that evening, he was teased that this was just a chickadee checkoff and that it was unnecessary. He kept reintroducing the nongame checkoff language multiple times that night whenever a tax amendment was introduced. Finally, about two on the morning of April 1, 1980, he introduced the checkoff amendment again. The other committee members said, "You are just going to keep introducing this bill until we pass it, aren't you." Collin said, "Yes," so they passed the checkoff.

I woke up in the morning of April 1, 1980, to read about the new Nongame Wildlife Checkoff in the *Minneapolis Star Tribune*! Thank you, Collin Peterson and Diane Vosick. You made a historic and innovative contribution on behalf of Minnesota's wildlife with a tax checkoff that has generated over forty million dollars for our state's nongame wildlife since its passage.

When I became president of the Nongame Wildlife Association of North America in the early 1980s, I realized that I had another whole new set of publics to address because Minnesota was one of the first states to create and begin development of a new nongame wildlife program. It was one of the first states to generate significant income from our new Nongame Wildlife Checkoff—over a half-million dollars in its first year. The Nongame Wildlife Program supervisors from other states looked to Minnesota for leadership and help in designing their new programs—especially relating to promotion of their new income tax checkoffs.

I provided national guidance for the development of other state nongame wildlife diversity programs throughout the 1980s and 1990s. I presented the keynote presentation for the first conference of the fledgling Minnesota Nongame Wildlife Program in April of 1981. This created a demand from other states with newly created nongame wildlife programs for sharing my guidelines and perspectives for developing their new programs. I traveled to twelve states from Alaska to Florida. I gave keynote presentations at nongame conferences and national conferences to guide them in creating, publicizing, and developing their new nongame wildlife programs. I also gave a comprehensive presentation on strategies and techniques for promoting Minnesota's Nongame Wildlife Checkoff at the North American Fish and Wildlife Conference in Boston in 1984 to help state Nongame Wildlife Program managers understand how to promote their state nongame wildlife tax checkoffs at state and national conferences.

Those twelve presentations took place in: Alaska (June 1981); Iowa (September 1981); Kansas (December 1981); Virginia (March 1983); Florida (November 1983); Illinois (December 1983); Michigan (March 1984); Oklahoma (April 1984); North Dakota (October 1984); the North American Fish and Wildlife Conference in March of 1984 in Boston, Massachusetts, where I gave a presentation on Publicity Strategies and Techniques for Minnesota's Wildlife Checkoff, Interfacing with the Public in Toronto, Ontario, December 1985; and the Northeast Fish and Wildlife Conference in West Virginia (March 1988) where I gave a paper on Trends in Wildlife Resources, Use and Impacts on Future Program for Nongame Wildlife Conservation. In May of 1989 I also gave a presentation on Wildlife Management—"Past and Future Perspectives for the Organization of Wildlife Planners" in Duluth, Minnesota.

I encouraged people to "Look for the Loon" on their Minnesota tax forms. I put my taxidermy skills to work by mounting a loon that had been found dead. I photographed it on a large tax form to promote the new Nongame Wildlife Checkoff.

I became actively involved in promoting the new Nongame Wildlife Checkoff by writing news releases about the checkoff, doing radio and television appearances about the projects that would become possible with the new tax checkoff, and posting public service billboards along Twin Cities metropolitan highways.

Implementing my new Five-H concept for wildlife conservation over the past forty-one years provided many opportunities to help wildlife in Minnesota and beyond. I also synthesized twenty Life Lessons learned from my experience in the DNR and incorporated them into Appendix A at the end of this book. These life lessons helped verbalize my conservation strategies, and it enriched my life in the process. Those life lessons can hopefully help high school and college students and other natural resource professionals as they embark on their own conservation careers.

Highlighting the accomplishments of the Nongame Wildlife Program on Minnesota Public Radio.

A highway billboard promoting the Nongame Wildlife Checkoff.

Women in Wildlife Conservation

There was one other public that had been sadly ignored by the Department of Natural Resources for wildlife conservation management and biologist positions prior to 1980—women. A new perspective on nongame wildlife was a professional conservation career opportunity for managing lands for the benefit of eagles, loons, herons, grebes, turtles, snakes, frogs, toads, salamanders, bats, warblers, bluebirds, purple martins, hummingbirds, butterflies, dragonflies, moths, bees, minnows, mussels, and hundreds of other nongame wildlife species that had been ignored by the DNR within the traditional realm of game management.

When I was hired, there were no women working as biologists or wildlife managers in the Department of Natural Resources' Section of Wildlife. There were few women interested in managing habitat for production of deer, ducks, pheasants, and other game species.

My first hiring priority when funding became available from the Nongame Wildlife Checkoff was to hire a nongame staff of five regionally based biologists. I hired two current DNR wildlife staff, including Jack Mooty, a wildlife researcher from Grand Rapids and John Schladweiler, the area wildlife manager from Madison in western Minnesota.

I advertised the remaining three positions nationwide for regional nongame wildlife specialist positions. I hired three extraordinary women with impressive credentials: Joan Galli was the Nongame Wildlife Program supervisor from New Jersey; Pam Skoog Perry, from St. Paul, Minnesota, was experienced with successful Nongame Wildlife Program projects in Florida; and Katherine "Katie" Hirsch Haws had considerable experience with nongame wildlife research and surveys in Alaska and Washington state. I don't think I realized the significance of this hiring process at the time—women in wildlife conservation! This was the first hiring of women wildlife biologists in the history of the DNR Section of Wildlife.

Stories began trickling in about their accomplishments and performance in helping wildlife as employees of the DNR. When Pam Perry gave presentations in school classrooms about wildlife in central Minnesota, young girls were amazed to see a woman in a professional DNR uniform. They did not know that a woman could have a job like that. Many thought their only career option was to become a housewife or perhaps a schoolteacher. Pam Skoog Perry, Katie Hirsch Haws, and Joan Galli did an exceptional job working with DNR staff in their advocacy for great blue herons, common loons, bald eagles, turtles, and bats, not only in the field but also when they made hundreds of radio and television appearances promoting conservation of nongame wildlife and the Nongame Wildlife Checkoff. The photos below show our initial nongame field staff of 1983, including Joan, Katie, and Pam. Those three pioneering women wildlife biologists in the Minnesota DNR served a cumulative total of approximately ninety-years in the Nongame Wildlife Program until retirement.

Our Nongame Wildlife Program staff of regional nongame wildlife specialists in 1983, including myself, Joan Galli, Katie Hirsch Haws, Pam Skoog Perry (front row) and Jack Mooty and John Schladweiler (back row).

The chapters in this book cover some program highlights including special memories, strategies, and credits to nongame wildlife movers and shakers, conservation organizations, and donors to the Nongame Wildlife Checkoff. They made successes possible. Unfortunately, space does not allow covering many initiatives within the Nongame Wildlife Program carried out by our regional Nongame Wildlife Program specialists and researchers under contract with nongame funding. They benefited dragonflies, mussels, bats, Blanding's turtles, five-lined skinks, Topeka shiners, Karner blue butterflies, northern cricket frogs, and mink frogs, among many others. There is undoubtedly enough material for another book.

Kristin Hall now serves as the DNR Nongame Wildlife Program supervisor and is doing an exceptional job of continuing to grow the program, expand its coverage on a broad array of invertebrates, and increase efforts for preservation and management of priority nongame wildlife habitats. The Nongame Wildlife Program staff is completing its new State Wildlife Action Plan, covering its conservation strategies, to be implemented for the ten-year period from 2025 through 2035.

Our DNR Nongame Wildlife Program staff at a statewide meeting in 2015, which included fourteen women in a staff of twenty.

Chapter 3

There "Oughta be Otters" in Southern Minnesota

River otter eating a frog at the Big Stone National Wildlife Refuge, Ortonville, Minnesota. Photo by Rob Rakow

The phrase "I have an idea!" became a classic Henderson catch-phrase during my career. Every time I used that expression, it would freeze my staff in their tracks, and I knew they were thinking *Here we go again!* However, these were the ideas that provided our program with elements of inspiration and creativity that resulted in a series of conservation success stories. Deciding to reintroduce river otters to southwestern Minnesota was the first "I have an idea" moment in my nongame wildlife career.

When I conceived of the otter restoration project, I did it as a scientific effort to reintroduce river otters as a native furbearer and a missing link of the state's biodiversity in southwestern Minnesota. My subsequent experiences taught me that river otters are much more than a furbearer. They are a charismatic symbol for Minnesota's lakes and rivers—like loons. They thrive best in clear and unpolluted water. They possess exceptional doglike intelligence, boundless curiosity, a fondness for play, and remarkable agility and grace both on land and in the water.

River otters are one of Minnesota's most fascinating, intelligent, and amazing wild mammals. Their long, slender bodies, agile swimming abilities, and widespread distribution across the state are not widely known or appreciated because they are mostly nocturnal. Otters can measure up to five feet long and weigh over thirty-pounds. They are Minnesota's largest aquatic mammal. Otter diets include fish, frogs, salamanders, crayfish, and other aquatic creatures. They are so adept at catching prey that they spend little time foraging and therefore have considerable time for play among family members and to explore their lakeshore and riverbank habitats. Otters may travel up to twenty miles a day exploring their territories.

Otters were originally found throughout most of Minnesota. However, they were trapped for their pelts during the era when voyageurs trapped beavers, otters, and other furbearers with no trapping regulations or limits. The demand for beaver pelts in the fur trade caused significant numbers of otters also to be taken incidentally in the late 1800s and early 1900s. As beavers were trapped out in much of northern Minnesota, the beaver pond habitat they had created also became less common and likely caused a significant decline in habitat for otters. Drainage of wetlands and environmental pollution also contributed to a decline in beavers and otters in Minnesota during the past century.

By 1900, beavers had been largely eliminated in northern Minnesota. In 1901, beavers from Canada were reintroduced to Minnesota in Itasca State Park, but no similar efforts were made for restoration of otters. By that time, they had become extirpated from southwestern Minnesota along the Minnesota River and its tributaries. A statewide trapping season on otters was closed from 1917 through 1944. The trapping season reopened in 1945, but only forty-six otters were taken. An annual trapping season on otters was established in northeastern Minnesota in 1955 and has continued to the present except for 1977 when it was closed. The number of otters taken annually from the 1950s to 1970s ranged from about three hundred to five hundred. The number of otters in the state has steadily increased with stricter trapping laws requiring registration of all otters taken, improved water quality, and wetland restoration. Otters have spread southeasterly in Minnesota along the Mississippi River, but they were still missing from southwestern Minnesota when I began working at Lac qui Parle Wildlife Refuge in 1974.

As the assistant manager of the Lac qui Parle Wildlife Refuge from 1974 through 1976, I never observed river otters along the Minnesota River or on the Lac qui Parle Wildlife Refuge. After being hired as the DNR's statewide Nongame Wildlife Program supervisor in 1977, Roger Holmes assigned me the responsibility for managing Minnesota's furbearer tagging efforts for pelts of river otters, lynx, and bobcats trapped in Minnesota. This was required by federal regulations for complying with the Convention on International Trade in Endangered Species of Wild Fauna and Flora. To comply with those regulations, I prepared reports to assure the U.S. Fish and Wildlife Service that Minnesota's furbearer management for river otters did not endanger the state's otter population.

All Minnesota trappers who caught otters had to record how many otters they took each year and report their results to me. As I prepared the river otter status report for 1977, I wondered about the absence of otters in southwestern Minnesota. While the otter was traditionally considered a furbearer under existing regulations, their absence in southwestern Minnesota left them administratively ignored under existing furbearer management. Then I had an idea! Maybe I could initiate a project for restoration of river otters along the Minnesota River valley. The river otter was an important mammal missing from the rivers of southwestern Minnesota. I realized if I didn't do it, it wouldn't get done.

After reviewing the habitat requirements and dietary needs of otters, I felt there was enough natural habitat and fishery resources to support a population of river otters. I developed a restoration plan and submitted it to DNR Section of Wildlife Chief Roger Holmes, DNR Section of Wildlife research group leaders, and the DNR Division of Enforcement for review. The plan was approved.

One of the biggest challenges for this project was that there was no playbook for restoring an otter population in the Midwest. There were other states in the Midwest that were buying wild otters from trappers in Louisiana for restoration, but I didn't like the idea of using southern otters that likely did not have genetic adaptations for surviving Minnesota winters. I decided it was ecologically more appropriate to use wild otters from northern Minnesota. I needed a source of wild otters for release, and I needed to recruit experienced trappers to catch the otters. I needed an efficient means of restraining and transporting the otters in a humane manner for their release along the Minnesota River, and I needed money to make it happen. I found ways to make it happen.

I knew the state's most proficient otter trappers based on the trapping records they had submitted to me to comply with the federal Convention on International Trade in Endangered Species (CITES) regulations. I knew how many trappers had ten years or more of otter trapping experience based on their CITES reports. I offered to recruit them to live-trap otters for the project by offering $150 for each live unhurt otter they caught.

I had trapped furbearers as a youth in Iowa, so I had a working knowledge of furbearers, basic trapping equipment, and trapping techniques. I required the trappers to use No. 1½ coil spring mink traps for catching the otters. This is a trap smaller than recommended for otters. A large male could easily pull its foot out of this trap, but smaller females and young-of-the-year otters could be held without significant foot injuries. There was a benefit for catching and releasing females as part of this project. A female otter breeds in the spring shortly after giving birth to its young. The fertilized eggs then go into a period of delayed implantation in which the fertilized blastocyst does not attach to the uterus until mid-winter. If the female otter is captured in the fall, it does not place undue stress on the fertilized eggs. Females could be captured in the fall with minimum risk to the female and to the health of her unborn pups.

I still had one more challenge—there was no budget for the restoration. No problem. I used my networking skills to appeal to Ben Thoma of the Willmar Sportsmen's Club, the St. Paul Audubon Society, and the Minnesota Archery Association for a $600 donation from each group. Each $600 donation would cover the costs for introducing four otters. Their $1800 covered the costs for capturing and transplanting the first twelve otters from northern Minnesota to the Lac qui Parle Wildlife Refuge. Conservation groups are much more willing to make donations for conservation projects if they know exactly what they will get for their donation: for example, four otters for $600.

Up to this point, I had approached otter restoration as a wildlife biologist because of the biological significance and ecological importance of river otters as an integral part of southwest Minnesota's fauna. I felt otter restoration was an element that needed to be addressed from a holistic point of view. However, I was about to learn much more than I anticipated about the private lives of otters—their personalities, intelligence, and disarming appeal.

Our first otter to be released was a most unusual otter. It had begun life as a pup near Flag Island Resort in Lake of the Woods. The otter lost its fear of humans that summer as it played with kids along the resort shoreline. The kids named the otter "Crazy" because of its amusing antics. Sometimes it would climb into a fishing boat and race around, looking for minnow buckets or stringers of fish. The lodge owners were afraid the otter would be taken for its pelt that fall, so they tried to smuggle it across the Canadian border back to their home in Warroad. They got caught at the border. The local conservation officer called me to ask what I would like to do with the otter. I was told this otter was very tame and not aggressive. It was a young male about thirty inches long. I agreed that I could release the otter as part of our restoration effort in southwest Minnesota. It was transported to the Twin Cities where I would care for it for a day until I could drive it to Lac qui Parle Wildlife Management Area. In the meantime, otter-sitting would become a new and challenging opportunity.

Oscar in our bathtub, pursuing minnows.

After picking up the otter, I went to a local bait shop and got an ice cream bucket filled with dozens of minnows. When I arrived home my wife, Ethelle, was still at work and our eight-year-old son Craig was still at school. Unfamiliar with the techniques for otter-sitting, I filled our bathtub and fed the otter by dumping minnows into the tub. With the bathroom door closed, I cautiously opened the crate. The otter emerged and loped around the bathroom. It was my first exposure to the behavior of otters. His movements were incredibly fluid and graceful, and it demonstrated extreme curiosity. It tried to open the door of the clothes chute with its nose. I had to grab it. It tried to open the towel closet with its nose. I had to pull it out. Then it tried to go down the toilet. Disaster averted. Again, I grabbed the otter and released it by the bathtub. Every time I picked it up, it went limp and was incredibly gentle. The otter looked at the bathtub filled with minnows and dove in. It swam back and forth, swallowing one minnow after another until only one was left. It swam back and forth in the tub, nudging the hapless minnow with its nose. Tiring of this game, it swallowed the fish. I was sitting on the edge of the tub watching the otter, totally entranced. Then it climbed out of the tub and curled onto my lap, circling several times to dry itself off before resting.

In the wild, otters use regular toilet sites along the shores of lakes and rivers. Oscar must have felt right at home as he paused on the closed lid of the toilet. The otter's antics were not over. It looked up at the ice cream bucket filled with minnows on the sink counter and leapt onto the counter as I tried to grab the bucket. The bucket spilled onto the bathroom floor. The minnows were flopping all over. The otter dove to the floor and started slurping up the minnows. Meanwhile, I was trying to grab them so there would be some surviving minnows to feed it the next day. That was about the time when Ethelle got home and discovered pandemonium in the bathroom. Then Craig got home from school, and he thought the otter's antics were hilarious. Craig and I decided the otter needed a name. We chose "Oscar."

Every time I picked Oscar up, he went limp like a tame puppy and allowed me to carry him around. While the otter was quite imprinted on people, the area I selected for his release was in a no-trespassing sanctuary, and I had faith that his previous experience foraging and surviving in the wild would prevail.

Before I headed for Lac qui Parle the next day to release Oscar, I decided to take him on a visit to Craig's third-grade classroom at Eisenhower Elementary School in Coon Rapids. Craig loved the idea of Dad bringing Oscar the Otter to his class for show and tell. Upon arriving at the school, I asked the principal if it would be OK to take an otter into the classroom to show the kids. I'm not sure he knew what an otter was, but he agreed.

Once I was in the classroom with Oscar in his crate, I told the children about otters and explained that I was beginning a DNR project to release otters in southwestern Minnesota where they had been missing for a hundred years. This would be the first otter released as part of that project. I explained that this otter was quite tame, and they didn't need to be afraid. I took Oscar from his crate, released him, and watched as he loped around the perimeter of the classroom. He climbed up the radiator by the window, disappeared behind the venetian blinds, and then peeked out through the blinds. The children squealed in delight. Oscar descended from the radiator and darted across the classroom, racing under the desks of the students as they popped up from their seats like human popcorn.

A teacher out in the hall heard the commotion and opened the classroom door to peek inside. Oscar darted for the door and into the hallway, where students from an art class were lying on their tummies, drawing on large sheets of paper and surrounded by containers of pencils and crayons. Oscar loped down the hallway among the kids. Pencils and crayons went flying everywhere. In hot pursuit, I managed to capture Oscar with a diving catch. He went limp and allowed me to carry him back to the classroom among the amazed students and teachers in the hall.

Once back in the classroom, I sat on the floor with Oscar in my lap and allowed each child to come up to see the otter and ask questions. The kids loved it, and the teacher was very impressed by my impromptu, memorable, and unscripted visit. Oscar may not have received a passing score in deportment, but if awards were ever given out for show and tell, Craig would have won the prize at Eisenhower Elementary that year.

The author holding Oscar before his release. Photo by Cindy Dorn of the Milan Standard

My time with Oscar was coming to an end. It was time to take him to the Lac qui Parle Wildlife Refuge. After a brief stop at the refuge headquarters, we headed to Rosemoen Island, a protected 600-acre sanctuary where Oscar would be free of human disturbance. I took Oscar to the water's edge on Lac qui Parle Lake and released him. He swam out a few feet, caught a bullhead, and promptly came back on shore to munch and crunch the bullhead at my feet.

I returned to my car and sat inside watching Oscar. Then he amazed me one last time. He returned to

Lac qui Parle Wildlife Refuge manager Arlin Anderson and refuge technician Dan Zimmerman releasing an otter. Photo by Cindy Dorn of the Milan Standard

the back of my car, climbed up the bumper, over the trunk, and onto the top of my car. When he reached the front edge of the roof, he peered down at me, upside down, through the top of the windshield. Then he scrambled back to the trunk, jumped to the ground, and loped to the lake to begin his new life. Oscar left me with one memorable calling card—muddy footprints across the top of my car. My last upside-down view of Oscar was most fitting. Oscar had turned my perception of otters upside-down because they were such amazing and intelligent mammals.

The rest of the otters released for this project were all wild-caught otters from northern Minnesota. The first wild otter trapped that fall was captured by Helge Lundmark of Clearbrook, Minnesota. After Helge had put the otter in a homemade wooden crate, he contacted the local DNR conservation officer, a pilot, who flew the otter to Montevideo. Lac qui Parle Wildlife Refuge manager Arlin Anderson (Andy) and I were waiting there to greet our first otter captured in the wild.

We took the otter to the sanctuary on Lac qui Parle WMA's Rosemoen Island along with a videographer from WCCO-TV, newspaper reporter and photographer Cindy Dorn from the Milan Standard, and local citizens interested in following the project. I cautiously opened the crate. The contented otter was sleeping in the grassy bedding that Helge had provided. The otter raised its head and laid down again.

I needed to know the sex of the otter, so I put on some heavy-duty chopper mitts, slowly placed my hands over the otter's chest and grabbed it. I pulled the otter from the crate and pinned it to the ground. The animal's tail began spinning around. I yelled,

An otter family exploring Big Stone NWR. They are likely the descendants of otters we originally released on that refuge. Photo by Rob Rakow

"Andy, the tail, hold down the tail!" As he did, the otter slipped from my grasp and bit me on the thumb as I peeked to determine the sex. I exclaimed, "It's a female! It's a biting female!" The otter did not injure my thumb, but it did provide a hilarious touch to the news on WCCO-TV that evening.

This project was accompanied by a huge media effort with statewide news releases with photographs of the release and extensive television coverage. The otter restoration project generated statewide publicity and awareness for the DNR's new Nongame Wildlife Program. It helped create appreciation for this little known and seldom-seen Minnesota mammal. This was my first success with the high-profile restoration of a wildlife species that had been regionally extirpated. It helped encourage my instincts for innovation, self-confidence, networking, budgeting, media promotion, and planning skills for carrying out future restoration efforts for Minnesota's wildlife.

Following the release of the otter caught by Helge Lundmark, I raised $3,180 with which I was able to fund the capture and release of twenty-two more otters from the fall of 1980 through the spring of 1982. Those otters were released along the Minnesota River, including the Lac qui Parle Wildlife Refuge, Lac qui Parle Lake, Marsh Lake, and the Big Stone National Wildlife Refuge (NWR) near Ortonville where I initiated a partnership with the U.S. Fish and Wildlife Service.

In the forty years that have elapsed since the release of the otters in southwestern Minnesota, river otters have pioneered along the Minnesota River and its tributaries throughout southwest Minnesota from Ortonville to Mankato.

The DNR estimates that the statewide otter population is now about 12,000, and it appears to be increasing at a time when the annual number of otters trapped is decreasing. In recent years an average harvest of 2,000 otters taken per year decreased to 1,050 in the fall/winter season of 2019-2020, 1,304 in 2020/2021, and 1,155 in 2021/2022. Trappers reported taking only 855 otters in the fall/winter of 2022/2023. This was likely due to a winter with extremely deep snow conditions in northeastern Minnesota. In the 2023-2024 season the harvest was 1,700 otters. The population has continued to expand and increase across the state. Regulations have changed to allow otters accidentally taken by beaver trappers in southwestern Minnesota to be legally registered whereas they may have previously been unreported.

River otters are still managed as game species taken during annual trapping seasons. A trapping season was reestablished in 2010 in southwestern Minnesota. However, that was a reasonable decision because of the need to provide an annual season for beavers in southwestern Minnesota. Beavers often become nuisances because they cause damage by flooding croplands and cutting shoreland trees. Otters are vulnerable to being caught in beaver traps, so this avoids a problem for trappers who need to deal with assisting landowners for help in controlling beaver damage on flooded land but accidentally catch otters in the process. An incidental catch of otters will not damage the restored otter population. The river otters are back, and their future is assured.

Meet the river otter face-to-face. Otters have been restored to the rivers and wetlands of southwestern Minnesota by the Nongame Wildlife Program after an absence of perhaps a hundred years. Photo by Rob Rakow

Chapter 4

Canada Lynx

Lynx, up Close and Personal

With all the new information available about the ecology, movements, and reproduction of Canada lynx, and considering the role that the DNR Nongame Wildlife Program had played in funding research by Dr. Ron Moen, I decided to produce a new Nongame Wildlife Program poster featuring the lynx in 2006. I spent several weeks trying to locate a good photograph of a Canada lynx. I failed to locate an acceptable photo, so I contacted Peggy Callahan at the Wildlife Science Center at the Carlos Avery Wildlife Refuge near Forest Lake, Minnesota. She had a pair of female lynx that had been rescued as orphaned kittens and raised at the Wildlife Science Center with a state permit.

I asked if I could take photos of the lynx. She agreed and said that would be no problem. I anticipated taking photos through the fencing of their enclosure, but imagine my surprise when Peggy took me inside the outdoor lynx enclosure and said I could just sit down inside and photograph the lynx up close. Not knowing what behavior to expect, I sat on the ground of the brushy fenced enclosure with some trepidation. I awaited this lifetime opportunity to photograph the lynx.

It did not take long to view their catlike qualities as they silently padded around the enclosure and passed by within several feet of me. Their paws were like huge furry booties as they passed by on long legs; their faces had a mystical appearance with their long, tufted ears, piercing yellow eyes, and furry sideburns featuring black highlights. Over the course of my thirty-seven years of nature tourism travels in Africa, Latin America, and the United States, I have observed many species of wild cats in Africa and Latin America. However, I had never seen any cats in the wild that even closely demonstrated the silent and flowing movements of lynx. They move with stealth-like grace.

My face-to-face encounter with the lynx was an enchanting experience.

My most intriguing observation that morning was a lack of eye contact from them. The lynx paid little or no attention as they passed me. Perhaps I did not look enough like a snowshoe hare to bring out their hard-wired predatory instincts. I have heard that when lynx are encountered in the wild, they do not perceive humans, cars, or trains as a threat or a danger. They have an innocence about anything they encounter that is beyond their world of the boreal forest. That is a quality that frequently results in their demise.

I sincerely appreciated the opportunity provided by Peggy Callahan to view and photograph the lynx at the Wildlife Science Center. They have done impressive research and made contributions for the conservation of gray wolves, red wolves, and Mexican wolves. More information about the Wildlife Science Center can be obtained from their website at www.wildlifesciencecenter.org.

The Canada Lynx is one of Minnesota's most distinctive, memorable, and least known mammals. It is one of three wild felines native to Minnesota. Others are the cougar (mountain lion) and bobcat.

Adult Canada lynx. The lynx is a medium-sized member of the cat family. It inhabits boreal forests of northern and northeastern Minnesota.

Lynx have conspicuously pointed ear tufts and a black-tipped tail. Lynx appear larger than bobcats because they may stand up to two feet tall at the shoulders. Moen et al (2008) documented mean weights of adult lynx captured and released in northeastern Minnesota as 21.2 pounds for three females and 22.5 pounds for five males. Lynx primarily inhabit the Arrowhead region of northeastern Minnesota including Cook, Lake, and St. Louis Counties.

In times of lynx abundance, their presence reflected their response to increasing populations in the snowshoe hare cycle. At such times, they wandered southward, even to agricultural regions of southern Minnesota, but they were never abundant anywhere in the state. Lynx prey primarily on snowshoe hares. Snowshoe hares live in northern coniferous forests. They undergo seasonal changes from white fur in winter to brownish fur in summer to help camouflage them against predators. They get the name snowshoe from their large hind feet that help support them while traveling through snow. Lynx will take an occasional red squirrel, ruffed grouse, or spruce grouse. However, Canada lynx depend so heavily on snowshoe hares that their abundance and reproductive success are tied primarily to the abundance and reproductive success of snowshoe hare populations.

Lynx are a northern boreal forest wildlife species whose status is closely tied to poorly understood ten-year cycles of boreal wildlife like snowshoe hares, ruffed grouse, snowy owls, lemmings, great gray owls, and voles. There is a mystique about lynx because of their reputation for living on a population pendulum that has swung back and forth between boom years of population abundance and bust years of scarcity from the 1820s through 1974. That cyclic population phenomenon for lynx appears to have dampened since the mid-1970s, but informal reports of lynx sightings still appear to increase somewhat on a ten-year cycle of frequency.

Canada lynx were originally trapped and hunted by the voyageurs. As early as 1829, fur buyers of Canada's Hudson's Bay Company noted that in some years lynx numbers increased greatly. This was referred to as a population irruption. State furbearer harvest estimates in more recent times showed that from 1933 to 1975 there were irruptions in 1940, 1952, 1962, and 1972. In the 1949 book by Wallace Grange entitled *The Way to Game Abundance*, the author generalized that cyclic species peaked in each decade in the year ending in two and bottomed out in each decade in the year ending in seven, give or take one or two years.

After being hired as the DNR's statewide Nongame Wildlife Program supervisor, Roger Holmes assigned me the responsibility for managing Minnesota's furbearer tagging efforts for pelts of river otters, lynx, and bobcats trapped in Minnesota. This was required by federal regulations for complying with the Convention on International Trade in Endangered Species of Wild Fauna and Flora. To comply with those regulations, I prepared reports to assure the U.S. Fish and Wildlife Service that Minnesota's furbearer management for Canada lynx did not endanger the state's lynx population.

All Minnesota trappers who caught lynx had to record how many lynx they took each year and report the results to me. I published a twenty-two-page DNR report in 1977 that summarized the history of what we knew about the status of lynx in Minnesota. Until 1975, the lynx was an unprotected species that could be shot or trapped at any time. There were no state agency concerns about its status, management, or conservation. Lynx numbers declined in that unprotected era. Lynx became a protected species in 1975. In 1976 a season was established for taking lynx and that included bag limits. I took the opportunity to share my understanding of lynx by writing an article for the Minnesota DNR *Conservation Volunteer* in 1978. It was entitled "The Lynx Link." Our understanding and appreciation for lynx has come a long way since then.

I prepared a status report on the results of statewide trapping efforts for river otters, bobcats, and Canada lynx beginning in 1977. No lynx were reported taken by hunters or trappers in Minnesota in 1975 or 1976. My report to the U.S. Department of Interior reassured the federal government that Minnesota's regulations complied with the Convention on International Trade in Endangered Species rules. It was also apparent that the boom-and-bust patterns of population fluctuation had changed—or ended. There was a season limit of five lynx or five bobcats or a combination thereof. In 1982, the expected lynx boom did not occur. In 1983, the lynx bag limit was reduced to two. The Minnesota DNR required that the carcasses of lynx be turned over to the DNR so research could be conducted to determine the age and sex of the animals. In 1984, the Canada lynx season was closed in Minnesota, and lynx became protected as a federally threatened species in 2000.

Research and Discoveries

After being unofficially considered as an extirpated species or an occasional vagrant from Canada in the 1980s and 1990s, lynx began to show up in the Arrowhead region. It finally received some long overdue attention as a resident breeding mammal deserving of management attention from county, state, and federal land management agencies and wildlife managers. Reliable reports stimulated a new interest in determining the status of the state's lynx population. From March of 2000 through March of 2006, there were fifty-three verified lynx sightings, and 153 probable lynx sightings were reported to the DNR. Amazingly, thirty-three of those sightings documented reproduction. The lynx was no longer just a vagrant species from Canada.

Dr. Ron Moen (right) and his Canada lynx research team, including Dave Danielson (left) and Dan Ryan (center) - June 13, 2006. Photo by Richard Baker

Beginning in 2003, a new project began: Canada Lynx Ecology in the Great Lakes Region. This ambitious research project involved the U.S. Forest Service, University of Minnesota Natural Resources Research Institute (NRRI), University of Minnesota-Duluth, Minnesota DNR, and the U.S. Geological Survey (Biological Resources Division).

The project was initiated by Dr. Gerald Niemi and led by Dr. Ron Moen of NRRI of the University of Minnesota. Graduate students on the project included Christopher Burdett and Nicholas McCann.

The Nongame Wildlife Program played an integral part in this effort with funding provided by the DNR Nongame Wildlife Research Program. DNR Endangered Species coordinator Richard Baker supervised nongame research. He felt that this was an ideal opportunity to help advance our knowledge of this very special mammal. Researchers captured thirty-three lynx and equipped them with radio transmitters. This effort provided new revelations about the movements, home ranges, and international travels of this species. Some of the radio-collared lynx were even tracked to their dens where kittens were observed.

DNR endangered species program coordinator Richard Baker with a lynx kitten tagged at its den. June 13, 2006. Photo courtesy of Richard Baker

This verified a resident population of lynx in northeast Minnesota and validated the need for state and federal agencies to manage and perpetuate their numbers in Minnesota's northeastern boreal forest. Minnesota's lynx population is now (2025) considered to be the largest population in the continental United States—somewhere between two hundred and three hundred individuals.

Two other significant revelations resulted from Dr. Ron Moen's research. First was the behavior of Minnesota lynx as great travelers. A lynx captured and equipped with a radio collar in January of 2004 had traveled about two hundred miles from Grand Marais northeast into Manitoba. Then it returned to Grand Marais by the end of 2004. Another lynx had traveled from Isabella four hundred miles to north-central Ontario. About 40 percent of the lynx radioed in Minnesota traveled long distances to Ontario and Manitoba. Male lynx outfitted with transmitters in northeast Minnesota ranged back and forth between Minnesota and Ontario, but it is unknown if they were originally from Minnesota or Ontario. Female lynx collared in Minnesota have stayed in Minnesota and maintained a resident breeding population, but some have traveled to Ontario and stayed in Ontario.

The other revelation from Dr. Moen's research was that lynx had been perceived as a wilderness species of the boreal forest. Radiotelemetry documented that lynx can benefit from logging because it creates younger boreal forest habitat which provides food and cover for snowshoe hares. When logging creates boreal forests in an age range from ten to forty years old, hares benefit from the habitat provided by younger forests of firs, pines, cedars, and spruces.

Since the completion of Dr. Moen's groundbreaking radiotelemetry research, the U.S. Forest Service has followed up with a lynx snow-tracking project that has documented the continuing presence and reproduction of lynx in Minnesota. Citizens have also provided additional photos and sightings of lynx to document their presence in northeastern Minnesota.

Is There a Future for Lynx in Minnesota?

The most recent developments relating to lynx in Minnesota involved fine-tuning trapping regulations for taking furbearers in the critical range of lynx habitat in the Arrowhead region, mainly east of MN Hwy 53. Trapping is still legal there for taking fisher, marten, and fox, but DNR state furbearer specialist John Erb has worked with trapper organizations and others to develop rules for taking furbearers without placing lynx at risk of incidental capture.

In 2021, the Center for Biological Diversity sought additional protection for Canada lynx in Minnesota to provide more restrictions on trapping furbearers in the DNR Lynx Management Zone east of Highway 53. Those restrictions were requested to reduce the potential for the incidental capture, injury, or death of Canada lynx due to trapping or use of snares for taking legal furbearers within that zone. From 2011 through 2021, sixteen lynx had been caught in traps set for other furbearers, of which six died.

In February of 2023, federal district court judge Eric Tostrud ruled that new restrictions were needed for taking furbearers with traps and snares to minimize the potential for accidental injuries or death to lynx in the Lynx Management Zone east of Highway 53. Those restrictions for reducing or eliminating incidental take of Canada lynx have been adopted by the DNR and published in the 2023 and 2024 DNR Hunting and Trapping Regulation booklets.

The latest development in Minnesota's Canada lynx saga is that on January 4, 2024, the U.S. Fish and Wildlife Service announced the implementation of a twenty-year Canada lynx federal recovery plan for Minnesota, Maine, Washington, and the Rocky Mountains to document lynx populations and implement management actions to protect and sustain those lynx populations. The goal for northeastern Minnesota is to sustain a population of one hundred lynx for the next twenty years. The plan calls for preserving at least 95 percent of current lynx habitat as forest lands. A total of thirty-one million dollars would be spent on monitoring populations and strengthening habitat management actions.

The protection, management, and conservation strategy for lynx has drastically evolved over the past fifty years. The lynx have gone from being totally unprotected and killed year-round for bounties as an undesirable predator to total protection by state and federal laws. However, there is one more wild card beyond the scope of state and federal laws that could severely impact the future of lynx in Minnesota—climate change. As climate change results in warmer temperatures across Minnesota and warmer climates shift northward, boreal forests are threatened with a transition to hardwood broadleaf forests. The range of boreal forests would shift northward into Canada, and a host of boreal forest plants and wildlife could disappear throughout Minnesota's Arrowhead region. Canada lynx could be one of the species lost due to this change.

We will depend on our forest biologists and ecologists to monitor this change and determine if there are strategies to preserve or maintain remnants of those boreal forest communities that have been such an integral part of Minnesota's cultural and natural heritage. They have sustained our state's Canada lynx populations. The last chapter of this story has yet to be written.

Chapter 5

A Dinosaur Among Birds Returns to Minnesota—Greater Sandhill Cranes

I am mesmerized by the sight and sounds of sandhill cranes. They provide a prehistoric eocene essence to foggy mornings in Minnesota's marshlands. Greater sandhill cranes are long-legged, stately, elegant water-birds characteristic of shallow wetlands and adjacent upland grasslands throughout much of Minnesota. Their calls can be heard long before they can be seen as cranes migrate overhead or trumpet from their marshy nesting areas.

The sandhill crane provides an important chapter in our conservation history. It was poorly understood, poorly known, and unappreciated until recent times. I am impressed with the historical and biological qualities of sandhill cranes. I also admire their intelligence. In 1949, Lawrence Walkinshaw wrote *The Sandhill Cranes* including a story about a young sandhill crane raised as a pet by a family in Florida in 1909. "Each day during horsefly season, the young crane would walk through the neighborhood to six neighbors' homes. It would walk onto the porch and make a chirping noise. When let into the house, the colt would peck and eat horseflies from the screen doors and windows. Then the neighbor would let the crane out so it could go to the next house. The crane only visited houses where it was welcome."

Fossil remains of cranes have been found in Nebraska dating back at least two and a half million years. Their prehistoric trumpeting calls can be heard up to three miles away. Aldo Leopold spoke reverently of them as a wilderness species in *A Sand County Almanac*, and he revered the sandhill crane in his essay "Marshland Elegy":

Sandhill cranes in wetlands of the Sherburne National Wildlife Refuge near Zimmerman, Minnesota.

"Our ability to perceive quality in nature begins, as in art, with the pretty. It expands through successive stages of the beautiful to values as yet uncaptured by language. The quality of cranes lies, I think, in this higher gamut, as yet beyond the reach of words."

The sandhill crane is an important component of Minnesota's fauna, but it was hunted nearly to extirpation during the pioneer settlement era when they were unprotected from shooting. The population was reportedly reduced to only several dozen birds in the Duxby area of northwestern Minnesota by the 1930s. As the DNR Nongame Wildlife Program supervisor, I was keenly interested in providing advocacy for protection of sandhill cranes as a nongame species and for the opportunity to promote their protection, survival, and enjoyment as an icon of wetland conservation.

Like loons, sandhill cranes have a strong pair bond and usually raise just one or two chicks each year. This pair was observed at the Carlos Avery Wildlife Refuge near Forest Lake, Minnesota.

I have an updated sense of sandhill cranes as a remarkably adaptive species in contrast to the vision that Aldo Leopold had for cranes as a wilderness species. A century ago wilderness was the last inaccessible place a species survived after it was killed off everywhere else where it was accessible to humans with guns. Sandhill cranes, whooping cranes, trumpeter swans, wolverines, wolves, elk, and woodland caribou were victims of that era. Sandhill cranes—and trumpeter swans—have since demonstrated their ability to return to their historic nesting habitats throughout the Midwest where they are no longer killed indiscriminately.

Over the past ninety years, sandhill cranes have staged a slow but steady recovery without the benefit of state or federal wildlife recovery efforts. They were protected by federal law during that period. They adapted to nesting in shallow, marshy wetlands with interspersed pastures and grasslands that were a low priority either for drainage or conversion to agricultural cropland.

In 1977, I responded to a suggestion by DNR wildlife manager Larry Bernhoft in Baudette to organize a volunteer observation program for greater sandhill cranes. I contacted field staff from: the U.S. Forest Service; U.S. Fish and Wildlife Service; U.S. Soil Conservation Service; DNR Divisions of Fish and Wildlife, Forestry, Ecological Services, and Enforcement, The Nature Conservancy; and wildlife and natural resource faculty members at the University of Minnesota in Crookston, Minneapolis, and St. Cloud State University.

The response from these volunteers was awesome. I received 135 observation cards for sightings of 2,440 cranes in 1977. The sightings portrayed the distribution of greater sandhill cranes in northwest Minnesota and a smaller population of greater sandhill cranes that was expanding into east-central Minnesota from the Crex Meadows Wildlife Area in western Wisconsin. I estimated the number of resident sandhill cranes in Minnesota ranged from 150 to 300 breeding pairs, which annually produced 150 to 300 young. The number of nonbreeding cranes was estimated at 300 to 600 birds, so the total state population was about 600 to 1200 cranes in 1977.

I continued the observation card program for two more years. Observers submitted 147 cards and reported seeing 1,545 cranes in 1978. In 1979, forty-seven observers submitted 114 cards and reported 5,931 cranes. The large number of cranes seen in 1979 was due to several large migratory flocks, most likely from Canadian breeding grounds. They were seen in the Borup area during fall migration.

I estimated that seventy-six pairs produced sixty-one colts in 1977, eighty-seven pairs produced forty-six colts in 1978, and seventy-five pairs produced at least nineteen young in 1979. Cranes were observed in seventy-eight townships in northwest Minnesota and in twenty-seven townships of east-central Minnesota. Eleven new townships were added to the sandhill crane range map in 1979, suggesting that the population was expanding its range in the state.

As I familiarized myself with Minnesota's sandhill cranes, I considered the sandhill crane as a holistic species worthy of preservation, but I realized most Minnesotans were not familiar with sandhill cranes. They were usually confused with great blue herons. Their grayish plumage is highlighted by reddish skin on their foreheads and long necks and legs. Their gray plumage may frequently have a rusty tinge because of iron staining from the wetlands where they live.

It was also obvious that Minnesotans did not perceive sandhill cranes as a game species to be hunted and shot. They are a species whose calls and sightings engender awe and appreciation as an integral native species of our wetlands that was nearly extirpated by unregulated killing in the past. There has been increasing popularity for crane-watching during their spring and fall migrations. They have become a **High Profile** species popular with birders in the spring and fall. The Sherburne National Wildlife Refuge, for example, recorded 29,000 cranes staging in November during fall migration in 2022. In 2023 the peak count was 17,979 on November 1, and on October 15, 2024 a peak of 12,933 cranes was observed.

I got my introduction to the charm and innocence of cranes on a visit to the International Crane Foundation at Baraboo, Wisconsin, in the 1980s. It was late summer, and I was in a pasture where flightless crane colts were free to roam. Over three feet tall, the birds came running up to me and gathered around like a group of excited school kids. I was startled when I felt nudges at my side. The colts were sticking their heads into my trouser pockets! My guide explained they were looking for kernels of corn which their keepers routinely kept in their pockets for feeding them.

Restoration of sandhill cranes has been achieved through what I would call passive restoration. They showed great adaptability to nest in diverse marshy habitats and adjacent agricultural croplands that were not a high priority for conversion to agricultural croplands. The cranes demonstrate strong parenting qualities for raising their young. My restoration strategy was to promote cranes as a valuable watchable wildlife species that benefits from protection of their shallow wetland nesting habitats and from support by wildlife watchers who wish to see them protected. I now consider greater sandhill cranes to be in the **High Profile** conservation category that help in advocacy for preserving Minnesota's shallow wetlands.

A greater sandhill crane calling to defend its young.

A sandhill crane colt hiding several yards from its parent.

After completing my volunteer project for citizens to report sandhill cranes from 1977 through 1979, I wrote a feature story, "Last Call for Cranes" in the *DNR Conservation Volunteer*. In the *Traveler's Guide to Wildlife in Minnesota*, published in 1997, I also highlighted five areas where sandhill cranes could be seen and enjoyed by the public. In 2015, I contracted with birder Bob Janssen to write *Birds of Minnesota State Parks*. Bob identified six state parks and a state recreation area where birders could observe sandhill cranes. These were new locations where cranes had not been seen for many decades.

I have seen the enormous interest by citizens over the past several decades in visiting the Platte River in Nebraska every March to experience the sandhill crane migration there. Other closer areas now have their own unique appeal during the fall crane migration. Major concentrations can be observed from mid to late October and early November at the Sherburne National Wildlife Refuge, the Carlos Avery Wildlife Refuge, and the Crex Meadows Wildlife Area in western Wisconsin. As crane populations have increased, they have become very popular for their captivating appeal, elegance in flight, memorable calls, family bonds, and popularity among wildlife photographers.

Among recent developments for crane-watching have been significant increases in springtime concentrations of thousands of cranes in northwestern Minnesota on expansive areas of prairies and shallow wetlands. Those areas include lands recently acquired through the federal Conservation Reserve Enhancement Program (CREP). One of the best sites to view, photograph and hear the calling of the cranes in springtime is the Neal Wildlife Management Area complex in the third week of April, according to John Voz, the regional CREP program coordinator and land acquisition specialist. He told me that the calling of the cranes then is so loud that it even drowns out the sound of booming prairie chickens in the area.

For a nesting species that lays only one to two eggs per year, the increase in sandhill crane numbers has been impressive. The U.S. Geological Survey Breeding Bird Survey counts for Minnesota have shown a thirty-fold increase in crane numbers from 1967 through 2019. In the past five years, cranes have been observed in eighty-six of Minnesota's eighty-seven counties and documented as nesting in sixty counties. Cranes have adapted to nesting in small shallow wetlands and marshes, mixed farmland with scattered

Sandhill cranes in a V-shaped flight formation during fall migration.

wetlands, pastures, and even suburban backyards with adjacent marshes. One important source of support for long-term protection of sandhill cranes came from the DNR Nongame Wildlife Program in 2005.

I decided to help fund research by the International Crane Foundation to develop Anthraquinone (*Avipel*) as a non-toxic deterrent that farmers could use to coat seed corn kernels. *Avipel* is distasteful to cranes, so they will not pluck seed corn kernels from the soil as they sprout in the spring. Without this deterrent, farmers would request permits to shoot depredating cranes in the spring. A hunting season in the fall, requested by farmers, would not have been effective because shooting cranes in fall would not decrease spring crop depredation problems. That is because the local population of cranes in the spring would be different from the larger population of migrating Canada-origin cranes present in the fall.

As cranes spread southeastward from northwestern Minnesota, the separate Wisconsin population has spread westward into central Minnesota. The northwest population, a part of the mid-continent sandhill population, is comprised mainly of the migratory subspecies of lesser sandhill cranes that winter mostly in Texas. There are also some larger cranes that nest in the Canadian prairie provinces and northwestern Minnesota. They were formerly referred to as a separate subspecies, but they are now lumped with greater sandhill cranes.

Most of the east-central crane population winters in southeastern states including Indiana, Kentucky, Tennessee, and Florida. Recent sandhill crane telemetry research, funded by the Legislative Citizens' Commission on Minnesota Resources (LCCMR), carried out by Dr. David Wolfson, Dr. John Fieberg, Jeff Lawrence, Tom Cooper, and Dr. David Andersen, revealed that the two crane populations have merged in north-central Minnesota—mainly in Becker and Mahnomen counties. Their research revealed variability in migration patterns between cranes using the mid-continent flyway from northwest Minnesota wintering in southern Kansas, Oklahoma, and primarily in Texas and sandhill cranes using eastern flyway migration routes. On a few occasions, radio-marked cranes diverged from their traditional migratory wintering sites in the southeastern states to utilize mid-continent flyway destinations in Texas.

The only issue that has arisen within the management regime for cranes is that the northwestern population of greater sandhill cranes nests in seven northwestern Minnesota counties and primarily migrates to Texas. It was placed under management of the mid-continent population of sandhill cranes by the U.S. Fish and Wildlife Service. In 2010, a hunting season was established for those seven northwestern counties of Minnesota as part of the hunted Central Flyway population—largely without any citizen input from

Minnesotans or Minnesota conservation groups—until it was too late for them to respond to the proposal. The first crane seasons were so early in September that the Minnesota population of cranes was over-harvested. It took several years to recover after the season framework was finally shifted to a later time in the fall when the proportion of Canada-origin cranes was significantly higher during the hunting season.

The season has seen declining interest by Minnesota hunters over the past fifteen years. From 2010 through 2019 there were about 490 hunters who annually participated in that hunt, and the average harvest was 373 cranes.

In 2021, there was an effort to expand the hunting zone for cranes throughout northern and central Minnesota where crane-watching has become extremely popular among Minnesota birders. It would have created a serious conflict between crane enthusiasts and crane hunters at a time when the number of waterfowl hunters and interest in waterfowl hunting in Minnesota is declining. The idea for an expanded crane season was defeated by DNR leadership.

It is quite apparent that the recovery of the greater sandhill crane is an important wildlife conservation success story to be celebrated. We can expect to see sandhill crane numbers expanding as they adapt to more nesting habitats, and there will likely be increases in migratory concentrations of sandhill cranes, providing more viewing and photography opportunities. The future for sandhill cranes in Minnesota is obvious—as a nongame species. It belongs in the skies and on the wetlands of our state to be experienced and enjoyed by our citizens just as we enjoy bald eagles, loons and trumpeter swans and just as people enjoy the annual passage of sandhill cranes every spring along the Platte River in Nebraska. Sightings of crane families in those habitats and in great seasonal concentrations are a highlight for birders, photographers, and conservationists. It is another success story for wildlife conservation.

Chapter 6

When Exploring in a Great Blue Heron Colony—Don't Look Up—and Beware of Falling Fish

Great blue heron on the shoreline of Muskrat Lake, Detroit Lakes, Minnesota.

Don't overlook the role that serendipity can play in the success of important conservation initiatives. Serendipity played a major role in helping save one of the largest and most significant heron colonies in Minnesota—the Lamprey Pass heronry near Forest Lake. In July of 1979, DNR Section of Wildlife chief Roger Holmes and assistant chief Tom Isley were flying from St. Paul with a conservation officer pilot to a meeting in Grand Rapids, Minnesota. As they passed over the eastern shore of Howard Lake near Forest Lake, they spotted a nesting colony with hundreds of great blue heron, great egret, black-crowned night-heron, and cormorant nests.

When they returned to St. Paul, they asked me if I was aware of a former hunting club property that encompassed a large heron colony on the east shore of Howard Lake since I had been developing an inventory of the state's heronries. I told them I was not aware of a heronry there. This opportunistic sighting of the colony led to the acquisition of the most important heronry ever acquired as a DNR Wildlife Management Area.

The hunting club was purchased by prominent St. Paul attorney and politician Uri Lamprey in 1881. This property originally included over three thousand acres of hunting club property, including Howard Lake and Mud Lake where a row of ten pit blinds for duck hunting was positioned on a historic duck pass between the two lakes. It operated from 1881 through the 1940s.

The Lamprey Pass Wildlife Management Area is shown in this photo. Mud Lake is at the top center of the photo, and Howard Lake is at the lower right corner of the photo.

The heronry discovered in 1979 was in the forest along the shoreline of Howard Lake at the bottom center of the above photo. I made a visit to the colony on May 2, 1980. It revealed 237 great blue heron nests, 118 great egret nests, 40 black-crowned night-heron nests, and twenty double-crested cormorant nests.

This was one of the seven largest heronries in Minnesota out of 172 colonies. The land had Hopewellian burial mounds on the property. This Native American culture flourished along rivers in what are now eastern and midwestern states from about one hundred BC to 500 AD. The burial mounds at Lamprey Pass date back about two thousand years. The Minnesota Historical Society considers the Lamprey Pass burial mounds to be one of the most significant archeological sites in Minnesota.

Then I discovered that the gun club property was for sale. I explored the land and was amazed by the variety of wildlife present: ruffed grouse, pileated woodpeckers, common loons, wood ducks, mink, muskrats, beaver, and deer. I also discovered a cemetery with headstones for the dogs of duck hunters who had been members of the Lamprey Pass Club.

However, a developer had designed a plan for creating an eight-hundred-unit recreational vehicle (RV) park under the heronry. I don't think he had ever camped beneath active heron nests. He took his plans to a Columbus Township board meeting for approval. The board voted down the request because they were concerned about preserving the heronry. The developer came back with a second request for a modified plan that reduced the number of recreational units to 350. Meanwhile, a local farmer, Don Steinke, and a local homeowner, Mary Ann Hoyt, rallied local citizens to attend a public hearing to vote on the fate of the heronry. About a hundred people showed up. It was the largest public hearing ever held in Columbus Township.

At the public hearing, I explained that I had surveyed the heronry. I described the sensitivity of heronries to disturbance and the biological importance of herons and egrets in our wetland ecosystems. I suggested that the loud guttural squawking and grunting in the heronry, the smell of heron feces, and the problem of dead fish dropping from nests onto campers would discourage even the most avid RV enthusiasts. I explained that the developer wanted to locate the RV campsites under the heron nests. At the conclusion of my testimony, one of the Columbus township attendees got up and said, "You know what we need to do?

We need to get behind the DNR and help them save this area!" The people stood up and cheered.

I did not have a budget for acquisition of Lamprey Pass. Then a remarkable thing happened. Call it a miracle if you wish. On April 1, 1980, the Minnesota legislature created the Chickadee Checkoff on state income tax forms that allowed citizens to donate funds for protection of nongame wildlife. Citizen donations for 1981 exceeded $523,000 giving us enough funding to acquire Lamprey Pass! The Minnesota Chapter of The Nature Conservancy arranged to purchase and hold the property for the DNR until the checkoff donations became available in 1982. We paid $200,000 from our first year of checkoff donations in addition to $196,000 that was provided in partnership with the DNR Division of Fish and Wildlife. They allocated game and fish funds to complete the purchase of the area and designate it as a Wildlife Management Area. The 1277-acre Lamprey Pass WMA became a biological and historical gem in Minnesota's legacy of wildlife management areas, and it is within an hour's drive from the Twin Cities.

After we had purchased the Lamprey Pass WMA, I took reporter Nancy Besse from New Ulm to the heronry so she could write a story for the DNR Conservation Volunteer about the saga of how this area was saved. It was while visiting the heron colony that we learned an important lesson. Don't look up! While we were standing at the edge of the colony, a smelly and partially digested falling fish plopped down onto Nancy's shoulder from thirty or forty feet above us. An upset young heron had just barfed up the fish in response to our presence. We brushed off her shoulder and later went into Forest Lake for lunch. Nancy went into the restroom where she tried to wipe off fish juice from the back of her shoulder. A woman entered the restroom and exclaimed, "Oh my, do you have an infant?" Nancy chose not to share the whole story. She simply said, "Yes."

On one of my subsequent visits to the heronry, a windstorm had passed through the colony, and I found a half-grown chick that had fallen from its nest. I decided to take the chick to the Wildlife Rehabilitation Center in Roseville the next day, but first I needed to catch a fish to feed the bird. I had fishing tackle in my car, so I drove to nearby Forest Lake to see what I could catch from shore. On my first cast, I caught a walleye. Should I keep the walleye and try for a bluegill to feed the heron chick instead? No, the chick needed a break. The chick dined on a filet of walleye that evening.

Great blue heron in shoreline habitat at Eagle Lake near Crosslake, Minnesota.

Like common loons and bald eagles, great blue herons are among Minnesota's most conspicuous birds. About three feet tall, these long-legged wading birds nest in tree-top colonies where they raise their young in stick nests.

Great blue herons frequently stalk along the shorelines of lakes, rivers, and wetlands in search of small fish, frogs, snakes, and small mammals. The great blue heron is the epitome of avian elegance, like a long-legged bird in a tux. In breeding plumage, their blue, gray, and white plumage is highlighted by slender black plumes flowing from the back of their head and dozens of narrow whitish plumes draped over the chest, back, and wing coverts. They may fly from their treetop colonies over fifteen miles to forage for prey in lakes, wetlands, and along rivers.

The newly created Nongame Wildlife Program needed to identify and protect sites used by nesting colonial waterbirds like great blue herons. Having no field staff, I approached this challenge by sending out news releases requesting volunteers to report colonial waterbird nesting sites by mail. In 1977, the volunteers were asked to report the nest counts and species composition for waterbird colonies throughout the state. That effort resulted in identifying 191 sites, including 94 great blue heron colonies. I repeated the volunteer survey in 1978. A total of 92 citizens submitted data that included 116 great blue heron colonies.

In 1980, I organized a volunteer survey of heron colonies with DNR regional nongame wildlife biologist Katie (Hirsch) Haws. We estimated there were 151 great blue heron colonies in the state. All the heronries were either in dead trees in beaver ponds, on islands or peninsulas in lakes, or on the edges of lakes and rivers. In 1985, 127 colonies were reported in forty-six counties. During the Minnesota Breeding Bird Atlas project conducted from 2009 to 2013, only ninety great blue heronries were identified in forty-seven counties although herons were observed in all eighty-seven of Minnesota's counties.

The great blue heron is a **High Priority** species within my Four-H ranking categories since it is commonly seen by boaters and anglers across the state, but they are usually seen singly along shorelines. People do not realize that the populations have been in a long-term decline. This heron should also be considered in the **Habitat** category because their colonies are extremely vulnerable to destruction by land developers, homesite construction, and long-term decline of the colonies due to trees dying from accumulated fecal deposits under the trees. Those sites need protection. Great blue herons also depend on preservation of lake, marsh, and shallow wetland edges with both clean water and healthy populations of frogs and salamanders as well as fish.

Sandhill cranes could be mistaken for great blue herons because they are similar in height, but cranes are uniformly gray, and they don't perch in treetops. Cranes nest as solitary pairs in shallow marshes and are much more vocal than herons, which are typically noisy only in their treetop nesting colonies. Cranes fly with their necks extended forward while great blue herons fly with their heads and necks recurved back over their shoulders.

Like pelicans and raptors, great blue herons were once the target of anglers and hunters who persecuted them because they ate fish. They were shot and vilified. It has taken many decades for that bias to diminish among people who considered any creatures that ate fish to be competing with them for the sport fish they sought.

Great blue herons are usually shy and difficult to approach. Ask any photographer. A century ago, duck hunters would shoot great blue herons and have them stuffed by a taxidermist. They would then place the stuffed heron near their duck decoys as a confidence decoy to reassure ducks that the area was safe for landing. Great blue herons are federally protected and cannot be killed or mounted for use as a hunting confidence decoy. Now there are companies that manufacture and sell life-size great blue heron decoys for duck hunting.

In northern Minnesota, great blue herons benefit from the presence of beaver ponds. When beavers make a dam and create a pond, they kill the trees impounded in the pond. Great blue herons prefer those dead and dying trees as colony nesting sites. They forage for fish and amphibians in the shallow waters of beaver ponds. In northwestern, central, and southern Minnesota, great blue herons typically nest on islands in larger lakes or along lakeshores and rivers.

Great blue heron on its treetop nest in a heron colony.

One of our first nongame program efforts to preserve a heronry was at Kabekona Lake in Hubbard County. The colony was on a DNR reservoir on state land. It had about forty pairs of herons from 1977 through 1980, but the flooded trees in the reservoir were dead and beginning to decay. The colony was visible along the west side of Highway 371, several miles north of Walker, Minnesota. Katie Haws and Dave Johnson constructed nesting platforms on power company power poles with assistance from the local power company. They drove out on the ice in winter, bored holes through the ice and into the reservoir bottom, fastened platforms on the power poles, and then placed the poles through the ice among nesting trees in the colony. It worked. It extended the life of the great blue heron colony.

Great blue heron in flight.

Great blue herons provide an incidental benefit for other birds. At Marsh Lake near Appleton, great blue herons nesting on an island in the lake moved to a nearby lakeshore willow grove after all the nesting trees on the island died and fell. I observed common grackles nesting within the masses of sticks underneath the heron nests. Perhaps they were finding fish remains that the heron chicks had missed. Even more intriguing were observations of heronries where bald eagle pairs took over a heron nest—usually on the periphery of a colony. There have been no studies on whether the eagles were preying on the herons or chicks or on how they interacted with the herons in the colony.

The U.S. Geological Survey federal Breeding Bird Survey has revealed that the state's great blue heron counts have declined by an average of 1.32 percent every year since 1967. The population is now only 47 per cent of the numbers counted in 1967. The decline is attributed to a combination of land development of shoreland habitats, wetland drainage, loss of feeding areas used by herons, and perhaps declines in frog and salamander populations that herons previously depended upon as prey.

Land developers have also resorted to use of blatant misinformation about great blue heron colonies. One developer recently hired a consultant who claimed that DNR sightings of single herons in southeastern Minnesota were actually heron colonies, so he fooled the local town board into believing herons were abundant throughout the region and that herons were common. This resulted in a vote for destruction of the only known colony in Olmsted County.

Then developers were told by federal biologists that they could begin cutting down the nesting trees as soon as young fledged from the nests in the late summer and before herons returned to nest in the spring. The heronry was abandoned the following spring.

While great blue herons are not yet threatened or endangered in Minnesota, this decline is troubling and could result in their being listed as a state threatened or endangered species. It is unfortunate that even though long-term trends are declining, there has been inadequate concern for additional protection to help the species. Heron colonies are used for multiple years, sometimes decades. However, the protection afforded by the federal government through the Migratory Bird Treaty Act of 1918 is inadequate. It does not provide protection for nesting trees used for multiple years by great blue herons, or bald eagles. Those nesting trees need year-round protection including months outside of the nesting season. In the case of the heronry near Rochester, the nesting trees on the proposed development were cut in the winter, and the colony was lost.

Another unusual threat for herons was the discovery that raccoons learned how to exploit great blue herons by climbing nesting trees at night and eating chicks in the nest. Research was initiated by DNR regional nongame wildlife biologist Joan Galli and carried out by Andrew Von Duyke in 2004 and 2005 at Peltier Lake in Anoka County. It documented the decimation of heron nesting efforts by a few raccoons that learned to prey on nestling herons. The guilty raccoons were subsequently controlled.

One of the largest heronries in the state in the 1970s and early 1980s was on a ten-acre island in Long Lake north of Willmar. In 1979, 1,494 great blue heron nests were reported. In 1980, the great blue heron nest count dropped to 440. There were also 330 great egret nests, 300 double-crested cormorant nests, and 424 black-crowned night-heron nests in this mixed-species colony. The heronry was acquired at the initiative of DNR regional Nongame Wildlife Program biologist John Schladweiler for $9,600 on October 23, 1992, with Reinvest in Minnesota critical habitat matching funds. The property was posted and protected by the DNR as the Wig Wildlife Management Area.

On June 16, 2023, DNR Nongame Wildlife specialist Michael Worland checked the site and observed no nesting activity by colonial waterbirds. Other declines of previously huge colonies are concerning. There was apparently no nesting effort in the Pigs Eye colony in St. Paul in 2022 or 2023. It was formerly one of the largest multi-species heronries in the state.

Like loons, herons are an indicator of healthy lakes and waters. Unfortunately, they are now seen in such low numbers that it is difficult to assess how seriously their populations are declining. There needs to be a regular periodic update of heronry nest counts. The DNR needs to learn if the cause of these continuing declines can be determined and recommend any remedial actions to assist in the recovery of the state's great blue herons. Funding has been approved for a statewide survey of heronries in 2025 by the Natural Resources Research Institute with funding from the Environment and Natural Resources Trust Fund, which is derived from the Minnesota lottery.

The future of great blue herons will be written where they nest in the treetops and stalk the shorelines of Minnesota's lakes and rivers in search of prey. They add an extra element of avian beauty to our lakes and wetlands. We need to step up our colonial waterbird monitoring, management, and protection efforts to keep them from declining further.

Chapter 7

Hawks and Bald Eagles

Bald eagle at its nest. Minnesota can pride itself on its recent record of raptor conservation and restoration.

The national recovery of bald eagles is a fantastic wildlife success story. Bald eagles have made a dramatic recovery since the 1960s. Credits and appreciation are due over the past sixty years to the many biologists, researchers, foresters, wildlife managers, and employees of the U.S. Fish and Wildlife Service, U.S. Forest Service, and National Park Service, University of Minnesota Raptor Center, conservation organizations, National Eagle Center, and DNR Nongame Wildlife Program. They have all made this recovery a reality in Minnesota and beyond. There are now more nesting pairs of bald eagles in Minnesota than in any state in the continental United States. Peregrine falcons have returned to the skies of Minnesota, and all hawks and owls are once again protected from shooting since great horned owls were finally given federal protection in 1972.

During the past 150 years, however, bald eagles, peregrine falcons, hawks, and owls suffered from the perception that they were outlaw birds that preyed on domestic poultry, upland game birds, and waterfowl. Some hunters and farmers shot these birds at every opportunity as a public service. Other people shot raptors to have them mounted for display in their homes—even bald eagles. There was also a commercial demand for eagle, hawk, and peregrine eggs by egg collectors known as oologists. Collecting federally protected wild bird eggs became illegal in 1918. In 1929, however, the Minnesota legislature removed legal protection from all eagles, hawks, owls, and falcons and declared them as outlaw birds. They encouraged people to shoot raptors. The Minnesota legislature finally restored protection to most raptors in 1948, except for birds like great horned owls.

Duck hunters shot peregrine falcons because of their reputation as the duck hawk. Homing pigeon fanciers shot sharp-shinned hawks, Cooper's hawks, and American goshawks because they preyed on their pet homing pigeons. Migrating hawks were also shot by the hundreds for sport at fall migratory hawk passage sites like Hawk Ridge in Minnesota and Hawk Mountain in Pennsylvania.

Misguided raptor prejudices died slowly. In spring of 1977, a DNR game warden brought me a wrinkled, dirty grocery bag to verify its contents. It contained a dead broad-winged hawk and several dirty dead nestlings. He told me a cabin owner north of the Twin Cities had discovered a nest of broad-winged hawks in a tree near the end of his driveway. He was so enraged at the presence of these killer birds that he took his shotgun, a shovel, and his children out to the nest to show them how to take care of hawks. He shot the adult hawk on the nest and climbed the tree to remove the chicks. Then he buried the chicks alive with the dead adult. The children were so traumatized that they told their school teacher. The teacher contacted the local game warden about the incident, and he arrested the shooter. I verified the identity of the hawk and chicks to secure prosecution in the case.

This was a sobering lesson. Protecting and restoring habitat and passing laws to protect birds is <u>not</u> the only conservation strategy to help wildlife. Environmental education, especially among children, is a vital component of wildlife conservation, helping citizens appreciate the role that all wildlife plays in the web of life. Unfortunately, environmental education is usually one of the first programs abandoned when DNR natural resource budgets are reduced.

Also, our attitudes toward the outdoors have sometimes played heavily in favor of game species—to the detriment of both predators and prey that all play an essential role in the balance of nature. We need to reflect a balance in our DNR programs for all wildlife and all nature enthusiasts—not just game species and hunters. We also need to ensure that hunters understand the importance and relevance of maintaining that balance by using non-toxic ammunition. They annually cause the death of bald eagles, golden eagles, and other raptors because many uncaring hunters continue using lead bullets or shotshells for hunting deer and upland game birds.

Hunters need to accept responsibility for the collateral damage they have caused for decades by poisoning America's raptors with spent lead ammunition in unretrieved game. How significant is that collateral damage to eagles? I estimate that during the past fifty years the use of lead ammunition for both waterfowl hunting and deer hunting in Minnesota may have been responsible for the death of about thirty eagles per year—perhaps over a thousand bald eagles!

Another issue of concern in my early days with the Nongame Wildlife Program was the problem of raptors getting injured by open bait trap sets where a dead animal was surrounded by concealed leghold traps to catch scavenging furbearers. That was where my trapping background helped with a solution. I collaborated with The Raptor Center at the University of Minnesota, the DNR Division of Enforcement, and the Minnesota Trappers Association to address the problem. Open bait trap sets were causing hawks and bald eagles to be unintentionally trapped. They frequently lost feet or toes, or they died from their injuries. Open bait sets were most likely to catch scavenging opossums or skunks which had little fur value. They were not effective trap sets for catching more valuable furbearers like foxes or coyotes.

The University of Minnesota Raptor Center, Minnesota Trappers Association, DNR Division of Enforcement, and the Nongame Wildlife Program collaborated to write legislation to prohibit placing traps within twenty feet of bait that could be seen by soaring birds. The bill passed and is still the law. I subsequently worked with the Division of Enforcement officer Joyce Minor Cieluch to produce an educational poster that explained how open bait trap sets were mainly used by inexperienced trappers. The poster showed them how to create a trap set that would not attract raptors. It was distributed to licensed fur buyers throughout Minnesota so they could distribute them to trappers to post in their fur sheds.

Minnesota's Bald Eagles—a Conservation Success Story

Bald eagles are one of the most well-known and highly regarded birds in the United States. As the national bird, it has long represented our country as a stunning and beautiful raptor found in all forty-nine of the continental United States and in Alaska. The total population of bald eagles has recently been estimated at over 70,000 eagles in the forty-eight coterminous states and 30,000 in Alaska. The population of eagles in Minnesota could approach 30,000, so the total population for Alaska and Minnesota alone could exceed 60,000 birds.

The bald eagle has suffered from a long history of persecution due to killing by some farmers, hunters, and ranchers, pesticide pollution, lead poisoning caused by use of lead ammunition for waterfowl and deer hunting, illegal poaching for sale of their feathers, egg collection by oologists, killing for payment of bounties by some state governments, and even being declared as outlaw birds by the Minnesota legislature in 1929.

However, bald and golden eagles have survived and increased over the past sixty years. Bald eagles have even adapted to nesting in Twin Cities suburban backyards and farmstead woodlots of southwestern Minnesota. Over that time the bald eagle has assumed the Four-H category as a **High Priority** species that deserves a high level of attention for protection and management since there is still a negative element in our society comprised of some deer hunters who continue to use lead bullets for deer hunting at a time that non-toxic ammunition for deer hunting is readily available, very effective for taking deer, and sometimes cheaper than lead bullets.

Bald eagles take about four years to reach reproductive maturity. A pair of eagles will often maintain two to three potential nests within their defended territory. The pair will usually select one of those nests and begin construction or maintenance of an existing treetop nest in late summer so it will be ready for nesting by January. Two or three eggs are laid usually in February and hatch in March. The chicks are provided prey, including small- to medium-sized fish, birds, and mammals through the early summer, and they usually fledge by late June. Eagles may use the same nest for many years and add new sticks and branches to the nest annually. Some nests can weigh more than a thousand pounds. Bald eagles mate for life or until the loss of a mate. The surviving eagle will select a new mate since there are usually unmated eagles present and available in the population.

National Bald Eagle Recovery and "Minnesota Bald Eagles to Go"

Minnesota's bald eagle population had steadily recovered from a low of about 40 nesting pairs in 1963 to about 150 pairs when I was hired. Unfortunately, many eastern and southeastern states had lost all their nesting bald eagles because of the toxic effects of DDT on their nesting success. DDT affected their calcium metabolism. The eggs became too fragile to withstand the weight of the adults, and they broke during incubation. There had been efforts in those states to obtain eggs from bald eagle nests from other states and hatch them for rearing and release, but those efforts were unsuccessful.

While serving as president of the Nongame Wildlife Association of North America in the 1980s and 1990s, I was contacted by nongame wildlife biologists in other states because their previous efforts to collect eagle eggs in the wild and hatch and rear the chicks for release had failed. We considered an alternative—capturing eagle chicks in the wild that were near fledging age. They could be transplanted to other states for hacking and then released in protected habitats where they had good chances for survival. Hacking involved keeping the chicks in elevated outdoor cages in good eagle habitat where they would be fed remotely and eventually allowed to fly free. Minnesota was producing at least one hundred or more chicks annually at the time. I believed that if a few chicks, no more than five per year, were donated for restoration efforts, it would not have a detrimental impact on Minnesota's eagle recovery. There was reluctance by some Minnesota eagle biologists to provide eagles to other states for restoration, and they opposed this idea. However, I decided to proceed with donating five chicks per year from Minnesota nests to other states in need of eagle restoration efforts.

The first state to request eagle chicks was New York. Biologist Peter Nye from the New York Department of Environmental Conservation came to Minnesota in June of 1977. We collected one chick from Puposky Lake in Beltrami County. It was hacked at the Montezuma National Wildlife Refuge in New York. Seven additional chicks were captured as nestlings in 1979 and 1980 with the assistance of expert tree climber Dave Evans of Duluth, DNR wildlife manager Jim Breyen, U.S. Fish and Wildlife biologist Jim Mattson, and my eight-year-old son Craig. Dave Evans climbed white pine trees to reach nests ninety to one hundred feet high. All the chicks captured for New York were released at the Montezuma National Wildlife Refuge. One bald eagle chick transplanted to New York was hit by a car while feeding on a roadkill at the age of thirty-eight in 2015. New York biologists estimated that this eagle could have raised as many as fifty young during its life.

The author and son Craig with an eagle chick captured for translocation to New York. The chick had jumped from its nest and glided down to this perch where we picked it up.

Bald eagle chicks were also provided for restoration projects in Tennessee (fourteen) Missouri (fifteen), Arkansas (three), and Georgia (fifteen) with assistance of regional DNR nongame wildlife specialists Katie Haws, Pam Perry, Jack Mooty, and DNR wildlife specialists Janet Boe and Dave Johnson. Five chicks were contributed each year through 1988. A total of fifty-five-bald eagle chicks were provided for this national endangered species effort over a period of eleven years. The eagle populations in those states have experienced substantial recoveries with eagles that were provided from Minnesota as well as from Alaska and Wisconsin. As Roger Holmes would have said "It was the right thing to do!"

Minnesota eaglets awaiting release from their hack tower at the Montezuma National Wildlife Refuge in New York. Photo by Peter Nye, New York Department of Environmental Conservation

The most recent estimates for bald eagle populations in the states we assisted for recovery are New York (426 pairs), Missouri (502 pairs), Georgia (extirpated by 1978, now 200 pairs), Arkansas (extirpated by 1930; now eighty pairs), and Tennessee (extirpated by 1961-now 175 pairs). These states also received additional eagle chicks from other sources, but it is gratifying to know that Minnesota was able to play a significant role in helping in the recovery of our national bird for states that had lost all or nearly all their original bald eagle populations.

Early Acquisition Efforts to Protect Bald Eagle Nests

Three bald eagle nests threatened by lakeshore development were saved through acquisition by the Nongame Wildlife Program and the Reinvest in Minnesota Program in 1988 as a Wildlife Management Area (WMA). The nests were on the eastern shore of Trout Lake near Bovey. Those fortunate eagles had survived and nested throughout the DDT era and had been nesting at that lake since 1948. The Trout Lake Eagle WMA was acquired with assistance from The Nature Conservancy on August 18, 1988, at a cost of $40,000. The WMA totals fifty-nine acres and is managed as a wildlife management area with seasonal sanctuary areas posted to protect the nesting eagles. Nowadays the proliferation of bald eagles would not justify acquisition of bald eagle nesting sites, but it was a priority at the time.

How Many Bald Eagles Live in Minnesota?

The U.S. Fish and Wildlife Service did an eagle survey several years ago, but it yielded a national estimate by region, not by state. A Minnesota DNR survey tallied about 2,300 nesting pairs in 2007, and the most recent estimate was 9,800 pairs in 2017. If we assume a conservative production of one-half chick per nest annually for 9,800 pairs, that adds about 5,000 chicks per year to the population. If 1,000 out of 5,000 chicks survive to adulthood from each year-class, about 500 pairs would be added annually to that previous count. I estimate the Minnesota population would now be about 12,000 nesting pairs—24,000 eagles. If we add four year-classes each of about 1,000 subadult eagles, that adds another 5,000 to 6,000 eagles to the state count.

My exercise of "voodoo eagle math" gives an estimate of about 30,000 bald eagles in Minnesota. As much as we might like to make a statistically accurate count of bald eagles for the state, it would be too expensive. Regardless, we can simply conclude that Minnesota's eagles are thriving. At a time when funds are limited and eagles are doing well, there are other wildlife species with higher priorities needing detailed surveys, management, and recovery efforts.

Eagles Were Still being Poisoned by Hunting with Lead Ammo

The danger of lead shotgun pellets causing lead poisoning in waterfowl was documented by George Bird Grinnell, editor of *Forest and Stream* magazine, in 1894. How long does it take

Bald eagle at its nest. Minnesota can pride itself on its recent record of raptor conservation and restoration.

hunters to admit that hunting with lead ammunition poisons wildlife? In the 1940s, famous waterfowl biologist, author, and artist Albert Hochbaum initiated research projects at the Delta Waterfowl Research Station in Manitoba about waterfowl mortality related to lead poisoning. Until then, the Wildlife Management Institute (WMI) in Washington, DC had been a strong supporter of the Delta Waterfowl Research Station. However, in 1948 one of the top research station officers affiliated with the WMI threatened to shut down Delta if they proceeded to study lead poisoning in waterfowl. The WMI was pressured by the arms and ammunition industry not to allow research that would incriminate waterfowl hunters for poisoning North American waterfowl. Thankfully, Minneapolis native James Ford Bell and Canadian businessman Colonel Arthur Sullivan stepped in and saved the Delta Waterfowl Research Station, but the lead poisoning research was discontinued.

During my career I have been an avid hunter. I hunted small game on our Iowa farm at age ten and began deer hunting at twenty. I was an avid waterfowl hunter for many years at Lac qui Parle as well as in Oklahoma, Georgia, North Dakota, and Manitoba. I left lots of lead shotgun pellets and .22 caliber lead rifle bullets scattered across the countryside. They are still there, and they are still toxic.

I am not an anti-hunter, but I am a hunter and conservationist who cares about all wildlife, not just game species. I do not wish to leave a toxic footprint on the wildlands and in the wildlife that I cherish. I switched to non-toxic ammunition over forty years ago. I am still amazed—and disappointed—that there are still so many hunters in denial that lead ammunition poisons wildlife. And there are still some deer hunters who refuse to believe that lead in venison threatens their health and their families' health. Non-toxic deer hunting ammunition alternatives for rifles, shotguns, and muzzleloading firearms are now readily available and affordable.

The curse of lead poisoning in wildlife followed me throughout my DNR wildlife conservation career—from 1974 to 2018 and into my retirement. I picked up a dying bald eagle on November 14, 1974, on the Lac qui Parle Wildlife Refuge where I was working as assistant manager of the refuge. It showed the symptoms that I later realized were symptomatic of lead poisoning. It stood on a field road with wings drooping and was unable to fly. I dropped my jacket over the bird, picked it up, and I carried it back to my pickup. I placed the docile eagle on the pickup seat beside me for the ride back to the refuge headquarters. I made plans to transport it to the University of Minnesota Raptor Center the next day, but it died overnight. I was a licensed taxidermist at the time, so I mounted the eagle, and it is now displayed at the DNR central office in St. Paul.

This immature bald eagle was found dying with lead poisoning symptoms in November of 1974.

It now serves to educate people about the dangers of using lead ammunition for hunting. In 1979, four years after I found the dying eagle, I read an article in the *Journal of the American Veterinary Medical Association* about a bald eagle that had died from lead poisoning at a waterfowl refuge in Maryland. That eagle had swallowed seventy-five lead shotgun pellets. The pellets were derived from the bodies of Canada geese killed or injured by hunters or picked up and eaten by geese in fields where the birds were hunted, injured, and then scavenged by eagles.

The dying eagle I found in 1974 was the first eagle I am aware of that showed the symptoms of lead poisoning in Minnesota. I wondered if eagles at Lac qui Parle were getting lead poisoning from dead and wounded Canada geese. This was an example of where I applied the strategy of connecting the dots between reading the scientific report of lead poisoning in an eagle in Maryland and realizing that the dying bald eagle I picked up in November of 1974 was apparently the first victim of lead poisoning from Minnesota. The federally threatened eagles at Lac qui Parle could be dying from lead poisoning.

"I had an idea!" I decided to propose a research project to investigate lead poisoning in bald eagles in Minnesota. At that time the bald eagle was a federally threatened species. The implications of goose hunting with lead ammo were huge because a lawsuit could shut down goose hunting at Lac qui Parle or even statewide in Minnesota if hunting with lead ammo was responsible for poisoning federally threatened bald eagles.

There was no money available either in the Nongame Wildlife Program or in the DNR Section of Wildlife to fund this research. However, I knew federal funding might be available for this project. I went right to the top in the U.S. Fish and Wildlife Service. I called Dr. Lucille Stickel, director of the Patuxent Wildlife Research Center for the U.S. Fish and Wildlife Service in Laurel, Maryland, to discuss my questions and concerns. She was immediately interested and concerned about the implications of federally threatened bald eagles being poisoned by eating Canada geese containing toxic lead shotgun pellets used in waterfowl hunting.

I explained my familiarity with the Lac qui Parle Wildlife Refuge and its staff. I described my connections with staff at The Raptor Center at the University of Minnesota (Dr. Pat Redig and Dr. Gary Duke), the wildlife faculty at the University of Minnesota (Dr. Dan Frenzel), and my ongoing collaboration with the Midwest regional endangered species coordinator for the U.S. Fish and Wildlife Service (Jim Engel). Networking was the key to making this idea and proposal a reality.

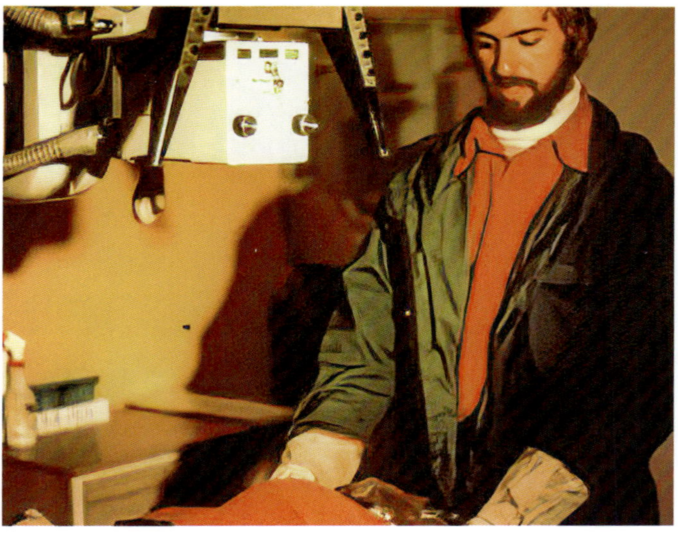

University of Minnesota graduate student Steve Hennes getting an X-ray of an eagle captured for lead analysis at the Lac qui Parle Wildlife Refuge. DNR file photo

We discussed having a University of Minnesota graduate student work under the supervision of professor Dr. Dan Frenzel. The student could live-trap eagles at the refuge to have their blood checked for lead, and they would be X-rayed for the presence of lead shotgun pellets in their digestive tracts. The student would collect regurgitated eagle pellet castings under eagle roosting trees to examine them for lead shotgun pellets. The student would also collect dead and unretrieved Canada geese on the refuge to determine the presence of lead pellets in their carcasses.

I told Dr. Stickel we could do the project for about $10,000 over two years. Within a couple weeks she approved the project and a budget of $10,580. I was very impressed by her efficiency, dedication, and quick response. She sent Dr. Oliver Pattee from the Patuxent Wildlife Research Lab to Minnesota to review the project planning among our team of researchers. University of Minnesota graduate Steve Hennes was selected to carry out the study which began in the fall of 1978. Steve caught and released twenty eagles after performing lead poisoning analysis on them. He found about 1,000 regurgitated bald eagle pellets under eagle roosting trees. About 10 percent of the pellets contained lead shot. We also assembled our researchers and Lac qui Parle staff to search for dead waterfowl after the goose season closed. We picked up 301 dead geese on the refuge in the fall of 1978.

In January of 1979, we organized a crew at the University of Minnesota and put on lead aprons as we X-rayed the dead geese. Our crew included Drs. Pat Redig and Gary Duke, Kate Durham of The Raptor Center, Steve Hennes, Young Adult Conservation Corps member Diane Vosick, and me. Twelve hours later we had shocking and unexpected results. We thought we would find lead shot that had been fired into the bodies of the geese. However, out of 301 geese, 153 geese had lead shot in their gizzards or crops. They had eaten lead shotgun pellets that had fallen to the ground in crop fields surrounding the wildlife refuge where the hunting blinds were located. They apparently misidentified the lead pellets laying on the ground as grain or grit.

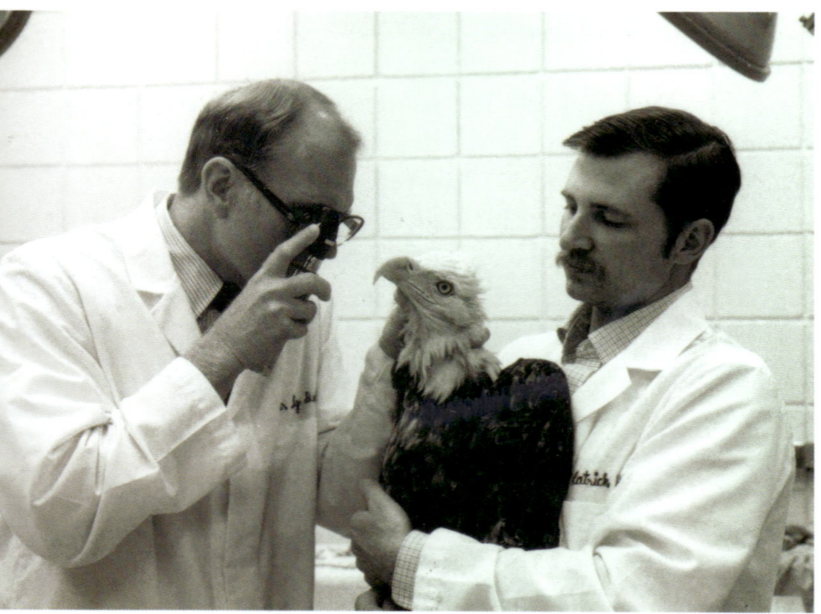

Drs. Gary Duke (left) and Pat Redig (right), co-founders of the University of Minnesota Raptor Center, checking a bald eagle for symptoms of lead poisoning.

On the following Monday I took our lab results to DNR Section of Wildlife chief Roger Holmes and told him "We have a problem! When word gets out that lead poisoning in Canada geese is impacting the survival of federally threatened bald eagles, a federal court action could close goose hunting at Lac qui Parle—or even across Minnesota."

Roger consulted with DNR commissioner Joe Alexander. After considering their alternatives, they decided to announce a pre-emptive action to impose a seven year phase-in period beginning in 1980 to require non-toxic ammunition for all waterfowl hunting in Minnesota, beginning in the fall of 1987. Additional federal funding for this project allowed University of Minnesota graduate student Fred Bengston to follow up Steve Hennes's research with another two years of research at Lac qui Parle to study and reaffirm the data and the problems posed by continuing use of toxic lead shotgun ammunition.

Bald eagles feeding on a dead deer. If the deer had been wounded with lead ammunition but not retrieved by hunters, the eagles would have been exposed to lead poisoning from bullet fragments.

The documentation developed from the research at Lac qui Parle helped convince the U.S. Department of Interior to require non-toxic ammunition for all waterfowl hunting in the United States beginning in 1991 because lead ammo was nationally causing mortality of federally threatened bald eagles. I wrote up this story for the *DNR Minnesota Volunteer* to alert Minnesota citizens to this threat to our national bird.

Dr. Pat Redig of the Raptor Center at the University of Minnesota and I assumed that the incidence of lead poisoning in bald eagles would decline with the requirement for waterfowl hunters to use non-toxic ammunition. It didn't happen. Research by Dr. Luis Cruz-Martinez, Dr. Pat Redig, and John Deen of The Raptor Center at the University of Minnesota included an analysis of 1,277 bald eagles that were admitted to The Raptor Center from January of 1996 through December of 2009. A total of 334 eagles had debilitating symptoms caused by elevated lead levels. They discovered that lead fragments in deer gut piles and from lead in deer carcasses unretrieved by hunters were the sources of this lead poisoning when eagles consumed the remains.

Some hunters claimed the lead was from sources unrelated to deer hunting. However, the incriminating factor was that there were small concentrations of copper in the blood analyses of the eagles that were derived from the copper jackets surrounding the lead bullets. Most lead poisoning occurs from two to eight weeks after the beginning of the fall firearms hunting season. There was also a smaller peak of lead poisoning when snow cover melted in the spring and exposed remaining lead-tainted gut piles and unretrieved deer carcasses.

This pivotal study validated the fact that lead bullets used for deer hunting were poisoning our national bird. The use of lead ammo continued to be defended by some national gun rights organizations and hunters who had been brainwashed by those organizations to believe that any advocacy for non-toxic ammunition would lead to guns being confiscated and the second amendment being repealed. That propaganda was a totally misguided excuse to scare the base of these organizations into donating money to them.

Human Consequences of Lead Ammunition Use

When lead ammunition is used for deer hunting, there is also a human health consequence. In 2008, a private physician in North Dakota X-rayed one hundred samples of venison that had been donated by hunters to food shelves. Most of the samples had been taken with lead ammunition. He discovered that sixty of the one hundred samples contained lead fragments. That venison was being provided to families in need of food shelf assistance! Why were public agencies, including Departments of Natural Resources, allowing citizens in need to be exposed to lead poisoning? A follow-up random sample of 238 packages of venison was analyzed from venison donated to the Minnesota food shelf. Radiographic results revealed that 32 percent of the inspected packages from Minnesota contained metal fragments—presumed to be lead. The remaining venison in those food pantries was recalled and destroyed.

In July of 2008, researchers in the Minnesota DNR Section of Wildlife responded to this issue by designing an innovative study using sheep carcasses as surrogates for deer carcasses. The fragmentation effects of traditional lead bullets and non-toxic copper ammunition were compared. The results were dramatic. When lead rifle bullets struck a sheep carcass, they shattered into 28 to 498 pieces. The fragments from lead bullets penetrated as far as forty-five centimeters (about eighteen inches) from the wound channel.

In contrast, non-toxic copper bullets shattered into only one to four fragments, and they were not toxic. Most hunters only remove a couple inches of discolored meat along the bullet wound channel. Any other toxic lead fragments deeply embedded in the venison would be consumed by hunters and their families. Why would deer hunters knowingly feed toxic, lead-tainted venison to their families? Maybe they should ask their spouse or children if they are OK with eating lead-tainted venison.

Another major step forward on this issue was an update on the benefits of using non-toxic ammunition by DNR staff writer Mike Kallok. He wrote an article for the DNR *Minnesota Volunteer* entitled "The Case for Copper" which detailed the problems with lead ammunition that poisoned bald eagles and exposed deer hunters, their spouses, and children to lead poisoning when they ate venison containing microscopic lead bullet particles. He won the First in Craft writer's conservation award from the Outdoor Writers Association of America for his article. The award was sponsored by the Pew Charitable Trust.

Welcome to the Era of Non-toxic Ammunition

Bald eagles are smart. Over the past several decades bald eagles learned to fly to sites where they heard gunfire during deer season. They were looking for the gut piles of deer that had been harvested and field-dressed. When they consume lead-tainted gut piles left in the field, they can get lead poisoning from lead bullet fragments. National and international ammunition manufacturers now make copper, bismuth, tungsten, tin and other types of non-toxic ammunition to avoid this problem.

Human Impacts of Lead on People Who are Not Deer Hunters, Especially Women and Children

The Minnesota legislature funded a program in 2010 with the Minnesota Department of Agriculture (MDA) to X-ray all venison packages donated by hunters to the state food shelf program. The MDA was required to destroy any venison packages that showed the presence of lead or metal bullet fragments. The program has been underway from 2011 through the 2024 deer hunting seasons and continues to the present. We are thankful that the Department of Agriculture has prevented Minnesota food shelf patrons from consuming lead-tainted venison.

In the fall of 2024-2025, Minnesota hunters harvested 170,544 deer, and 251 deer were donated to the state food shelf program. Those deer averaged thirty-six pounds of venison per animal. The Minnesota Department of Agriculture venison testing program determined the lead contamination rate in venison packages was 8.08 percent lead contaminated. If that contamination rate is applied to the amount of venison kept by Minnesota deer hunters, I calculated that 496,078 pounds of lead-tainted venison were eaten by deer hunters, their spouses, children, and friends after the 2024-2025 deer season. That is half a million pounds being consumed as part of our deer hunting tradition. There is a need for non-toxic ammunition to become mandatory for deer hunting because too many hunters continue to ignore the issue of feeding toxic lead-laced venison to their families.

On August 22, 2012, Lori Naumann and I organized what became the first Copper Roundtable meeting of persons concerned about this issue. Attending were Dave Orrick of the St. Paul Pioneer Press, Doug Smith of the Star Tribune, Ryan Bronson of Federal Cartridge, Dr. Pat Redig, Irene Bueno Padillo and Michelle Willette of the University of Minnesota Raptor Center, and Alex Gutierrez of the DNR Enforcement Division.

Staff from the DNR Section of Wildlife were not allowed to attend because they had been placed under a DNR Division of Wildlife mandate not to discuss issues related to lead ammunition. The mandate prevented them from discussing lead ammo and non-toxic ammo alternatives after the results of the 2008 research project on lead ammo fragmentation revealed the extensive fragmentation of lead bullet fragments into the deer muscle tissue that could affect the health of deer hunters and their families. DNR leadership had apparently been bullied by gun rights advocates to prevent any discussion of this issue. Where were their concerns about the potential impacts on deer hunter families consuming lead in their venison?

The roundtable was an encouraging success in which the participants were able to discuss what they knew about this issue and find common ground where it could be discussed publicly in an objective and professional manner. Subsequently, news stories about the lead poisoning issue and the significance and importance of non-toxic ammunition alternatives were published for the first time in the *Star Tribune*, *St. Paul Pioneer Press, Duluth News-Tribune*, and the *Grand Forks Herald.*

We were finally making progress. Wildlife program director John Moriarty at Three Rivers Parks began requiring all shotgun hunts on Three Rivers Parks property to use non-toxic ammo, beginning in fall of 2017. This was a first for Minnesota. In 2022, the U.S. Fish and Wildlife Service required non-toxic ammo for all hunting on National Wildlife Refuges in Minnesota. More progress! In the fall of 2023, DNR Commissioner Sarah Strommen required that non-toxic ammunition be used for all hunting on state Scientific and Natural Areas and for youth-mentored deer hunts in Minnesota's state parks. For the deer season of 2024, the DNR expanded the requirement for non-toxic ammunition to be used for all special deer hunts in DNR state parks as well as in Scientific and Natural Areas. Hopefully the DNR will soon expand that requirement to state Wildlife Management Areas. Increasing numbers of deer hunters are trying non-toxic ammunition for deer hunting every fall as they discover that copper/non-toxic ammo is more effective and as accurate or more accurate than lead bullets. But the rate of change is still not acceptable if Minnesotans are still eating a half million pounds of contaminated venison every year. National outdoor writers like Ron Spomer are publishing excellent articles about the effectiveness of copper/non-toxic ammunition for big game hunting both in North America and Africa.

Shooting clinics for deer hunters were sponsored by the Minnesota Chapter of The Wildlife Society. They provided dramatic evidence of the fragmentation of lead bullets when striking a deer. The bullets fracture into tiny toxic bullet fragments both in the venison and in the resulting deer gut piles that could subsequently poison eagles.

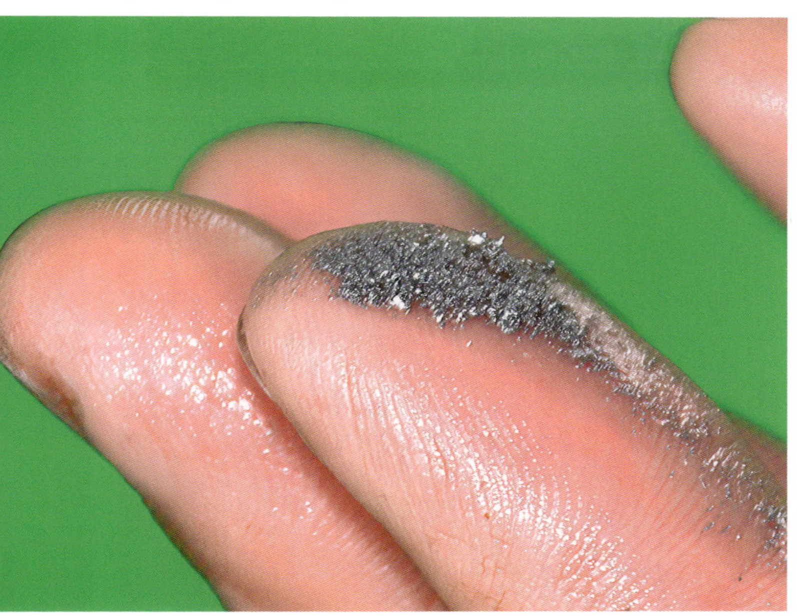

These are the microscopic lead bullet fragments that occur when a lead bullet shatters upon striking its target, like a deer. They become embedded in the venison that is consumed by the hunter and the hunter's family and in the entrails where it can be consumed by raptors like bald eagles.

A solid copper bullet does not shatter into small fragments upon impact. It is not toxic to wildlife and is not a health threat to humans.

In 2015, The Raptor Center drafted a bill for educational efforts to inform deer hunters about the problem associated with lead poisoning. Funding would be derived from the Legislative Citizens' Commission on Minnesota Resources using Environment and Natural Resources Trust Fund dollars (lottery proceeds), but it was defeated. The funding was defeated annually for six years, but the appropriation was remarkably approved in 2021 for $133,000. Dr. Juli Ponder formed a Get the Lead Out working group to develop projects and strategies for advocating use of non-toxic ammo for hunting and non-toxic small jigs and sinkers for fishing to avoid poisoning loons.

There have been substantial developments in non-toxic rifle ammunition over the past fifteen years. It does not cause secondary poisoning of raptors like bald and golden eagles. Copper bullets will typically penetrate 20 percent deeper into a deer than a lead bullet. Many hunters using non-toxic ammo report one-shot kills. While some hunters complain that the copper ammo is too expensive, a price check in October of 2023 revealed that the cost of a box of twenty copper/non-toxic bullets ranged from $39-$61. That price was comparable, and in some instances cheaper, than the cost of a box of twenty lead rifle bullets ($49-$60). A price check in fall of 2024 showed a price of approximately $1.75 to $1.90 per non-toxic shell.

When people buy guns and ammunition in the US, they pay an 11 percent federal tax. Most of that money is rebated back to state wildlife conservation departments using a formula based on the state's land area and the number of licensed hunters. This law was passed in 1937 and was named the Pittman-Robertson Act. Contrary to some claims, there is no credible information that a lead ammo ban would negatively impact Pittman-Robertson excise tax revenue funding for conservation. In 2023, more national and international ammunition manufacturers began making non-toxic copper big game hunting ammunition. Fiocchi, Sako, Remington, Norma, Winchester, and Federal all offer non-toxic big game hunting ammo.

According to the results for the North Central region of the U S for the National Survey of Hunting, Fishing, and Wildlife-Associated Recreation by the U.S. Fish and Wildlife Service in 2022, big game hunters spent an average of $1,352 a year for big game hunting in the West North Central region of the country which includes Minnesota. If a hunter uses about six copper/non-toxic bullets for a deer hunting season and if they cost about two dollars each, the total cost for ammunition for a deer season would be less than fifteen dollars. That would be just over 1 percent of the cost for all deer hunting expenditures per hunter per year.

Sadly, the continuing use of lead ammo for deer hunting paints deer hunters as uncaring polluters of our wildlands who defend the use of lead ammo for the sake of national gun rights groups who care nothing about the health of either deer hunters or their families. Hunters using lead ammo for deer hunting add more lead to our nation's outdoor environments every year—including public lands like DNR wildlife management areas, wildlife refuges, and state and national forests. The mandatory use of non-toxic ammunition for deer hunting could restore the image of hunters as conservationists who care about the health of their families and all wildlife.

Bald Eagle Webcam

In 2012, DNR Division of Ecological Services supervisor Jim Japps, Lori Naumann, and I decided that both the technology and funding were available to equip a bald eagle nest in the Twin Cities metropolitan area with a webcam. It would be a great use of that technology to allow eagle enthusiasts to watch the nesting behavior of a pair of local bald eagles laying eggs, incubating their eggs, raising their young, and to encourage donations to the Nongame Wildlife Checkoff.

Lori Naumann took over the challenge of selecting a local bald eagle nest that was accessible for installation of a webcam. She found a way to attach the camera high in the chosen nesting tree. She became a master at the complex networking needed to implement this plan. Lori obtained a federal permit for placing the camera near the eagle nest. She selected a metropolitan bald eagle nest about ninety feet high in a cottonwood tree and arranged for running electrical lines to the camera. Lori also arranged for Excel Energy to provide voluntary use of a bucket truck for attaching the camera near the nest. Mission accomplished. The Minnesota DNR Nongame EagleCam went on the air in January of 2013.

Excel energy bucket truck staff installing the EagleCam in 2012.

Bald eagle webcam of parent feeding chick. Photo courtesy of Lori Naumann, Minnesota DNR EagleCam manager.

The pair of eagles nesting in 2013 seemed young and inexperienced because they laid three eggs in January which exposed the eggs to freezing weather. The eggs did not hatch. However, the eagles garnered a huge following on the EagleCam. It became a big hit in school classrooms around the world where students enjoyed learning about eagle conservation and natural history. In 2014, the same pair of eagles returned and laid three eggs. Three chicks hatched and two survived.

Over the past eleven years bald eagles have annually occupied the EagleCam nest. The nest featured two females and four males over that time. Of twenty-seven eggs laid: twenty hatched and fifteen fledged. *Minnesota Volunteer* staff writer Keith Goetzman wrote an article in 2015 entitled "Learning on the Fly," which provided a historic overview of the bald eagle in Minnesota and promotion of the DNR's bald eagle webcam.

The EagleCam is about more than statistics. It is about the intimate opportunity to observe the day-to-day life of bald eagles as they court, mate, incubate their eggs, and raise their young. The EagleCam provides a nature study opportunity that teaches more than ever anticipated. Sometimes people learn there are not happy endings in the life of bald eagles, their eggs, or chicks. Sometimes an adult will disappear, and the parenting role must be taken over by the other parent. Sometimes the eggs freeze or break during incubation, and sometimes the chicks die on camera as happened in 2022 when a larger chick pushed its smaller nest mate out of its nest. The chick died of injuries from the fall.

In recent years, the EagleCam was updated with a newer model that takes infrared images throughout the night. People can also see the prey taken by eagles that they feed their chicks: fish, cottontail rabbits, rock pigeons, ducks, and songbirds. There is also a new microphone that allows viewers to hear the vocalizations of adults and chicks as well as bird calls near the eagle nest. There are many teachers who use the EagleCam for teaching their students about the life history and conservation of our national bird and how the eagle represents a dramatic recovery from rarity to common in our lifetime.

The EagleCam has been the most successful promotional effort ever undertaken by the Minnesota DNR. Each year the EagleCam is turned on in November and remains on until the following August. The number of webcam watchers has increased annually. When the nesting season began in 2022, the EagleCam had 341,828 viewers from all 50 states and 127 countries. The EagleCam also motivated about 33,000 people to sign up for the Nongame Wildlife Program newsletter, and there were 36,000 people following the Nongame Wildlife Program on Facebook. EagleCam viewers were shocked when a heavy, wet snow storm caused the bald eagle nest featured on the webcam to fall, killing the chicks.

The eagles have since relocated to another site near the old nest. They began rebuilding a new nest in the fall of 2023, and they resumed nesting again in 2024. Because of the inaccessibility of the new nesting tree, Lori Naumann has worked with Excel Energy to have the EagleCam camera and microphone installed at a new nesting tree with another pair of metropolitan area eagles. The new DNR Nongame Wildlife Program nesting pair premiered on November 22, 2024. The local pair of eagles, however, selected a different nest nearby and did not initiate nesting in the nest with the camera for the 2025 nesting season. However, the nest gained national news attention when a hen mallard duck took over the huge eagle nest in the treetop and laid eggs in the nest. Stay tuned for the next chapter in this continuing story of Minnesota eagles and the DNR Eagle Webcam.

The bald eagle is a stunning symbol of our country and a symbol of our determination to protect them from unnecessary threats to their survival, including lead poisoning.

Chapter 8

Minnesota's "Other Eagle"—The Golden Eagle

Golden eagle at Camp Ripley, later captured, outfitted with a transmitter, and named Kungsorn. Golden eagles have an imposing and regal appearance. Photo credit: Anthony Housey, Camp Ripley Public Affairs

When I became the DNR's Nongame Wildlife Program supervisor, the migration routes and wintering grounds of the golden eagle in the Midwest were unknown. I was determined to solve that migration mystery. As assistant manager at the Lac qui Parle Wildlife Refuge from 1974 through 1976, I saw golden eagles once or twice each winter at the refuge in western Minnesota in the company of bald eagles that preyed on dead or injured Canada geese that had been shot during the hunting season. I assumed those golden eagles had migrated eastward from western states where they were a regular breeding species.

Historically, golden eagles were highly regarded as a bird of royalty. They were considered the "king of birds." When falconry traditions were observed in Europe, golden eagles could only be possessed by kings for falconry purposes. Even now they are still used for hunting by falconers in Mongolia. Golden eagles hunt by circling high in the sky, diving at high speed and striking prey like deer or foxes.

It has taken a long time for golden eagles to be acknowledged or correctly identified as a winter resident in Minnesota. After starting my work as Nongame Wildlife Program supervisor, I was made aware of golden eagles by DNR state park naturalist Dave Palmquist. He told me they were routinely observed wintering in Whitewater State Park and adjacent Whitewater Wildlife Management Area. Where were those eagles coming from? It did not make sense that they would migrate across Minnesota from the western states to the Whitewater River valley. There were also golden eagles nesting in northeastern Canada and wintering in eastern states, but it did not make sense that those eagles would be migrating southwest to winter in Minnesota. It was a migration mystery.

Golden eagles get their name from the golden feathers, called hackles, on the back of their head and neck.

Several Canadian provinces list the golden eagle as threatened or endangered, so it seemed appropriate to learn more about this remarkable raptor even though it was not a native breeding species in the state. Adding to this mystery was confusion about accurate identification of bald eagles and golden eagles. Immature bald eagles are all brown or mottled brown for their first three years. Birders can confuse them with golden eagles. I received many calls from citizens over the years to report sightings of golden eagles, but there were usually no photos to verify the sightings, and most of them were undoubtedly immature bald eagles. When someone reported a golden eagle, many of their birding peers did not believe them. It was assumed that they had mistaken a bald eagle for a golden eagle.

I found some interesting historical information that documented golden eagles nesting in Manitoba. In the 1892 book *Bird-Nesting in North-West Canada*, noted oologist Walter Raine from Toronto commented on a visit to Winnipeg in 1891 when he was invited to travel north of Winnipeg along the Winnipeg River to collect specimens of golden eagles nesting on a cliff. Raine declined to make the trip, but the taxidermist from Winnipeg was an experienced naturalist and hunter acquainted with distinguishing bald and golden eagles.

Interesting records of wintering golden eagles also came from Fillmore County, Minnesota, where country doctor and noted naturalist Johan Hvoslef recorded twenty-eight sightings of golden eagles between 1881 and 1897. His daily journals documented birdlife from Fillmore County from 1881 through 1917. The sightings were wintering eagles seen between the dates of October 26 and April 19.

Scott Mehus, director of the National Eagle Center in Wabasha, was intrigued by the presence of golden eagles in the Whitewater Valley. He began looking for them in forested, hilly habitats and goat prairies of southeastern Minnesota and western Wisconsin. He found wintering golden eagles and initiated a volunteer survey to document the presence of wintering golden eagles in 2005. He trained volunteers to distinguish golden eagles from bald eagles and recruited over two hundred volunteers to survey eagles wintering in western Wisconsin, southeastern Minnesota, Illinois, Kentucky, and northeastern Iowa. The volunteers have counted from 62 to 145 golden eagles each January from 2018 through 2025.

On February 20 of 2008, I joined Scott Mehus of the National Eagle Center, Dr. Martell of The Raptor Center, retired University of Minnesota ornithology professor Dr. Harrison B. "Bud" Tordoff, DNR Nongame Wildlife Program raptor permits coordinator and publicist Lori Naumann, and DNR endangered species coordinator Richard Baker. We traveled to

This immature golden eagle provided a dramatic and startling appearance as it passed over us on our scouting trip with Scott Mehus on February 20, 2008.

western Wisconsin and the Wabasha area. We located several golden eagles including one immature eagle that flew right over us. Encouraged by our success, we collaborated over lunch to create the Golden Eagle Project. We had verified the presence of golden eagles wintering in the area, but we still didn't know where the eagles nested. We needed to capture golden eagles and attach satellite transmitters to identify their nesting areas, migration routes, and wintering ranges. We set a goal of capturing and outfitting six eagles with satellite transmitters.

We got a breakthrough toward solving our mystery in the fall of 2008. A coyote trapper in western Wisconsin accidentally caught a golden eagle in a trap. The injured bird was transferred to The Raptor Center at the University of Minnesota for treatment and rehabilitation. I offered to pay for satellite transmitters and the satellite data subscription service with Nongame Wildlife Program funds if the eagle survived and if we could capture more eagles. The eagle survived and could be released after rehabilitation.

This is the satellite transmitter that allowed the eagle to be tracked for up to five years.

The satellite transmitter would provide about five years of data on the eagle's travels. The radiotelemetry data yielded some amazing information on the migratory traditions of this awesome raptor. The first eagle, named "Whitey," was outfitted with transmitter #42 on March 25, 2009. It was released in western Wisconsin where it was originally trapped. The eagle, an unmated adult male, was subsequently tracked to the northern borders of Newfoundland and Labrador where it spent the summer.

National Eagle Center director Scott Mehus with our first golden eagle to be released with a satellite transmitter.

Whitey demonstrated an incredible sense of wanderlust during his life that could only be described as an odyssey. His life would make quite a novel. He returned in the fall and winters of 2009 to 2010 in Buffalo and Trempealeau counties of western Wisconsin. In spring of 2010, he followed his 2009 route up the western shore of Hudson Bay but turned around and went north along the eastern shore of Hudson Bay. He spent the summer in northwestern Quebec in a large area between Hudson Bay and Hudson Strait. In fall of 2010, he moved south where he spent the winter in Allegheny County, New York. In spring of 2011, he migrated eastward through Maine to the Gaspe Peninsula of Canada along the St. Lawrence Seaway and spent that summer in Labrador. Project biologist and migration specialist Mark Martell received Whitey's last signals as he began migrating south in the fall of 2011. This was one of the most interesting and puzzling birds of any species that Mark ever tracked.

A second eagle, an adult female, was live-trapped, outfitted with a satellite transmitter, and spent most of the following summer on the Labrador coast but died the following spring. A third eagle, #45, was caught in the winter of 2010 in Waupaca County, Wisconsin. She nested the following summer in the barren grounds of Canada and returned to Waupaca County the following winter. In spring, 2012, she traveled 1,650 miles to a nesting area north of Great Slave Lake. At last, we had discovered the previously unknown nesting grounds used by golden eagles. A fourth eagle with satellite #46 was a nonbreeder. It was trapped on January 17, 2011, near Wabasha, Minnesota. It wintered in the Whitewater Wildlife Management Area. The following spring it migrated to the Nunavut region of Canada northwest of Hudson Bay. It spent part of the summer north of the Arctic Circle on Igloolik Island.

A fifth male eagle, #53, was caught at Hawk Ridge in November of 2012 and again in 2013. It wintered in Ozark County of southern Missouri. In spring of 2013, it migrated to an area north of Lake Manitoba where it was presumed nesting. In spring of 2015, it migrated 2,482 miles from its wintering area in Minnesota back to its nesting grounds.

At a Nongame Wildlife Program staff meeting in 2014, Camp Ripley's DNR wildlife biologists Brian Dirks and Nancy Dietz mentioned that golden eagles were coming to camera trap sites focused on dead deer. The cameras had been placed to study local packs of timber wolves. I encouraged them to join the Golden Eagle Project by capturing the eagles and outfitting them with satellite transmitters.

Golden eagle named Kungsorn at the moment of release at Camp Ripley. The satellite transmitter is visible on its back. Photo credit: Anthony Housey, Camp Ripley Public Affairs

On March 11, 2015, Brian Dirks and Nancy Dietz captured an adult female golden eagle and outfitted it with transmitter #54. The eagle migrated 1,975 miles to the Northwest Territories east of Great Bear Lake in spring. Three additional eagles have been captured since then—one in 2019 and two in the winter of 2020. Those two eagles have been tracked to summering areas north and east of Lake Manitoba, and one subsequently summered primarily in the Apostle Islands area of Wisconsin. Mark Martell of Audubon Minnesota managed the data being collected by the satellite transmitters. A total of nine golden eagles were captured and monitored with satellite transmitters for this project.

We have learned much about the winter food habits of golden eagles. In fall and winter, they scavenge on deer gut piles left by hunters and on unretrieved deer carcasses resulting from the hunting season. Unfortunately, this exposes golden eagles to lead poisoning caused by lead bullets when they consume deer gut piles. The extent of mortality caused by that poisoning is not known. I was made acutely aware of this threat when DNR state park naturalist Kurt Mead contacted me about a deer hunter, Eric Husevold, who had taken a deer in Tettegouche State Park on November 9, 2014. Eric had noticed that deer gut piles from previous hunts had usually disappeared within twenty-four hours of when the deer was taken. He set up a trail camera to photograph the scavengers that showed up to devour the gut pile.

Eric was excited to share the photos he had taken with a trail camera. Two ravens showed up at the gut pile within forty-five minutes of when Eric left the site to drag his buck back to the park headquarters. A rough-legged hawk and a red-tailed hawk showed up a half-hour later. Two adult bald eagles arrived a couple hours later and then a golden eagle came to compete for the remains. The entire gut pile was gone within three hours. Sadly, a lead bullet had been used to take the deer. All those raptors and ravens, including the two bald eagles and the golden eagle, had been exposed to potential lead poisoning in the gut pile from just one deer and one bullet. Thanks to Eric for helping bring attention to this problem.

In the bluff country of southeastern Minnesota and western Wisconsin, golden eagles have benefited from the long-term increase of wild turkeys which have become a major prey item. They also prey on fox squirrels. Fox squirrels are the only mammal that can digest the toxic seeds of cockleburs, which are typically exposed above the snow cover in winter. Fox squirrels do not hibernate, and they are typically seen feeding on cockleburs exposed above the snow on sunny winter days. That is when they are vulnerable to being taken by golden eagles.

Our collaboration with the National Eagle Center has been a wonderful partnership. On September 11, 2022, I received this note from Scott Mehus, Conservation Director of the National Eagle Center in Wabasha, Minnesota:

"I fondly remember that day (2007) that you all came down to go out and look for golden eagles with me. I remember how Bud Tordoff mostly just sat there and was not too interactive until we started seeing golden eagles and we started talking about studying this population. It was like seeing a kid in a candy store, as he was so lit up and full of life, ideas, and excitement. To witness you, Mark, Bud, and everyone coming together with ideas and support was something that I will always cherish and remember!

"I am so grateful for all you were able to do to get us transmitters! Once that was started it has opened so many new doors, and we have gained so much valuable information on this species in this area and in the Eastern States. Thank you so much for your part and your support in all of this!"

He continued, "We need to be concerned about the golden eagle as it's relying on Minnesota for habitat to get them through winter. Most wildlife managers had no idea the bird was here, let alone what its habitat requirements were, but now they can share their findings to develop habitat management guidelines."

I have previously suggested that the golden eagle be listed as a special concern species by the Minnesota DNR, but some biologists responded that it was inappropriate since it was not a native breeding species. I still felt that golden eagles were deserving of a closer review of their status and hazards to survival since use of lead ammunition for deer hunting was exposing both golden and bald eagles to lead poisoning, and the extent of that poisoning is unknown.

This Golden Eagle Project has been a wonderful collaborative effort by the National Eagle Center, Audubon Minnesota, University of Minnesota Raptor Center, Minnesota Army National Guard environmental office, and the DNR Nongame Wildlife Program. This cooperation has filled in major gaps in our knowledge of the migratory patterns of the golden eagle, which until now had been a neglected raptor in Minnesota. It is an international resource to be valued, protected, and conserved both in Canada and the United States. This project has enriched our knowledge of how Minnesota is significant as an international migratory bird flyway crossroad. That flyway extends from the Arctic Circle to coastal areas of Peru and Chile, east to the rainforests and coastal areas of Brazil and Argentina, and across the United States from the Pacific Ocean to the Atlantic coast. People interested in signing up to participate in the mid-winter golden eagle count should contact scott@nationaleaglecenter.org.

Chapter 9

Monarchs, Hummingbirds, and Chickadees, Oh My!

My blue ribbon 4-H insect collection, 1963. Photo by Curtis Henderson

Wildlife conservation is not just a conservation endeavor for restoration and habitat management of threatened and endangered species. It is an opportunity to teach people how to bring joy, natural beauty, and inspiration from nature into their lives. It is an opportunity to help citizens discover nature in their own backyards and share those experiences with their family. They can observe the beauty, songs, nesting behavior, and parental care provided by birds, butterflies, bees, and other creatures through landscaping for wildlife, bird feeding, and providing nest boxes for wildlife.

Much of my appreciation for backyard wildlife was grounded in my farmland experiences as a child. In the 1950s, most Iowa farmland weed control was accomplished by cultivators, not herbicides. Farms in the 1950s were ecologically diverse. Fields of corn and soybeans were rotated with oats and nitrogen-fixing legumes like alfalfa. There were pastures, farm groves, small gardens, orchards, woodlots, grassy waterways, grassy terraces, roadside ditches with prairie grasses, and odd corners with native wildflowers, grasses, and shrubs. It was a world with surprisingly diverse birdlife, mammals, frogs, toads, turtles, and lots of butterflies, bees, moths, fireflies, grasshoppers, beetles, and other invertebrates.

I delighted in the variety of insects I observed and collected on our farm for my 4-H insect collection. I got blue ribbons for my entomology collection in 1963 at the Story County 4-H fair and the Iowa State Fair. I continued my interest in insects with undergraduate studies at Iowa State University in entomology and zoology. I carried out a National Science Foundation undergraduate research project in the summer of my junior year on the flight periodicity of *Aedes vexans* mosquitoes. I published the results of that study in my first scientific publication: Knight, K. L. and C. L. Henderson. 1967. Flight Periodicity of *Aedes vexans* in the *Journal of the Georgia Entomological Society*.

After I was selected for the DNR Nongame Wildlife Program supervisor position, my wife Ethelle and I moved to Blaine, a northern suburb of Minneapolis, where we began landscaping our backyard to attract wildlife. I wanted to attract some of the wildlife diversity I had enjoyed as a child. While trying to develop a landscaping plan for our yard, I recognized the need for a book specifically for Minnesotans about landscaping for butterflies, hummingbirds, songbirds, and other wildlife. Information about attracting pollinators was particularly lacking. This was the beginning of a ten-year odyssey for planning, writing, and publishing a book for the DNR that I would call *Landscaping for Wildlife*.

This hands-on landscaping challenge provided continuing joy for Ethelle and me with the discovery of each new butterfly, bee, and moth that appeared in our backyard. I studied what trees, shrubs, grasses, annuals, biennials, and perennial plants could be beneficial for wildlife plantings. As our plantings matured, we enjoyed, documented, and photographed visits from monarchs and other butterflies in our yard and songbirds like cedar waxwings, eastern bluebirds, tree swallows, American robins, house wrens, black-capped chickadees, brown thrashers, mourning doves, and gray catbirds.

The joy of discovering the diversity and beauty of Minnesota's pollinators can be captivating. Children are drawn to the presence of caterpillars and the chance to see their metamorphosis into adult butterflies and moths. It is a great opportunity to connect children to nature. This approach includes learning about both the host plants necessary as food for caterpillars and the nectar plants needed by adult butterflies and moths.

The monarch butterfly was an ideal poster child for promoting both pollinator conservation and the concept of landscaping for wildlife. Monarch butterflies symbolize hundreds of lesser-known bee, butterfly, and moth species that benefit from hands-on gardening experiences and larger scale habitat conservation. Gardeners, public and private agencies, and conservation organizations needed to get involved with plantings of host plants and nectar plants—not just pretty flowers that are often invasive and not native.

Adult monarch butterfly visiting a swamp milkweed blossom.

Monarch caterpillar feeding on swamp milkweed leaves.

The popularity of the monarch butterfly is legendary, but ironically, their populations have been declining for the past several decades. Their numbers are estimated to have declined eighty percent from 1999 to 2016. In the winter of 2023 to 2024 the number of monarchs wintering Mexico dropped dramatically. This is an ecological tragedy. What has happened to our ecological conscience since our observation of Earth Day in 1970?

My connections with a monarch butterfly became personal on a late summer trip back from visiting my parents in Iowa when I was writing *Landscaping for Wildlife*. Ethelle and I had stopped at an I-35 Interstate rest stop in southern Minnesota when I noticed a live monarch butterfly on the asphalt beneath the front bumper of a parked car. It appeared to have fallen from the radiator of the car. I carefully picked up the butterfly and placed it on the dashboard of our car. It had no apparent wing damage or injuries. When Ethelle and I got home I placed the monarch on the blossoms of a large *Sedum* plant by our front door. I knew *Sedum* was a popular nectar plant for monarchs during their fall migration. Every day I moved the butterfly from one blossom to another. About five days later, I checked on my patient in the morning, and it was gone…I would like to think—en route to Mexico.

I used a hybrid approach to my choice of flowers in our yard. In addition to native pollinator species, we used some nectar-producing flowers that were not native but not invasive. Some of these plants made especially good container plants for use on our deck to attract butterflies and hummingbirds. This gardening adventure began my effort to share what I learned from our gardening experiences. I did not want to write that book simply citing references from other books. I wanted to provide the best information available for Minnesotans based on our own personal experience and the gardening successes of our gardening friends.

Following is a list of plants that Ethelle and I used to attract butterflies, moths, bees, and hummingbirds: common milkweed, swamp milkweed, purple coneflower, pale purple coneflower, black-eyed Susan, columbine, butterfly plant, narrow-leaved coneflower, rough blazing-star, meadow blazing-star, northern blazing-star, and Joe-Pye-Weed.

Henderson backyard in Blaine in 1977.

Backyard photographed from the same spot in 1993.

My wife Ethelle is the gardener with the green thumb who has brought our landscape plantings to life and turned our yard into a haven for songbirds and pollinators.

Additional plants used to attract pollinators were boneset, *Monarda fistulosa*, northern blazing star, *Pentas*, showy goldenrod, aromatic aster, cardinal flower, columbine, coral bells, *Salvia* (including many cultivars for hummingbirds), cosmos, *Tithonia*, zinnas, showy goldenrod, scarlet runner bean, cardinal climber, *Fuschia*, *Phlox*, firecracker plant (*Cuphea*), *Sedum*, *Lantana*, and rosy periwinkle.

Native wildflowers attract many pollinators besides butterflies. A hummingbird clearwing moth (*Hemaris affinis*) visits a swamp milkweed blossom.

A bumblebee (*Bombus* sp.) visits a lupine blossom.

Most landscaping references from the DNR at that time informed readers how to attract game species like deer, grouse, pheasants, ducks, and geese. Plants recommended by the DNR included non-native Russian olive, Ginnala maple, Black Hills spruce, and Tatarian honeysuckle. They were exotic species, and some were even invasive. There were many ecological issues that needed to be addressed by the DNR Section of Wildlife. Invasive trees like Russian olive and Black Hills spruce were being planted on DNR wildlife management areas that had previously supported native prairie communities. I helped plant hedges of those trees and shrubs while working at Lac qui Parle from 1974 through 1976.

There were also exotic plant issues within the DNR Division of Forestry. Every year they sold wildlife packets of five hundred bare-root trees and shrubs to citizens who wished to create wildlife habitat on their land. The packets typically included ten species of fifty plants each. Some of the packets included exotic species, and some were invasive. I provided regular feedback to the forestry staff on species that would be more appropriate for future wildlife plantings, and I saw progress on the native plant composition of their wildlife tree and shrub packets. I was especially pleased to see their interest in growing native oak tree species at their state nurseries.

One year the Division of Forestry offered to buy oak acorns from citizens so they could propagate oaks at their Moose Lake nursery. The DNR Forestry Office in St. Paul was swamped with people bringing in sacks full of acorns. Then I got a call from the DNR commissioner's office. The Forestry Office had run out of funds to buy the acorns. They needed to know if I had money to help buy grocery bags of oak acorns from a single mom who had gone out with her children to raise enough money to buy groceries. I said "Sure. They can bring the bags to my office." I paid her for the acorns, and I was happy to help resolve this dilemma. However, when I came into the office the next morning the secretaries were in a panic. Hundreds of acorn maggots had emerged from the acorns that night and were crawling all over my office and surrounding office area! I had to do some immediate maggot control to get rid of the problem, but it was days before the clerical staff entered my office again.

Natural resource managers and Minnesota gardeners needed to eliminate the use of exotic invasive plants from landscape and wildlife plantings. They also needed to recognize the importance of using local-origin native plants from Minnesota instead of native plant species that originated in other states or regions where they were not adapted to the shorter growing season of a northern Minnesota climate. For example, seed from prairie grasses like switchgrass was collected in states like Kansas and sold for planting in Minnesota. The Kansas switchgrass needs a longer growing season for seeds to mature. In Minnesota, the growing season was too short for the Kansas seeds to mature and become viable. These problems resulted in the need for collecting and using seeds of local origin plants for habitat restoration efforts. Also, some supposedly native plants originated in the Midwest, but they had been exported by horticulturalists to other regions or countries to genetically alter them to create different cultivars, sizes, forms, or colors. Genetic modifications for these cultivars may have eliminated the nectar or pollen-producing qualities of the flowers, so now they had little or no appeal to pollinators. For more information on local origin native plant sources of Minnesota plants from Minnesota nurseries, go to the Minnesota DNR website and enter Minnesota DNR Native Plant Nurseries to locate nurseries that can provide local origin native plants

Another problem is that landscaping books to benefit backyard wildlife are usually written from a national perspective. Authors wrote those books to maximize their income through national sales. Many plants recommended in those books were inappropriate for Minnesota's plant hardiness zones or native plant communities. It is also important for Minnesota gardeners to realize that the US map of plant hardiness zones was modified in 2024 to show that the boundaries of those zones have shifted northward. However, this is usually just an issue if non- native exotic plants are being considered. Minnesota gardeners and wildlife enthusiasts needed a landscaping book written specifically for Minnesotans—with primary emphasis on native plants and benefits for native pollinators and songbirds. I wrote *Landscaping for Wildlife* on behalf of the DNR for the benefit of Minnesota citizens. All the royalties went to the Nongame Wildlife Program.

I also approached *Landscaping for Wildlife* from an artistic perspective. Minnesota has an abundance of artists who paint beautiful images of wildlife. I felt that even if a person is not blessed with artistic skills, their property can become a living canvas that will attract real butterflies, moths, bees, cardinals, bluebirds, and hummingbirds.

A landscaping for wildlife project usually includes four principles—providing food, water, shelter, and space for wildlife. That was not enough. I added five more guidelines: 1) include plants that provide the ecological functions provided by plants; 2) ensure that plantings provide a diversity of wildlife benefits in all four seasons; 3) arrange plants to provide protection from prevailing winds, snow drifting, and provide adequate sunlight exposure; 4) protect songbirds from unnecessary predation; And 5) utilize local-origin native plants whenever possible (exotic plants may be used if they are not invasive).

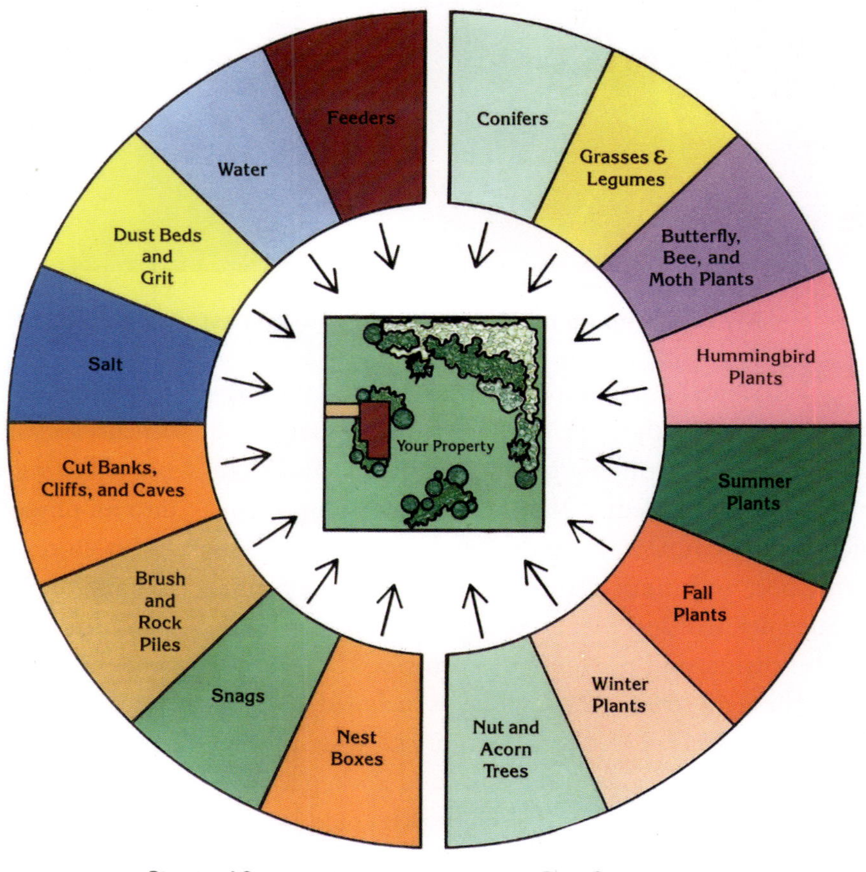

My diagram of sixteen habitat components.

My *Landscaping for Wildlife* book with an eastern bluebird providing a literary endorsement.

I designed a new model for ecological landscaping for wildlife that included sixteen habitat-based components: eight living plant components and eight structural components. The living plant components included 1. conifers, 2. grasses and legumes, 3. butterfly, bee, and moth plants, 4. hummingbird plants, 5. Summer fruiting plants, 6. Fall fruiting plants, 7. Winter plants, and 8. Nut and acorn trees.

The eight structural components included: 9. Feeders; 10. Water; 11. Dust beds and grit; 12. Salt; 13. Cut banks, cliffs, and caves; 14. Brush and rock piles; 15. Snags; and 16. Nest boxes. This approach could be used for any rural or urban wildlife habitat development plan.

Landscaping for Wildlife contained a thirty-eight-page spreadsheet in the appendix that listed eight categories for plants, grasses, sedges, trees, shrubs, vines, annuals, biennials, and perennials. Within each group the plant characteristics were lumped into three groups for their relative benefits for wildlife—excellent, good, and fair.

Writing this book morphed from a pet project into an obsession. I worked on it evenings, weekends, and even on vacation, to the exasperation of my wife. I estimate that I spent over two thousand hours researching and writing this book, mostly on my own time outside of work hours. When the book was completed, my wife Ethelle said, "If you ever do that to me again, I will divorce you!" I never did it again.

Published in 1987, *Landscaping for Wildlife* was written for urban homeowners, farmers, woodlot owners, wildlife managers, soil conservation specialists, foresters, landscape architects, horticulturalists, and nursery managers. One of the most important topics I dealt with in my landscaping for wildlife effort was the inclusion of pollinators to benefit butterflies, bees, moths, and hummingbirds. That was long before pollinators became a buzzword. The public response was amazing. I developed a slide program with my photographs to portray the joy and techniques associated with landscaping for wildlife. It was a big hit. My staff and I presented it hundreds of times over the past thirty-seven-plus years to garden clubs, bird clubs, garden centers, 4-H clubs, boy scouts, nature photographers, camera clubs, photography businesses, and conservation groups.

This ecological approach to landscaping changed a traditional backyard from a bluegrass desert treated with herbicides and insecticides to habitat supporting an ecologically diverse community of butterflies, songbirds, hummingbirds, bees, dragonflies, and other invertebrates. Among the state's well-known butterflies that have responded to these more diverse backyards are the monarch, mourning cloak, viceroy, red-spotted purple, tiger swallowtail, question mark, comma, and painted lady. Hummingbird moths and sphinx moths were also conspicuous and welcome pollinators at our backyard plantings.

A total of 90,398 copies of *Landscaping for Wildlife* have been sold. The project was embraced by gardeners and wildlife enthusiasts throughout the state. One of the most rewarding compliments I ever received came at a state bluebird conference in 1996 at a church in Marine on St. Croix. A priest attending the conference brought a well-worn copy for me to autograph. The priest told me "When it comes to helping wildlife, *Landscaping for Wildlife* is my bible." I was speechless. That comment alone helped justify the years of effort I had put into that book.

Regional Nongame Wildlife Specialist Pam Perry and the author at the Uppgaard Wildlife Management Area.

One of the other rewarding responses to the publication of *Landscaping for Wildlife* was the donation of a beautiful 110-acre natural area with forest land, marshes, and a lake in central Minnesota near Crosslake in 1988. The land was donated by conservationists Bob and Barb Uppgaard. After donating the property, Barb Uppgaard told DNR regional media rep C.B. Bylander "Rather than keep the property for our children and grandchildren, we decided to give it to everybody's children and grandchildren… We're just enlarging our family." In 1989, the *DNR Conservation Volunteer* published the story of the Uppgaard donation by author C. B. Bylander.

Hidden Pond at the Uppgaard Wildlife Management Area. A gift from Bob and Barb Uppgaard to nature lovers everywhere.

The whole donation process began when the Uppgaards contacted Pam Landers from the Minnesota Environmental Education Board. She referred them to me. After learning about the amazing biodiversity and habitats of the area, I suggested that they donate the property to the DNR for designation as a Wildlife Management Area and that the Nongame Wildlife Program then create the state's first Landscaping for Wildlife woodland habitat demonstration area. The Uppgaards needed to split their donation over a two-year period, so Don Davison of the Minnesota Chapter of The Nature Conservancy stepped in to accept the donation. They split the value of the donation over two calendar years and then transferred the land to the DNR. The land was designated as a DNR Wildlife Management Area. It was valued at $100,000, and it generated a one-to-one Reinvest in Minnesota match of another $100,000 for purchase of additional wildlife areas of benefit to Minnesota's nongame wildlife. Two bald eagle nesting sites on the pristine eastern shore of Trout Lake near Bovey were threatened by development. A portion of the Uppgaard donation RIM match ($40,000) was used to purchase that property.

Pam Perry realized that the Uppgaard area, north of Brainerd, was unique because it contained fifteen of the sixteen habitat components described in my book. There was a great variety of wildlife on the Uppgaard WMA: common loons, great blue herons, river otters, beavers, deer, wood ducks, eastern bluebirds, tree swallows, pileated woodpeckers, ruffed grouse, painted turtles, bats, hawks, and owls.

After the Uppgaard Wildlife Management Area (WMA) was designated as Minnesota's first Landscaping for Wildlife Demonstration Area, a local group of volunteers decided to develop the habitat potential of the site and designated themselves as the Grub Club. They met every Friday afternoon throughout the spring and summer for many years to provide walking trails, habitat improvement, and signage to interpret and enhance the habitat components present on the WMA.

Pam Perry and DNR wildlife technician Kevin Woizeschke coordinated improvement of the WMA with the Grub Club to teach interested citizens how they could develop their own forest and wetlands for wildlife. The Grub Club helped attract butterflies, moths, and hummingbirds by planting wildflower gardens and butterfly meadows. Other wildlife features included an osprey nesting pole and platform, a dusting bed for birds, dead trees which provided nesting cavities for birds, nest boxes, brush piles for birds and mammals, a wildlife viewing blind, and a prairie planting. Other Landscaping for Wildlife Demonstration areas were subsequently designated throughout the state at regional DNR offices and at the Brainerd Landscape Arboretum.

Barb and Bob have passed on, but their generosity and legacy continues as a wonderful example of how citizens can make a difference in promoting wildlife conservation through donations of land. Estate donations have also become an increasingly important and popular way for conservationists to designate the Minnesota DNR Nongame Wildlife Program as a beneficiary as part of their estate plans. Those donations are matched two-to-one from the Critical Habitat Matching Fund. Donations to the Nongame Checkoff are also matched two-to-one by the Reinvest in Minnesota Critical Habitat Matching Fund from conservation license plate sales. This loon license plate is one of the most popular choices of critical habitat license plate designs. This photo of a showy ladyslipper was donated by the author for use as a Reinvest in Minnesota critical habitat license plate design.

Critical Habitat Matching Program conservation license plates feature our state flower—the showy ladyslipper.

Our Minnesota state bird, the common loon, is one of the most popular conservation license plate designs.

A Minnesota pollinator in action: Milbert's tortoiseshell feeding on a purple coneflower at the Brainerd Landscape Arboretum.

A New Conservation Ally: The Pollinator Friendly Alliance

The Pollinator Friendly Alliance was created in 2016, and they are headquartered in the St. Croix River Valley. The alliance was created to respond to continuing survival problems for butterflies, moths, and bees caused by habitat loss and pesticide contamination. Their national mission is to protect pollinators, conserve the environment, help restore ecosystems, improve water quality, and to care for our planet. They sponsor an impressive annual pollinator conference which includes contributors and speakers from throughout North America and beyond. They also initiate many conservation initiatives for planting local origin native plants. For further information, contact their website at www.pollinatorfriendly.org.

Hummingbird Helper: Saving Hummingbirds from a Shocking Fate!

Ruby-throated hummingbird visiting a cardinal flower.

The smallest bird in Minnesota, hummers have remarkable powers of flight. They can fly forward, backward, up, down, and upside down as they approach flower blossoms to feed on nectar. A hummingbird will make about 1,000 flower visits daily and consume one-and-a-half to eight times its weight in nectar daily—the human equivalent of a person eating 3,500 pancakes per day. Their hearts beat about 1,200 times per minute, and their wings can beat from 50 to 200 times per second. Ruby-throated hummingbirds are the only Minnesota bird that is a pollinator.

Hummingbirds provide a joyful sight for gardeners when they arrive in early May. A pair of hummingbirds will typically raise two young annually and migrate in September. Ruby-throated hummingbirds are protected by state and federal laws.

Their annual migration takes them from Minnesota to destinations as distant as the tropical dry forests of northwestern Costa Rica. Minnesota gardeners treasure the visits of ruby-throated hummingbirds as they visit native wildflowers like beebalm, cardinal flower, Canada lily, and spotted jewelweed. They are also attracted to plantings of *Salvia*, flowering tobacco, petunias, impatiens, rosy periwinkle, cigar flower, *Lantana*, *Hosta*, and black-eyed Susan (*Thunbergia* sp.) vines.

In June of 1983, DNR regional nongame specialist Pam Perry got a call from DNR conservation officer Harris Mills about a landowner near McGregor who had discovered dead hummingbirds hanging by their feet from an electric fence wire around his horse pasture. Each hummingbird was hanging upside down adjacent to red plastic electric fence insulators called *Red Snap'rs*. The birds apparently had mistaken the red insulators for flowers, perched on the electric fence wire, and probed the insulators with their bills to seek nectar. If they touched the steel post, they were elecctrocuted. They twitched every time the current surged through their little bodies, even after they were dead.

Red Snap'r insulator with a dead hummingbird.

The black replacement version of the "Red Snap'r" that does not lure hummingbirds to their death.

I called federal migratory bird specialist Mark Shaffer in Washington, DC. He told me that the ruby-throated hummingbird was not endangered, but the species had been declining range-wide in recent years. This unusual electrocution threat was caused by a local company in Minnesota that was manufacturing millions of these insulators and marketing them internationally.

This was not just a Minnesota problem. The insulators could be killing hummingbirds throughout the United States, Canada, and even in Latin America. I was serving as president of the Nongame Wildlife Association of North America at the time, so I contacted state nongame wildlife biologists throughout the United States and inquired if there were similar problems in their states. I got responses that Anna's and Rivoli's hummingbirds were also being electrocuted in Colorado and California. The resulting national media coverage included articles in the *Miami Herald* and *New York Times*. There was immediate attention and concern expressed by U.S. Fish and Wildlife Service biologists in Washington, DC.

Many dead hummingbirds and Baltimore orioles were found electrocuted by Red Snap'rs in Missouri in the fall of 1983. It was a very dry fall there, and few red flowers were available to provide nectar for migrating hummingbirds. Instead, they were attracted to pastures with electric fences and red insulators. I contacted the company CEO and suggested that the problem could be avoided by changing the color of the insulators to a color that did not attract hummingbirds, like black.

At first, the CEO denied that the insulators were causing a problem, but after the story was reported in *Birdwatcher's Digest* magazine, the company was deluged with mail from outraged bird lovers criticizing them for killing hummingbirds. An elderly man in Ohio wrote to the company president saying that he was old and confined to a wheelchair. Watching hummingbirds come to the feeder by his picture window was the only enjoyment left in his life, and now the company was going to kill his hummingbirds. That was the point at which the CEO relented and decided to change Red Snap'rs to black by the summer of 1984. The crisis was resolved by providing a polite and thorough assessment of the problem, good communications with the company president, and application of national media savvy. I followed up by presenting the company president with an award for conservation of hummingbirds.

Chickadees and Bird Feeding

Wildlife Conservation Begins with Children Watching Chickadees at the Feeder

The Nongame Wildlife Program is well-known for its success stories associated with trumpeter swans and peregrine falcons, but an important foundation of that success story comes from understanding the bond that Minnesotans have with birds in their everyday lives—chickadees. Black-capped chickadees are not endangered and are beloved by Minnesotans. They are daily visitors at Minnesota backyard bird feeders.

Our neighbor children, Nicholas (left), Josh (center), and Haley (right) Matilla, in our front yard filling a bird feeder.

Males begin their familiar "fee-bee" song in the mid-winter doldrums of January. It is a welcome if not slightly early harbinger of spring, followed later by the chicka-dee-dee calls as the nesting season progresses. Chickadees are hardy, year-round residents that defy Minnesota's harsh winters.

Chickadee Wins Contest as Minnesota's Favorite Bird!

Early in my career with the Nongame Wildlife Program, I realized that the program must be well-balanced among efforts to help wildlife species, ranging from species like the bald eagle, peregrine falcon, and bluebird to more common and adaptable wildlife like chickadees, robins, and blue jays. I developed a contest with publicist Dorothy Molstad at the Minnesota Zoo. We asked people to send us postcards listing their three favorite birds in 1982. We received over six hundred postcards. The winner was the black-capped chickadee. The tiny chickadee beat the bald eagle, cardinal, robin, and loon.

Black-capped chickadee at a feeder.

People sent postcards and notes demonstrating the depth of their interest and passion for birds. For example, Betty and Will Snyder of Winona commented: "To choose just three birds as our favorites is mighty hard—each brings so much joy. Their colors, songs, and actions bring back memories that mean something to each of us. Our list would be: 1) the chickadee. Its friendly, happy nature without fear and its energetic movements; 2) the bluebird. It brings the promise of happy spring days and thrills with its color; and 3) the cardinal. Its song, sometimes even on a nice winter day, inspires happiness year-round and its colors give joy."

The postcard survey provided an important lesson. It resulted in a short list of the birds that Minnesotans most cared about. If we wished to appeal to the broadest spectrum of Minnesotans, we needed a program that would help threatened or endangered wildlife like the bald eagle, peregrine falcon, and trumpeter swan. But we also needed to address the desires of people to attract and enjoy wildlife in their own backyards and in their daily lives. A well-designed and balanced Nongame Wildlife Program needs to get conservationists excited about helping rare species while touching the daily lives of citizens from two to 102 years of age with the beauty, songs, and behavior of chickadees, robins, goldfinches, hummingbirds, and butterflies in their own backyards.

I published *Landscaping for Wildlife* in 1987 and *Woodworking for Wildlife* in 1991. They were wildly popular, but many species of wildlife could also be attracted by a well-planned variety of bird foods and feeders in a backyard setting. It was time to complete my trilogy of books for Minnesotans to attract wildlife by landscaping, placing nesting boxes, and maintaining feeders. Many citizens subsequently became involved in a broader spectrum of wildlife conservation activities. *Wild About Birds* became my "pet project" over the next several years, but I needed to learn more about bird feeding before I began writing the book. I needed to consult with bird feeding enthusiasts throughout Minnesota.

One of my friends at the DNR heard of my forthcoming project. He asked, "Why do we need another book about bird feeding?" I was a bit puzzled but then realized it was an excellent question. I bought many bird feeding books and reviewed them. They included bird species not found in Minnesota, and they did not have enough information about winter bird feeding or coverage of some birds that came to feeders in the state. Most authors wrote their books for a national audience because they wanted to maximize their profits or royalties from their book sales. I didn't need to worry about that. All the royalties from my DNR books went to the DNR Nongame Wildlife Program. I estimate that my books provided over $250,000 in royalties to the Nongame program over the course of my career. I had the luxury of writing my bird feeding book specifically for Minnesotans about birds in Minnesota.

In December of 1993, I developed an outline of everything to include in my new bird feeding book. It included: 1) what birds might come to Minnesota bird feeders; 2) what were the best foods to attract those birds; and 3) what were simple bird feeder designs that bird lovers and woodworking enthusiasts could make at home. I needed more information on successful bird feeding techniques for Minnesota. As I planned my schedule for 1994, I scheduled presentations with bird clubs, garden clubs, and other conservation clubs throughout Minnesota. In each case, I asked the person in charge, "Who is the best and most successful bird feeding enthusiast in your town?"

I visited over forty families that year to interview them about their favorite bird foods, best bird feeders and techniques for attracting birds, predator protection, water use, and use of brush piles. I set up my cameras on tripods and focused on their bird feeders using fifty-foot cable releases for taking photos from my hosts' homes. Since I was taking many photos of birds at feeders in winter, I encountered temperatures as low as minus twenty-five degrees. I literally wrote the book with my camera that year based on the photos taken on my travels throughout Minnesota and in my own backyard. Dave Ahlgren subsequently helped by reviewing bird feeder designs that had been provided by my bird feeder experts across the state.

As I worked on my book, I realized that bird feeding in the 1980s and '90s was changing from a winter hobby to a year-round hobby. Previously, people set out bird food in winter and discontinued feeding in spring. I initially took advantage of this problem by contacting bird food stores and manufacturers and telling them that instead of letting the seeds get moldy over the summer, I would donate them to Minnesota Department of Transportation (DOT) rest areas for use in their bird feeders and to state DNR state park naturalists who would also use them to feed birds. They responded well to this offer by providing free bird food for DOT rest areas and state parks.

However, I sensed that people were missing a great opportunity to attract colorful and beautiful birds to feeders in the spring and summer. Yellow-rumped warblers could be attracted to feeders as they migrated north in the spring. Ruby-throated hummingbirds, bluebirds, orioles, goldfinches, indigo buntings, robins, brown thrashers, downy and hairy woodpeckers, and even pileated woodpeckers could be attracted to nectar and suet feeders in the summer. Grape jelly is an important food for orioles in summer. This was important information for wild bird specialty stores that benefited from increased bird food sales in all four seasons. Another missing ingredient for bird feeding was the opportunity to provide water year-round. Dripping, splashing pools of shallow water attract birds throughout the spring and summer, and a birdbath with a heating element and thermostat brings birds throughout the winter.

I realized that I could increase the joy and delight that Minnesotans derived from bird feeding. I began learning more about the business side of it. One day I saw a stack of bird food bags at a local grocery store. They were produced by a local company named Barzen International. Several days later I was arranging to give a presentation about the Nongame Wildlife Program for the University of Minnesota student chapter of The Wildlife Society. The president was a student named Jeb Barzen. I asked him if he had any connection to Barzen International bird food. Jeb said, "Yes, my father is the CEO."

Bingo! This was an example of how serendipity can become an essential element for success in making a networking connection. I asked Jeb if I could meet his father to learn more about his bird feeding business. His father, John Barzen, graciously shared his marketing strategy. He said that high quality bird seed mixes like sunflower, peanuts, and safflower attract high quality birds like cardinals, rose-breasted grosbeaks, goldfinches, orioles, woodpeckers, and chickadees. Low quality bird seed mixes like cracked corn, bread, and red millet attract nuisance birds like house sparrows, starlings, and cowbirds. Those foods should be avoided.

DNR area wildlife manager Bob Meyer and son Ryan stocking up on sunflower seeds for the birds.

I explained that I wanted to write a book to encourage bird feeding in Minnesota. He was enthusiastic about this idea. I asked if he could help encourage donations to the Nongame Wildlife Checkoff on his company's bird food bags. He agreed. I printed rolls of stickers that his employees stuck on the company's bird food bags to promote the DNR Nongame Wildlife Checkoff.

Meanwhile, I learned that the Minnesota Department of Agriculture had an inspection fee assessed to bird food companies to cover the cost of inspecting bird seed products for noxious weed seeds. I thought perhaps a supplemental fee could be added to their fee to help promote the bird feeding industry. I decided that a fee of a penny per pound would be a modest amount. I called a meeting of major companies marketing bird food in Minnesota, and my idea did not go well. I learned that the profit margin on wild bird food was less than a penny per pound! I had much to learn about the bird feeding industry.

Jim Mallman was a commodities trader for Nature's Seasons wild bird food that was produced by American Agco in St. Paul. He was brutally frank about the idea of a mandatory fee on the sale of wild bird food. Thankfully, Jim was willing to listen to my idea of why I felt a fee was desperately needed to help with the conservation of Minnesota's wildlife while including advocacy for the wild bird feeding industry. I described the fledgling efforts of the Nongame Wildlife Program to help Minnesota's wildlife. Our program was severely underfunded and in need of supplemental funds. Jim became a major inspiration for our nongame conservation efforts relating both to advocacy for bird feeding and promotion of a national effort to pass legislation referred to as the Conservation and Reinvestment Act that would provide matching funds for nongame wildlife conservation throughout the United States.

Jim helped me craft a marketing plan for developing a strategy by which Minnesota bird food companies could enroll in a voluntary program for making tax deductible donations to the Nongame Wildlife Program. They could help wild birds by donating at a rate of $2 per ton of bird food sold in exchange for permission to use a colorful new DNR Wild Bird Food Conservation Program logo that I designed for use on their wild bird food bags. The donations could be matched with supplemental donations through the Reinvest in Minnesota Critical Habitat Matching Fund, and 10 percent of the donations would be used by the Minnesota Department of Agriculture to fund inspections of wild bird seed to ensure that the seed did not contain noxious weed seeds.

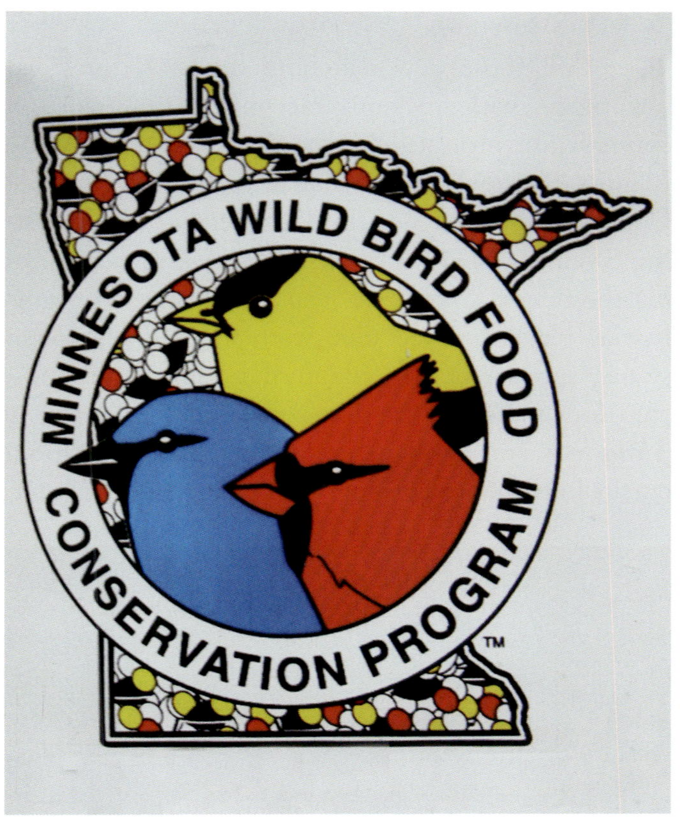

The Wild Bird Food Conservation Program logo.

The Nongame Wildlife Program agreed to promote *Wild About Birds* at book signing events at bird food stores and conduct an advertising campaign to encourage people to buy bird food carrying the new Wild Bird Food Conservation Program logo. I enrolled sixteen wild bird food manufacturers into the new program.

Our nongame operational budget was very lean in the mid-1990s, and we were urgently in need of supplemental funds. I was hopeful that the wild bird food donations would help fund nongame field operations. However, in the first year of operation, the voluntary donations from the wild bird food manufacturers totaled $6,100. It was not nearly as much as I hoped for, but "I had an idea!" I appealed to conservation groups like Wildlife Forever and The Bluebird Recovery Committee for donations to match the wild bird food manufacturer donations. They agreed. I subsequently got a match to those donations from the DNR Critical Habitat Matching Fund. Then I submitted a request to the National Fish and Wildlife

Foundation in Washington, D.C., to match the funds that had already been generated from the bird food industry and also matched by Minnesota's conservation groups. The consecutive matches were approved, and my nongame project budget ballooned tenfold from $6,100 to $60,000.

With those new matching funds, I developed a workplan with my nongame staff to fund thirteen conservation projects. We purchased the eighty acre Mentor Prairie Wildlife Management Area in Polk County, conducted a satellite telemetry study of nesting Swainson's hawks, carried out nesting surveys of red-shouldered hawks, boreal owls, northern goshawks, black-throated blue warblers, and trumpeter swans, sponsored five wild bird feeding workshops, paid for publishing the *Traveler's Guide to Wildlife in Minnesota*, and developed a Project WILD classroom curriculum about neotropical migrant birds.

These are the feeders featured in *Wild About Birds*, which I built and checked out in my backyard.

As I worked on the text for *Wild About Birds*, I wanted to ensure the woodworking instructions for the feeders were accurate, so I personally cut out and built the feeders to be portrayed in the book in my workshop. I set them up in my yard and on my deck to try them out over the next several years—twenty-six of them. I had some of the most well-fed birds in the neighborhood.

I covered sixty-eight bird species in my 1995 book *Wild About Birds, The DNR Bird Feeding Guide*. Following a book signing kickoff event sponsored by American Agco, *Wild About Birds* created such an enormous demand that I appeared at over sixty book signing events the following year at wild bird food stores, country grain elevators, bird clubs, Barnes and Noble bookstores, Audubon meetings, and nature centers throughout Minnesota. People were so excited to have a bird feeding guide specific to their own state. The book sold over 61,000 copies. On one occasion it was obvious that bird feeding provided far more than nutritional benefits for the birds. It provided people with an intangible and personal sense of joy and inspiration.

Jim Mallman and I were attending a book signing at a feed store in Mankato. A woman explained that she had purchased *Wild About Birds* and used its recommendations to buy feeders and bird food for her father who was in the final stages of Alzheimer's disease. The feeders were set up by the picture window in the living room where he could watch the birds. Even when the end was near and he was no longer able to speak, he still wanted to sit by the window. She said that every time a bird came to the feeders, he smiled.

Chapter 10

Bring Back Bluebirds, Wood Ducks, and Purple Martins

I recall how excited I was as a child when I watched house wrens raise a family in the wren house that Grandpa Holland built with my assistance in his basement workshop. I realized the same excitement was possible among children and nature lovers when they discovered the joy of attracting birds with their own homemade nest boxes. The eastern bluebird is a catalyst that could create the enthusiasm needed to help Minnesota wildlife through nest box conservation.

Nest box conservation is a science built upon understanding the needs for cavity-nesting birds that typically use tree-hole cavities as sites for laying and incubating their eggs. They subsequently leave the nest cavity soon after hatching or after extended parental care for up to several weeks. People can use their woodworking skills to create nest box boxes specific to the needs and dimensions of a particular species in need of conservation efforts, like bluebirds or wood ducks. These efforts can improve protection and fledging success of cavity-nesting birds from predators, parasites, or weather.

Citizens then need to learn what habitats are appropriate for placing nest boxes for their desired birds, what guidelines are necessary for building nest boxes, and how to build, erect, and manage nest boxes that deter predation by raccoons, house cats, hawks, owls, and snakes.

In addition to house wrens and chickadees, which respond to homemade nest boxes, the eastern bluebird is an iconic songbird that responds to well-constructed and managed nest boxes. My experiences with bluebirds taught me an important conservation lesson—bluebird enthusiasts are full of passion, boundless enthusiasm, patience, and an undying love for the bluebird of happiness. The efforts of the Nongame Wildlife Program brought joy to thousands of Minnesotans through their hands-on efforts to help bluebirds.

Male eastern bluebird at a nest box in the author's yard.

Dick Peterson and his wife Vi began attracting bluebirds with nest boxes in Sherburne County in the 1960s. Dick demonstrated childlike enthusiasm for his dedication to help bluebirds. He developed his own nest box design—the Peterson bluebird nest box. I met Dick soon after I was selected as state DNR Nongame Wildlife Program supervisor. He pleaded with me not to overlook bluebirds. He took me out on his bluebird trails, taught me techniques for attracting bluebirds, and showed me how to build a bluebird nesting box. An accomplished photographer, he took hundreds of wonderful bluebird photos that he graciously allowed me to use for creating slide programs about helping bluebirds.

Bluebird conservationist Dick Peterson with an orphaned bluebird chick he named Mabel. Dick was feeding it a mealworm. Photo donated by Dick Peterson

The charisma of bluebirds made them the **High Profile** species that could generate huge support for the Nongame Wildlife Program and help restore bluebirds. The eastern bluebird was still uncommon in Minnesota when the Nongame Wildlife Program began.

Dave Ahlgren assembling a Peterson bluebird house.

Dorene Scriven, pioneering head of the Minnesota Bluebird Recovery Committee.

I met Dave Ahlgren and his wife Jan at a bluebird workshop I presented at the Minnesota Zoo. They were volunteers at the Zoo. After my presentation, Dave and Jan expressed their interest in helping bluebirds and joined the newly formed Bluebird Recovery Committee that had been created by bluebird enthusiast Dorene Scriven. Dave was an accomplished carpenter and a pilot for Northwest Airlines. As I initiated a statewide bluebird recovery effort, I thought it would be a great idea to have the Nongame Wildlife Program sponsor six regional bluebird workshops in 1983 in cooperation with the Bluebird Recovery Committee. My regional nongame wildlife specialists would organize the workshops. I wanted a hundred bluebird nest boxes cut out and ready for assembly at each workshop—a total of six hundred Peterson nest boxes.

I called Dave and asked if he could cut out some nest boxes for bluebird workshops. He agreed. Then he asked how many. I told him six hundred. After a long silence, Dave said fine. We carried out eight workshops across the state from January through March for 458 participants. The workshops provided a statewide launching pad for promoting bluebird conservation. One memorable workshop occurred in Hutchinson where famed wildlife artist Les Kouba attended the workshop and encouraged the parents and children to become active in helping Minnesota's wildlife.

Dorene Scriven inspired me with her dedication to helping bluebirds. She was the catalyst who organized the Bluebird Recovery Committee in Minnesota. She was the driving force who organized their annual bluebird conference and published annual reports about the success experienced by the state's bluebird volunteers. She was so successful that she also motivated bluebird volunteers from Wisconsin, Iowa, and Nebraska. She wrote three excellent books on how to manage bluebird trails.

One of my first projects for helping bluebirds was to update an outdated eight-page DNR pamphlet, "Birdhouses in Minnesota" in 1979. This was the kind of **Hands-On** involvement that I was seeking to connect Minnesota's nature-loving citizens who loved woodworking and the satisfaction of helping birds. I asked Dave Ahlgren to review the designs in *Birdhouses in Minnesota.* He didn't like them. He said they looked like they had been designed by biologists. He suggested getting rid of angled cuts and converting the designs into simple, one-board designs whenever possible.

Conversely, I also realized that other nest box designs were too complicated for beginners because they had been designed by accomplished woodworkers with expensive equipment. The response to the pamphlet update was great. It encouraged me to embark on a more comprehensive book on nest boxes. I began reviewing books about building birdhouses, but they were generally inadequate. They had designs that could become death traps for the birds if they did not have appropriate predator guards for protection from raccoons and cats. The old tendency to put nest boxes on fence posts and trees attracted predators like house cats and raccoons. Newer recommendations included placing nest boxes for purple martins on predator-proof posts in water or placing large, inverted cones under nesting structures for bluebirds and wood ducks to prevent access by cats or raccoons.

Many books were written for national audiences that had nest box designs for species that did not occur in Minnesota. The books lacked information on monitoring practices, or they lacked explanations of what habitats were appropriate for benefiting the target species.

There was a need for a book for Minnesota citizens to benefit Minnesota wildlife. I sought expert naturalists and carpenters who I felt were the best authorities in the nation for nest boxes that would benefit each of the species I selected. *Woodworking for Wildlife* was published in 1984. It contained forty-eight pages detailing how to attract forty-three species of Minnesota wildlife. The DNR printed fifty thousand copies and distributed them free of charge by using donations to the Nongame Wildlife Checkoff. The book was a hit. It became an essential reference for wildlife enthusiasts across Minnesota.

***Woodworking for Wildlife* nest box parts with an impatient bluebird waiting for me to finish the box.**

The personal responses I got for my book were beyond heartwarming. One night I was giving a presentation to a 4-H club on how to build one-board bluebird nest boxes. I called on a girl who was about ten years old to help me. I coached her as she cut each of the lines on the board with my reciprocating saber saw. She drilled pilot holes for the wood screws and cut out the entrance hole. With an electric drill, she used deck screws to assemble the bird house. She completed the nest box within fifteen minutes. She shyly held up the nest box, and the 4-H parents in attendance applauded as I gave her the nest box to take home. After the meeting, one of the 4-H moms came up to me and said, "Do you know what you just did?" Puzzled, I responded, "No. What do you mean?" She said, "The girl who made the bird house has attention deficit disorder. You just made her look great among her friends!"

In 1994, I sent free copies of *Woodworking for Wildlife* to all the industrial arts teachers in Minnesota's schools. I subsequently got this letter from Helen Olson, Special Education Teacher from Princeton Junior High School in Princeton, Minnesota. "Mr. Thestrum, our industrial arts instructor, set up the building project, and once a week for eight weeks we went down to make the bluebird houses. It was an excellent project for our ten Educable Mentally Handicapped Students."

Creating a bluebird trail was also the ideal 4-H project for my son Craig. We selected the Bunker Hills Archery Range near our home for the bluebird trail. It was a perfect bluebird habitat—oak savanna with scattered burr oaks. With two dozen bluebird houses placed about one hundred yards apart, Craig's nest boxes produced an average of ten broods and thirty-eight chicks per year. After Craig graduated from high school, I took over the bluebird trail. Over the fifteen years that Craig and I managed those bluebird houses we raised 551 bluebirds. It was a wonderful and enormously satisfying conservation project.

One of the most interesting aspects of this effort was that nest box specifications provided by nest box experts from throughout the nation were being continuously improved. Management techniques were also dynamic. I kept up with these changes and wrote a revised 112-page second edition in 1992 to benefit forty-seven wildlife species. Then I wrote a third edition that was published in 2009. *Woodworking for Wildlife* sold 97,420 copies through Minnesota's Bookstore in addition to 50,000 copies of the 1984 edition that were distributed free—a total of 147,420 books. It was the most successful book ever published by the Minnesota DNR.

The collective enthusiasm and efforts of the Minnesota Bluebird Recovery Committee created a multiplier effect that spread widely to promote bluebirds and other wildlife. It increased awareness and statewide support for the Nongame Wildlife Program. In 1983, 233 volunteers reported they had fledged 2,968 bluebirds. From 1986 through 2000, approximately 400 to 500 people per year reported about 15,500 chicks fledging per year. Over a twenty-year period, over three hundred thousand bluebirds were fledged by these citizen volunteers. The Bluebird Recovery Committee also sponsored an annual conference to recruit new bluebird enthusiasts and teach them the basics of how to create and manage their own bluebird trail. The efforts of the Bluebird Recovery Committee continue to the present. According to the long-term results of the federal Breeding Bird Survey from 1979 through 2019, eastern bluebird populations in Minnesota have increased an average of about 1.3 percent annually during that period, and the statewide population estimate approximately doubled since those surveys began.

John Thompson, Bud Grant, and the author discussing bluebird conservation at the Minnesota Vikings practice facility.

We got another boost for promoting bluebirds when local bluebird enthusiast John Thompson contacted the Minnesota Vikings and encouraged them to put some bluebird nest boxes on their training facility in Eden Prairie. Bud Grant was already feeding deer on the facility, and he was sincerely interested in all kinds of wildlife, including bluebirds. John got permission from Bud to place bluebird nest boxes around the Vikings practice field. I subsequently visited with John and Bud to talk about bluebirds at the Vikings headquarters after I had previously met Bud when he was on a fishing trip in Costa Rica. He was excited to help bluebirds, and he also agreed to do a television public service announcement for the DNR, encouraging Minnesotans to donate to the Nongame Wildlife Checkoff on their state tax forms.

A clutch of five bluebird eggs in my backyard.

The last of five chicks ready to fledge from our backyard bluebird nest.

When giving presentations about bluebirds, I usually told people not to expect bluebirds to nest in their yards. Then in 1991, a pair of bluebirds made a liar of me. They nested in a Peterson bluebird nest box in our backyard in Blaine. The male showed up on May 25, and the pair began building their nest two days later. The first beautiful blue egg was laid on May 31, and the fifth egg was laid on June 4. Incubation began on June 6, and on June 19 the first three eggs hatched. Four chicks fledged on July 6, and the last chick fledged a day later. Every day was a backyard adventure that summer as Ethelle, Craig, and I enjoyed the enchanting beauty and songs of the bluebirds and watching the fluffy little chicks as they grew.

They became amazingly tolerant after they learned I would place live mealworms in small trays near their nest. The male even posed for me when I placed mealworms on my hammer and birdhouse boards for the cover photo of the 1992 *Woodworking for Wildlife* book. Local TV stations visited my backyard to photograph the bluebirds while I promoted the value of helping bluebirds and supporting the Nongame Wildlife Checkoff.

What do a 4-H shooting sports class, wood ducks, a timely complaint, and the Nongame Wildlife Program have in common? Millions of dollars, that's what.

My son Craig grew up with my wife Ethelle and me in a farmhouse on the Lac qui Parle Wildlife Refuge. He grew up surrounded by wildlife and helped each year releasing wood ducks, mallards, and Canada geese that we banded on the refuge. After we moved to Blaine, Minnesota, he became active with Anoka County 4-H activities in 1982. He later joined their 4-H Shooting Sports program. He took classes in archery and the use of a pellet pistol. With my background in wildlife biology and management, it was an opportunity for me to become an assistant instructor for shooting sports youths at classes that were held at the nearby Bunker Hills Archery facility.

There was another instructor with whom I felt an immediate bond of common interest in wildlife and hunting—Bill Stevens. Bill was the Federal Cartridge national marketing representative and premium ammunition manager. His job included promotion of hunting, shooting sports, and natural resource conservation. He helped pioneer the 4-H Shooting Sports Program and was instrumental in promoting conservation at Federal Cartridge. Bill's son, Andrew, was the same age as Craig, and he was also enrolled in the Anoka 4-H Shooting Sports Program. Bill and I served as instructors for several years for the Anoka County Shooting Sports Program. We spent many enjoyable evenings with our sons and with Anoka County 4-Hers teaching them gun safety, archery techniques, use of a pellet pistol, and wildlife conservation concepts like how to build wood duck nest boxes.

In 1990, Bill was selected to serve on Governor Rudy Perpich's Blue-Ribbon Committee for the Reinvest in Minnesota (RIM) program to improve wildlife conservation funding in Minnesota. At one of our 4-H Shooting Sports sessions, I was lamenting the problem that funds coming from hunters, like hunting license revenue, waterfowl stamps, and pheasant stamps, were matched three-to-one from Pittman-Robertson federal taxes for game conservation in Minnesota. However, when Minnesota citizens donated money to the Nongame Wildlife Checkoff on their tax forms, none of that money was matched.

Bill responded by saying, "I can take care of that! I have a Blue-Ribbon Committee meeting coming up." A few days later, he told me the Blue-Ribbon Committee had approved matching the donations of land or money to the DNR Nongame Wildlife Program, including donations to the Nongame Wildlife Checkoff and estate donations. They would be matched equally from the Reinvest in Minnesota Program. Funding would also eventually come from the sale of RIM Conservation License Plates. They would match checkoff donations by over one million dollars per year. In 2022, the Minnesota legislature approved increasing the RIM match to the Nongame Wildlife Fund to two-to-one. Donations from Minnesota citizens and the RIM match now total over three million dollars per year! Bill's creative idea resulted in millions of dollars for conservation of habitat and nongame wildlife across Minnesota over the past thirty-plus years. Thank you, Bill.

One evening at our 4-H Shooting Sports program I gave a presentation about wood ducks and then the 4-Hers worked in pairs to assemble wood duck nest boxes. After Craig and his buddy Jeff Stedman had completed their nest box, I contacted legendary waterfowl biologist Art Hawkins to learn if he had a place to put the nest box at Lake Amelia on his property near Hugo. Art was internationally known as a waterfowl and wood duck expert. He eagerly agreed. We met at his home and put up the box with Art. He kept meticulous records for Craig and Jeff's nest box. The nest box produced broods of wood ducks for the next twenty years. That single nest box produced over two hundred wood duck ducklings!

Wood duck expert Art Hawkins with Craig Henderson and Jeff Stedman ready to put up their wood duck box with Art.

Meet the All-American Wood Duck

Drake wood duck in spring plumage.

I believe the wood duck is the most stunning and beautiful of all American waterfowl. The iridescent plumage of the drake woody is a living work of art. The elegant greenish, bluish, and purplish crest of the drake is highlighted by white streaks and a brightly marked red, black, and white bill. The drake's body features stunning iridescence, streaks, and spots. The hen woody also has intricate plumage designs featuring more subdued tones of brown and gray as well as iridescent blues and purples.

The wood duck is a uniquely North American species except for a few woodies that nest in western Cuba. Like common goldeneyes, hooded mergansers, and buffleheads, they nest in tree cavities instead of on the ground or over water in marshes like most other ducks. Their primary habitat was originally in forested regions of the eastern half of the United States in habitats associated with rivers, lakes, forested swamps, and beaver ponds. Preferred foods include wild fruits, berries, and acorns. The tails of wood ducks are longer than those of most dabbling ducks because they live in forested habitat. The longer tails provide greater agility in flight to maneuver among the trees to reach their preferred nesting cavity entrances and perches. Wood ducks may be considered a game bird by waterfowl hunters, but the woody has many enthusiastic advocates including youths, nature photographers, and nature lovers who have no interest in hunting them. They appreciate the beauty of the ducks and the opportunity to help them overcome a lack of nesting cavities when they return to Minnesota in the spring.

Wood ducks nest in Minnesota and migrate to southeastern states in winter. One of the most interesting features of their migratory behavior is that hen wood ducks find their mates on their wintering grounds. The hens then return the following spring with their mates to the areas where they hatched. Providing wood duck nest boxes helps enhance wood duck populations since the females will return to their natal grounds and look for additional nesting sites and nest boxes in the area.

Wood ducks have a long history of both ornithological interest and severe overhunting by people who wrote about woodies and those who hunted woodies year-round in the 1800s and early 1900s. It was an era of rampant wildlife exploitation. There were no seasons closed to hunting and no bag limits. Wood ducks were hunted for their meat and their feathers. Trout anglers used their feathers for tying light and dark Cahill flies and Quill Gordon flies. They would pay three to four dollars for a prime drake wood duck skin. Wing feathers were used for salmon flies. In 1918, a closed season was declared on wood ducks throughout the United States and Canada. The overharvesting of mature eastern hardwood forests and over-trapping of beavers caused a reduction in beaver pond habitats used by nesting woodies. Those were also likely reasons contributing to the continental decline in wood duck populations.

Unfortunately, the exploitive attitude of some hunters toward wood ducks has not improved since the early 1900s. When I was a grad student at the University of Georgia, I hunted woodies several times in beaver ponds near Athens. On one occasion I went out with my hunting partner Dick Bailey from the University of Georgia Institute of Ecology on a late fall morning in 1972. We went to a wooded swamp hoping to bag some wood ducks. The pond was strangely quiet. I heard no wood duck howeeking calls as the sun rose. The woodies were gone. Someone had hunted there late the previous evening and shot wood ducks until it was too dark to see where they had fallen. Freshly shot woodies in stunning plumage were floating lifeless in the water around us. We picked up our bag limit of two dead wood ducks each and left the silent swamp without firing a shot.

The passage of the Migratory Bird Treaty Act in 1918 played a significant role in stopping the demise of this marvelous species. Until then, ornithologists believed the wood duck was destined for extinction. Following passage of the Migratory

Bird Treaty Act, the wood duck became protected in the United States and Canada until 1941. Wood ducks responded well to those twenty-three years of protection. Fifteen states opened a season for wood ducks in 1941 and allowed a daily bag limit of one wood duck. The seasons were expanded nationwide in 1942.

Nest Box Conservation

The era of the 1940s coincided with experimentation to develop nest boxes for wood ducks. Concerned waterfowl hunters and waterfowl biologists came to the rescue of wood ducks by advocating their protection. They began building nest boxes that simulated tree cavities that the ducks used for nesting. Experimentation with wood duck nest box design and management extends back at least eighty years. Nest boxes were initially built with one-inch by twelve-inch lumber and nailed high on tree trunks. Those nest boxes were hard to open and check because they opened at the top and required climbing a couple extra feet higher on a ladder, placing the person checking the box in danger of falling ten or twenty feet or more. When nest boxes were nailed to a tree, the box would eventually fall to the ground as the tree grew beyond the head of the anchor nail. Also, nest boxes were frequently taken over by raccoons, squirrels, or starlings.

The nesting ecology of wood ducks has long held the attention and fascination of waterfowl enthusiasts. Hen wood ducks pluck down from their breasts to line their nests. Wood duck eggs hatch after twenty-eight to thirty-one days. They typically lay ten to fifteen eggs in a clutch, but sometimes other hen wood ducks, hooded mergansers, and even common goldeneyes lay eggs in a wood duck nest. Some nests may ultimately contain over thirty eggs. This is called dump nesting.

Some naturalists once thought the newly hatched ducklings left their nest cavity by riding to the ground on the back of the hen. Not true. About a day after hatching, the hen flies to the ground below the nest in the morning and calls to the ducklings, including ducklings of other species that have also hatched. They climb up to the entrance of their nest cavity or nest box and leap to the ground to join the hen. Then they begin a hazardous journey with the hen to a nearby wetland.

A hen woody with her newly hatched brood of ten ducklings on Eagle Lake near Crosslake, Minnesota.

This hen wood duck is accompanied by a hooded merganser duckling. A hen hooded merganser had apparently laid eggs in her nest, and this hen was only successful in hatching one hooded merganser duckling.

I helped with wood duck nest box management during my three years at the Lac qui Parle Wildlife Refuge by managing wood duck nest boxes each spring. That job did not come without some excitement. On one spring day I came upon a nest box about nine feet above the ground on the trunk of a large tree. The roof was missing, and I did not have a ladder. Tom Gilbertson, a tall, husky refuge technician, was assisting me. He offered to lift me so I could stand on his shoulders to check the nest box. Once on his shoulders, I peered into the top of the nest box and found myself nose-to-nose with a very large and surprised raccoon that had been sleeping. I yelled and slid down Tom's back.

New DNR Research Revelations—Aspen Forest Conservation for Wood Ducks

While there is an impressive amount of effort spent to help wood ducks through building and managing nest boxes for them, there is another important dimension to their management and survival—managing forests that will provide older trees that have cavities accessible for cavity nesters like wood ducks. DNR wildlife researchers from Bemidji, Jim Berdeen and Ed Zlonis, are doing pioneering telemetry research on the nesting ecology of wood ducks in northern Minnesota forests.

The research is not yet completed, but there have already been significant revelations. Nests have been found from ten to sixty feet above ground, usually in the vicinity of forested wetlands. The trees primarily utilized for nesting were bigtooth and quaking aspen. Wood ducks rely on other wildlife species to create nesting cavities since they cannot create a nest cavity on their own. Unused nest cavities originally created by pileated woodpeckers in older aspen trees are preferred by wood ducks, and researchers have found virtually no use of nest boxes in their study area. The diameter of the entrance holes created by the pileated woodpeckers is an ideal size to accommodate wood ducks to the exclusion of larger nest predators like raccoons or fishers.

Stay tuned for further information from the DNR Wetland Wildlife Research Group researchers Jim Berdeen and Ed Zlonis for their final reports on this very significant study. Forest management planners will need to pay much closer attention and give a higher priority to managing and preserving older growth aspen sites for the benefit of wood ducks, pileated woodpeckers, and other wildlife like forest bats and nesting owls.

Over the past fifty years, Minnesota has had a dedicated core of wood duck enthusiasts. They created The Wood Duck Society. It mirrored the dedicated enthusiasm of the Bluebird Recovery Committee. Their website is www.woodducksociety.com. They have an annual meeting every spring in the northern Twin Cities metro area and have a newsletter called the "Wood Duck Newsgram."

When I began working on the best plans and advice for wood duck nest box construction and management in *Woodworking for Wildlife*, I had the benefit of five of the nation's top wood duck experts. Art Hawkins was a retired Mississippi Flyway Waterfowl Biologist for the U.S. Fish and Wildlife Service. He was a former grad student of famed ecologist Aldo Leopold. Art maintained many wood duck nest boxes on his Lake Amelia property near Hugo, Minnesota. Another wood duck expert was Lyle Bradley from Anoka. Lyle had a knack for raising wood ducks. He had a marsh abutting his backyard that connected with the Rum River. Early in the spring, dozens of wood ducks gathered on his lawn to eat shelled corn that he scattered for them. The ducks spent the early morning hours inspecting the wood duck boxes in trees around his yard.

Wood duck expert Roger Strand checking a wood duck nest box.

Roger Strand, from New London, was another inspiration for helping wood ducks. Instead of using nest boxes in trees, he placed nest boxes on used, surplus, eight-foot Department of Transportation highway signposts driven into the ground, usually along the shoreline of a lake, marsh, or river. The nesting post was outfitted with an inverted cone-shaped predator guard under the box. Raccoons could not raid the nest box, and the boxes could be safely checked from the ground by opening the side of the nest box. This design was easy to check with children because parents could hold their kids up to an open nest box, and the kids could see the eggs. Checking the nest box does not cause the woodies to abandon the nest. Roger made a big difference in improving wood duck nest box success and management. Don "the Duckman" Helmeke was another inspiration for me. He came up with a lighter weight nest box design using one-by-ten-inch lumber that was the basis for the updated design in the 2009 edition of *Woodworking for Wildlife*.

Native American students at the Windom Spanish Immersion School building a wood duck nest box.

Nest boxes for wood ducks have had an incidental benefit to other cavity-nesting waterfowl such as hooded mergansers, common goldeneyes, and buffleheads. Hooded mergansers have adapted to using wood duck nest boxes. In northern Minnesota common goldeneyes frequently use nest boxes intended for wood ducks. Buffleheads were once rare as a nesting species in northwestern Minnesota, but they have become more common as nesters in that region. I believe this happened when they began using wood duck nest boxes that were placed at the Agassiz National Wildlife Refuge.

Walter Breckenridge Teaches Me to "Talk to the Ducks"

Dr. Walter Breckenridge, my mentor, avid birder, ecologist, an inspiration for me, and an expert on wood ducks.

A friend of mine, Dr. Walter Breckenridge, once told me that when he checked the wood duck nest box in his backyard in Brooklyn Park, Minnesota, he would begin talking to the hen wood duck in a calm gentle voice as he ascended the ladder. When he opened the side door to the nest box, he could reach in, gently lift the hen, and count the eggs. He then gently lowered the duck onto her eggs and closed the box, still talking to the duck. Breck said wood ducks can live a long time, and he was sure the hen knew his voice. He also told me a predator never talks to its prey before it kills it, so the duck knew he meant her no harm.

Federal breeding bird surveys have shown that wood duck counts in Minnesota have approximately doubled between 1966 and 2023. Their population in Minnesota has shown an increase of about 1.4 percent per year over the past fifty-seven years. This is a cumulative increase of about 50 percent for wood ducks over that period. At least some of this increase can be attributed to the efforts of conservationists who provided nest boxes for woodies. It is also likely that a recovery in the state's beaver population has also helped with woody recovery since beaver ponds create ideal wood duck habitat. However, we still need more people to spend more time putting up nest boxes and "talking to the ducks" every spring.

Modern video technology has added another element of enjoyment for monitoring and watching the nesting activities in a wood duck nest box. A birdhouse spy cam can be attached to the inner roof of a wood duck nest box and provide live video to watch the progress of incubation in wood duck nests (birdhousespycam.com). It costs about one hundred dollars for the camera, and there are additional features for using this spy cam, either with cables connected to a television indoors, or it is also possible to get a wireless connection for the camera.

Purple Martins: Our Vanishing Swallow

The popularity of the purple martin goes far back into American history. Arthur Cleveland Bent had this to say about purple martins: "Even before the white man came to America's shores it was a dooryard bird in Indian villages... It is beyond all doubt the "bird-box" species of this country... Young and old admire it, encourage it, and protect it, and those who have a word of criticism for it are few and far between."

Native Americans on the east coast would trim saplings around their dwellings for placing gourds that they hollowed out for the martins to nest in. They also erected poles with crossbars for hanging the nesting gourds. They apparently enjoyed the presence of the martin families as much as modern-day lakeshore owners enjoy viewing the martins' family life.

The earliest records of purple martins in Minnesota were in northern areas where they nested in bro-

Purple martin male with dragonfly.

ken tree stubs, woodpecker holes, crannies in cliffs, and among the boulders of Spirit and Hennepin Islands in Mille Lacs Lake. They nested among those boulders in 1886, 1915, and in 1930 when there were three hundred pairs of martins nesting on Spirit Island and fifty pairs on Hennepin Island. Those boulder-strewn islands currently provide nesting habitat for double-crested cormorants and common terns. Now martins depend almost entirely on nesting boxes provided by homeowners who attract them either to plastic, gourd-shaped nests or to apartment-style nest boxes high on poles in backyards, lakeshores, over water near lakeshores, and on public parklands near water.

Purple martins are the largest member of the swallow family in Minnesota. About seven to eight inches long, the adult males are iridescent purplish black. The females have a purplish back, wings, and tail, but their breast and forehead are pale-grayish white.

The primary foods of purple martins are dragonflies and damselflies. Other insects caught on the wing include beetles, flies, butterflies, moths, wasps, bees, cicadas, and mayflies. Grasshoppers, crickets, and spiders may also be taken by martins foraging on the ground. Martins are often given credit for eating lots of mosquitoes. But mosquitoes do not comprise a significant portion of their diet. Dragonflies eat lots of mosquitoes and ironically dragonflies are a major component of the martin's diet. However, martins are not considered a serious threat to the mosquito control provided by dragonflies.

The Minnesota Breeding Bird Atlas Program, from 2009 through 2013, provided excellent documentation of purple martin colonies in Minnesota. They are found primarily in the lake country of central Minnesota. There are scattered colonies in southern Minnesota and in northwestern Minnesota.

Purple martins have long been associated with lakeshore homes and lifestyles since they forage for insects over meadows or over open water along lakeshores, ponds, and marshes. They are an enjoyable backyard neighbor that can provide hours of entertainment for homeowners who love to watch the aerial acrobatics of martins as they catch insects on the wing and return to their martin house to feed their young. Male martins are also famous for the spring serenades of their dawn song. After male purple martins have returned from Brazil to their colony in the spring and mated with the females, they begin morning serenades with their dawn song.

Every morning before sunrise they fly above their martin house with loud singing to attract migrating subadult martins to join the colony. Subadult martins that join the colony help ensure the long-term preservation and genetic diversity of the colony. Adult males mate with the migrant subadult females, and that increases production of young at the colony. Purple martin "landlords" have learned to play commercially available recordings of the dawn song to attract more martins to an existing colony and to start new colonies where they have placed new martin houses.

Helping purple martins has been a golden opportunity for our regional nongame wildlife biologists and their technicians to encourage purple martin conservation in collaboration with Minnesota's Purple Martin Working Group.

Kelly Applegate of the Mille Lacs Band of Ojibwe Wildlife Program was so inspired by purple martins that he formed the Purple Martin Working Group (PMWG) of Minnesota in collaboration with the National Purple Martin Conservation Association, U.S. Fish & Wildlife Service, Minnesota DNR Nongame Wildlife Program, Audubon Minnesota, and Minnesota Ornithologists' Union. Pam Perry and Kevin Woischeske of the DNR Nongame Wildlife Program in Brainerd and I served as members of the PMWG.

The PMWG was one of the most dynamic conservation groups I knew in my work at the DNR. They brought together a very special innovative and technologically creative grass roots conservation effort. Kelly Applegate was an inspiration and catalyst who captured the energy of this talented group of volunteers. They met every challenge for studying the life cycle, migration, staging, and wintering location mysteries surrounding this bird that was widely enjoyed and popular but poorly understood. His PMWG team included Larry Leonard, Dick Doll, Lee Bakewell, Mike North, and Tony Lau. Other team members included Mark Newstrom, Roger Everhart, Amber Burnette, Brian Hiller, Cathy Henry, Bridget Stutchbury, and Kevin Fraser.

This team brought together a mix of talent for remote photography, fundraising, weather radar expertise, data management, geolocator expertise, radio transmitter experience, banding experience, scientific perspective, and web page management. Additional volunteers served as meticulous colony managers, including Dr. Bill Faber, Jennifer Lust, Don Wilkins, Ray Sieben, Daryl Lindstrom, Ron Seekamp, Jerry Nelson,

Purple martin project leaders Pam Perry, Kelly Applegate, and Mike North, left to right.

Peggy Boike, Paul Schulte, and Randy Frederickson.

When this effort began, there were many unknowns about Minnesota's purple martins. Little was known about their status, distribution, movements, migration, and wintering sites. There were questions about the proper techniques for management of purple martin colonies and martin house management. There was information available from the national Purple Martin Conservation Association in Pennsylvania, but Minnesota's martin enthusiasts wanted to learn more about the specific natural history and conservation of Minnesota's purple martins.

They began with banding chicks in martin houses in the Brainerd area. From 2005 through 2021, volunteers banded 2,037 purple martins. In 2008 they began using numbered red bands in addition to the aluminum U.S. Fish and Wildlife Service leg bands so the martin landlords could identify the origin of martin colonies at lakes where they staged prior to migration in late summer. In 2009, they attached radio transmitters to twenty-four purple martins so their local movements from nesting colonies to fall staging areas could be identified prior to the martins's fall migration.

By 2012, the volunteers had color-banded martins at sixty-one colony sites and determined the location of the early fall staging areas at lakes in central Minnesota where tens of thousands of martins gather in mid-August before migrating to Brazil. The martins perch along power lines in the immediate area of the roosting lake in the afternoon. At sunset they begin circling over the lake and then settle into emergent stands of cattails or phragmites in the lake. Thousands of martins cling to the stems of these plants overnight where they are safe from nocturnal predators. Larry Leonard was the martin enthusiast who learned to utilize Doppler radar weather images to locate migrating concentrations of purple martins as they gathered in the evenings in mid-August and again in the mornings as they dispersed across the countryside for foraging.

Martins select different lakes each year for fall staging prior to migration. They have been documented at Big Swan Lake, Lake Osakis, and Big Spunk Lake. After a staging site is located, PMWG volunteers arrange for evening pontoon rides to observe the spectacular concentrations of martins. I have seen these staging spectacles at White Bear Lake, and in 2010 I went out on the pontoon sponsored by the PMWG to observe about seventy thousand martins as they circled over Lake Osakis before dropping into the phragmites plants to rest for the night. It was one of my most spectacular wildlife experiences.

Lee Bakewell initiated the next phase of PMWG technology with geolocators. A total of forty-one martins from four colonies were outfitted with geolocators

Purple martins at fall staging area in flight over Lake Osakis at sunset, 2010.

in 2011. This was part of a continent-wide effort involving attachment of 421 locators to purple martins. Geolocators were attached to martins at Brainerd, Forest Lake, Mille Lacs Lake, and Willmar. Geolocators are a wonderful tool to discover the migratory pathways and wintering areas of martins, but the martins must be recaptured the following spring after they return from migration so the data on the geolocators can be downloaded. Out of the forty-one Minnesota martins outfitted with geolocators in 2011, five geolocators were recovered the following spring, and the movements of the martins to Brazil and back were documented.

The martins departed Minnesota from August 9 to 27, 2011. Four martins flew south, crossing the Gulf of Mexico and reached landfall on the Yucatan Peninsula. They continued through Central America and Panama to Colombia and arrived at their wintering grounds of tropical rainforests in northern Brazil from late September to late October. In mid-April they retraced their fall migration route through Central America and the Yucatan Peninsula. They crossed the Gulf of Mexico to Louisiana and arrived in Minnesota from April 28 to May 7.

While it is exciting to learn the migratory details from the data revealed by geolocators, examination of US breeding bird survey data is sobering. It shows that purple martins in Minnesota have decreased by a huge 4.8 percent per year from 1967 through 2019. That amounts to a 92 percent population decline since 1967. This decline merits a significant conservation effort in central Minnesota lake country and a review of their conservation status as perhaps a threatened species in Minnesota.

While many people enjoy the presence of purple martins in Minnesota's lake country, they have failed to notice that martins are disappearing from Minnesota's lakeshores, and they need our help. If the purple martin is such a well-loved bird and accommodated by placement of nest boxes on lakeshore homesites, why are they in such serious decline? There are several reasons. Outdated purple martin houses with six-inch by six-inch nest compartments that were used twenty to thirty years ago are now death traps for martins. Cooper's hawks have learned that by visiting a purple martin nest colony during the day they can reach into a nest box and grab and eat the nestling martins. At night, great horned owls have learned to visit martin

Purple martin migration route for Minnesota martins, showing the location of their wintering area in the rainforests of northern Brazil. Source, Mike North

houses, reach into the nest boxes, and extract the martin chicks for a midnight snack.

Other problems have contributed to the martins's demise. Purple martin landlords who maintained lakeside colonies with wooden martin houses for many years have let their wooden martin houses deteriorate. Careless or negligent management allows martin houses to be taken over by house sparrows and starlings. Lakeshore yards where martin houses were erected years ago have "closed in" over the years because tree growth has reduced the larger open areas that martins require for their territorial flight displays.

New lakeshore homeowners may also inherit a decades-old and rotted-out martin house that needs to be replaced. They typically do not have the training, budget, or knowledge on how to install, manage, or afford a state-of-the-art martin house. They need to learn how to attract a martin colony, and they need to learn how to manage purple martins that colonize their martin house. Martin houses require continuous attention during the early spring and summer season to optimize martin productivity. House sparrows and European starlings must also be prevented from taking over martin houses in early spring before the martins arrive.

Some lakeshore owners are reluctant to invest in a state-of-the-art purple martin house on a pole equipped with a winch that allows the martin house to be safely lowered for easy maintenance—the cost may range from about $250 to $1,500. Information can be obtained from the Purple Martin Conservation Association at www.purplemartin.org. New martin landlords can also benefit greatly with coaching from experienced martin landlords.

Another reason for the demise of the purple martins is that newer generations of lakeshore owners often do not appreciate native wildflowers, shrubs, sedges, and grasses that the previous owners may have maintained along their property margins and lakeshores. New owners often replace native plants and remove emergent aquatic vegetation because their vision of a scenic lakeshore property includes an extensive manicured bluegrass lawn, boulder riprap along the water's edge, and no emergent lakeshore vegetation like cattails, phragmites, and sedges. They consider those plants to be weeds. The resulting lakeshore lawn and boulder riprap is a biological desert that produces few butterflies, dragonflies, or other insects—fewer insects to provide food for purple martins.

The other problem with a clean lawn mentality is that it is accompanied by use of herbicides and pesticides, often including neonicotinoids. This dependence on chemicals is detrimental to preserving healthy and diverse insect populations. This problem is exacerbated by use of

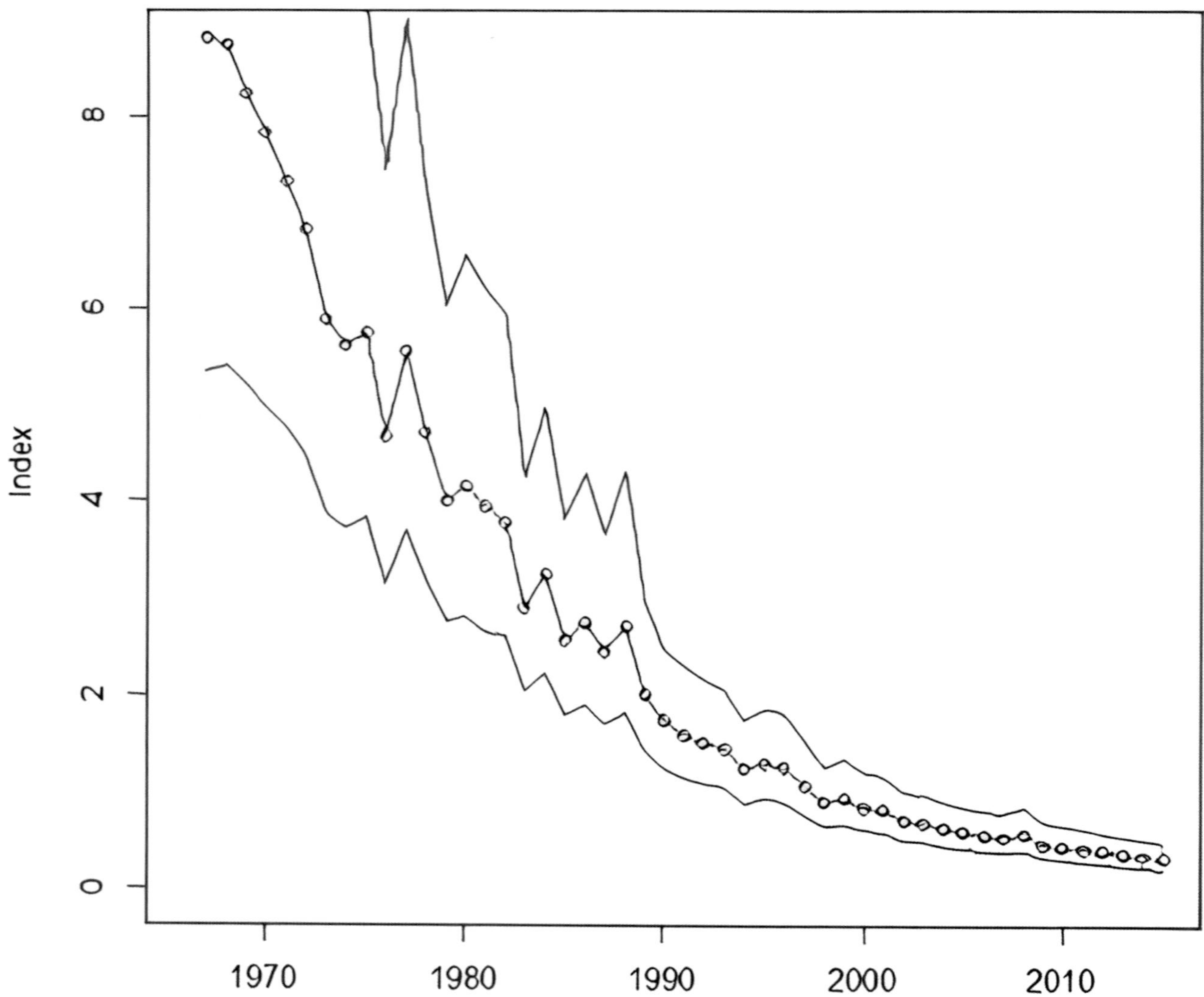

Federal Breeding Bird Survey population trend for the purple martins in Minnesota, 1967-2018.

herbicides and pesticides in the surrounding agricultural landscape. That further diminishes insect populations.

To address the problems being experienced by purple martins, and to complement the conservation efforts that were already underway, I felt I could contribute to purple martin conservation in two ways. First, I could provide more effective guidelines for construction and management of purple martin houses because existing information was outdated and detrimental to the well-being of martins.

Second, I could provide a new vision for how people could design and manage lakeshore property with native plants and provide a more ecological strategy for creation of native plant buffer zones, reducing the amount of manicured lawn, and producing more lakeshore frontage with native, local-origin plants. This strategy was incorporated into the *Lakescaping for Wildlife and Water Quality* book, which I co-authored with landscape architect Fred Rozumalski and limnologist Carolyn Dinndorf. That book was published in 1997, and over 27,000 copies have been sold.

One of my biggest challenges for helping purple martins was keeping up with the most effective guidelines for construction of a martin house. In my first update of the eight-page *Birdhouses in Minnesota* booklet in 1979, my design included the now-outdated one-story nest box with eight six-by-six-inch nesting chambers and two-and-a-half-inch-diameter entrance holes. The recommended height was fifteen to twenty feet above the ground. Those houses needed to be checked regularly during the nesting season with a ladder. Otherwise, the nesting pole needed to be hinged so it could be tilted down for maintenance after the nesting season. The hinged pole did not allow for monitoring the martin nest compartments during the nesting season.

I upgraded the martin house design in the 1984 edition of my forty-seven-page DNR book *Woodworking for Wildlife*. That edition featured eight six-by-six-inch nesting chambers and two-and-a-quarter-inch-diameter entrance holes. A new feature was a one-half-inch dowel fence around the perimeter of the nest box, two inches high. It kept chicks from falling from the martin house. Additional enticements for encouraging martin house use included placing a shallow tray of crushed and dried chicken eggshells near the house because female martins need calcium for egg development. Another beneficial feature was to create a shallow mud puddle on the soil below the martin house to serve as a source of water near the nesting pole.

My 111-page second edition of *Woodworking for Wildlife* was published in 1992. A new feature was the addition of partitions around the periphery of the nest box entrances separating each of the nest compartments. This prevented larger martin chicks from going into other nest compartments where they could prevent smaller martin chicks from being fed.

Two martin chicks begging for food.

Newer recommendations also included that martin houses should be in open sites at least thirty feet from surrounding trees to allow enough space for their aerobatic maneuvers and dawn song displays. Martin houses don't need to be as high as previously recommended. A twelve- or fourteen-foot long, four-inch by four-inch post could be anchored four feet in the ground so the house would be only eight to ten feet high. This makes it easier and safer to check the houses with a shorter ladder. Martin houses are also often successful if placed on poles or posts at the end of docks or in water near the docks. They only need to be a couple feet above the high-water mark. These can be checked by the martin landlord wearing chest waders.

Prior to the nesting season, a handful of sawdust can be placed in each nesting compartment along with a pinch of 1 percent rotenone to control mites and lice infestations on the martin chicks. The greatest changes for purple martin conservation were yet to come.

Dick Hjort lowering a martin house with a winch.

It was time for another edition of *Woodworking for Wildlife*. My new 164-page third edition was published in 2009. Among new features were designs for construction or purchase of martin nest houses or plastic gourd clusters to place on poles or posts that could be vertically raised and lowered with a winch or pulley. Options included commercially made martin houses or wooden house designs. Instead of eight nest compartments in the previous nest box design, the new design included four compartments that were six and a half inches wide and eleven inches deep. This discouraged predation by hawks or owls. The entrance hole should either be two and one-eighth inches in diameter and one inch above the floor, or it should feature starling-proof entrance holes shaped like the letter D on its back, three inches wide and one and three-sixteenth inches high at the center and one inch above the floor.

This type of martin house requires use of removable Troyer nesting trays. They are inserted into each nest compartment. People who do not wish to build their own nesting boxes or Troyer nesting trays could contact the Purple Martin Conservation Association or Andrew M. Troyer at the Purple Martin Place for purchasing martin houses, plastic nesting gourds, starling-proof entrance hole templates, and nesting poles with winches and pulleys.

A commercially available nesting gourd in use by martins. A cluster of these gourds can be suspended from poles to attract purple martins.

Another new feature for accommodating martins included a large tray on a post filled with white pine needles. Martins prefer white pine needles for making their nests because chemicals in the pine repel external parasites on the chicks. Mounting the purple martin house on a pole with a winch and pulley is recommended because it is safer and easier to service about once a week during the nesting season. As stated earlier, it is important to keep the entrance holes of the nest compartments closed until the martins arrive in the spring to prevent sparrows and starlings from taking over the colony before arrival of the martins.

A demonstration site for purple martins sponsored by Minnesota's Purple Martin Working Group. It includes nesting gourds, commercially available martin houses, and perching rods atop the nesting structures. Winches are used so the nests can be lowered weekly during the nesting season.

The Purple Martin Working Group has placed demonstration sites in public parks around central Minnesota to show people how the houses should be placed and managed. I developed an informational poster for the working group to display at those demonstration sites so people could see how the martin houses should be placed and managed at those demonstration sites.

Woodworking for Wildlife Goes Global

After completing my 1984 edition of *Woodworking for Wildlife*, I was contacted by DNR moose biologist Pat Karns from Grand Rapids. He had just returned from spending a year with Russian moose biologists learning about their techniques for moose research and management. He was inspired and impressed with the dedication and professionalism demonstrated by their wildlife biologists.

Pat liked my latest version of *Woodworking for Wildlife* and told me that there were lots of cavity-nesting birds in Russia. He said wildlife biologists there could benefit from the information in this publication. He asked if I could send a copy to Dr. Olga Chernova of the Severtzov Institute and Professor Valery Ilyichev who was president of the Laboratory of Birds' Ecology in Moscow. I sent them copies. I was pleased that the information in my book could potentially benefit birds on the other side of the planet.

On October 21, 1985, I got a letter personally co-signed by both Dr. Olga Chernova and Professor Valery Ilyichev:

"I thank you very much for sending me a copy of booklet *Woodworking for Wildlife, Home for Birds and Mammals*. I have given the book in the Laboratory of Birds' Ecology and Control of Birds' Behaviour and the All-Union Ornithological Society, where the analogous investigations are conducted."

On May 29, 1985, I received a purchase order from the Central Intelligence Agency in Washington, DC, requesting a copy of *Woodworking for Wildlife*. Of course, I sent them a copy. I didn't realize I may have been guilty of leaking bird house secrets to the Russians.

Woodworking for Wildlife Helps Cuban Birds, Including Cuban Martins

While leading a birding tour to Cuba in 2013, I met Cuban ornithologist Maikel Cañizares Morera from the Institute of Ecology and Systematics in Havana. I gave him a copy of my 2009 edition of *Woodworking for Wildlife*, thinking it could potentially benefit Cuban birds. Maikel tried the kestrel design with a three-inch diameter entry hole for use by Cuban parakeets, but the ungrateful parakeets chewed out the entry holes with their sharp bills until the nest boxes were non-functional.

Maikel would not be deterred. He replaced the wooden nest box plans with a cylindrical design made of cement and jute fabric. His idea was brilliant, and it was parakeet-proof. He installed clusters of the cement-fortified nest boxes on cliffs for Cuban parakeets. They were successful. He tried the same design in different habitats including the Zapata swamp, central Cuba, and northern Ciego de Avila.

The results were impressive. On the limestone cliffs of central Cuba the nest-boxes were occupied by Cuban martins. In addition, the Cuban parrot, West Indian woodpecker, bare-legged owl, and Cuban pygmy owl all used the cement nest boxes. The national bird of Cuba, the Cuban trogon, also used the nest boxes. I had no idea that my book could have provided such a breakthrough for helping endemic Cuban birds, but it did!

Cuban ornithologist Maikel Cañizares with some of his cement nest boxes that were used by Cuban martins.

Chapter 11

Meadowlarks, Bobolinks, and Upland Sandpipers

An upland sandpiper alighting on a fence post.

It was easy to tell what bird books I read as a child. The covers were worn off. I learned to identify the birds on our farm by studying my well-worn bird books. One spring morning in 1956 I was riding home on the school bus when I spotted a new bird standing on a fence post—an upland plover. At the time it was still referred to as an upland plover, but it is now called the upland sandpiper. I was only ten, but I knew it from an image in my bird books.

I was so excited that I told my family about it as soon as I got home. Sometimes they did not sense the same excitement I felt about my bird sightings. One time I told my mother I had just seen a horned lark. She said "That's silly. Birds don't have horns." End of discussion. There were other memorable songbirds that I discovered in our alfalfa fields and pastures, like the western meadowlark and bobolink. However, I didn't see another upland sandpiper near our farm for another forty-three years.

After being assigned to the Lac qui Parle Wildlife Refuge in 1974, I once again encountered upland sandpipers. I heard their distinctive wolf whistles on the prairies there. It became one of my favorite birds. On the Lac qui Parle prairies I also heard the musical songs of birds I had known as a child—the bobolink and western meadowlark, and I even heard the maniacal calling of marbled godwits for the first time. Those birds provided me with a choir of avian serenades.

One spring day in early May of 1975 the Lac qui Parle Refuge staff was carrying out a prescribed prairie burn on the Lac qui Parle Wildlife Management Area. During the burn, I discovered the nest of an upland sandpiper with four distinctive, speckled eggs in the path of oncoming fire we had started. Using my drip torch, I burned a ten-foot diameter circle around the sandpiper's nest and stomped out the circle of fire so it would create a circular firebreak when the burn reached the nest. I returned to the nest a day later, and the sandpiper was back on the eggs.

My upland sandpiper saga continued in 2003. My mother passed away that year, and I purchased half of our one hundred thirty-two-acre farm near Zearing, Iowa, from my siblings. I enrolled four and four-tenths acres into a Conservation Reserve Program (CRP) contract that year and planted a mix of prairie grasses and wildflowers. In spring of 2004, Ethelle and I hiked out to inspect our new prairie planting. We were welcomed by the distinctive wolf whistle of an upland sandpiper forty-eight years after my first sighting of one. In the twenty years that have passed since that first CRP planting on my farmland, I have increased my CRP enrollment to twenty-nine acres including a new prairie planting in 2023 on six acres. The Pheasants Forever seed mix I planted there included over seventy species of native wildflowers and grasses.

The loss of prairies in Minnesota has had a dramatic effect on the state's grassland bird life and prairie pollinators. The cumulative population trends in the federal Minnesota Breeding Bird Survey data for the fifty-two-year period from 1967 through 2019 showed average annual declines for many species of birds, including: the western meadowlark, 6.74%; grasshopper sparrow, 6.44%; dickcissel, 3.33%; savannah sparrow, 1.98%; bobolink, 1.62%; field sparrow, 1.56%; vesper sparrow, 1.55%; and upland sandpiper, 1.44%. Upland sandpiper numbers dropped about 50 percent over that fifty-two-year period.

Western meadowlark.

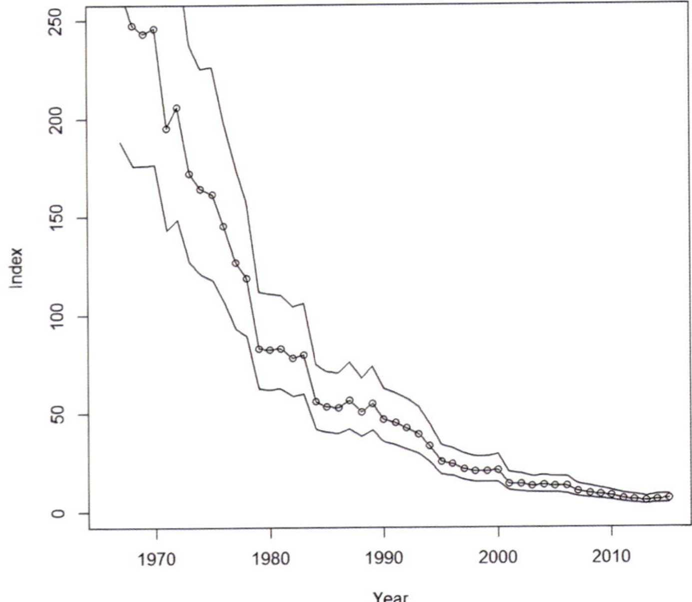

The U.S. Geological Survey Minnesota breeding population trend for the western meadowlark, 1967-2018.

The bobolink is just one of the grassland species that reflects this continuing decline in their numbers. The losses have continued as many farmers converted their Conservation Reserve Program grasslands back into row crop production in response to higher corn prices. Even virgin prairies disappeared as farmers removed boulders that had been deposited on prairies during the last glaciation so the land could be converted to croplands. The boulders were bought by landscaping businesses and sold as lawn decorations.

Bobolink singing on Touch the Sky Prairie near Luverne, Minnesota.

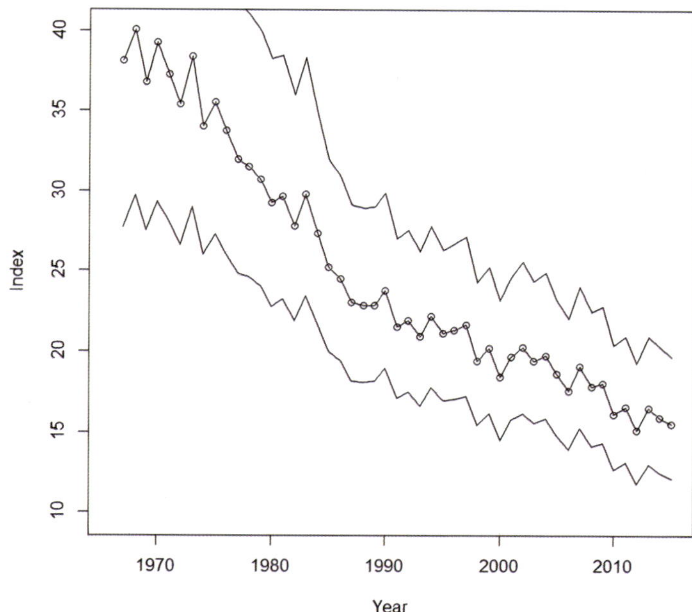

Population decline of the bobolink in Minnesota as determined by the U.S. Geological Survey Breeding Bird Survey, 1967-2018.

Those actions eliminated nesting habitats for many grassland songbirds as well as invertebrates. These birds were not only an important component of biological diversity on those original prairies, but they added inspiring elements of beauty and birdsong to the prairie landscape.

A dickcissel singing on the seventy-eight acre grassland remnant on the Battle Creek site in Maplewood, Minnesota.

Sadly, some of the chairs in that choir are now vacant. The richness and diversity of the resulting symphonies are greatly diminished. The Baird's sparrow and Sprague's pipit have disappeared as nesting species on Minnesota's western prairies, and the chestnut-collared longspur is rare except for occasional sightings on the Felton Prairie in Clay County. Western meadowlarks and grasshopper sparrows have become rare. They need to be considered for listing as threatened or endangered under Minnesota's endangered species law.

Providing benefits for birdlife on Minnesota's prairies has been a priority for the Nongame Wildlife Program. We provided funding from Nongame Wildlife Checkoff donations and critical habitat matching funds for acquiring prairie and grassland tracts, including the Dugdale WMA (160 acres in Polk County), Maple Meadows WMA (60 acres in Polk County), Mentor Prairie WMA (80 acres in Polk County), Wo Wacintanka WMA (553 acres in Freeborn County-some grassland), Mound Prairie WMA (17 of 346 acres in Houston County), Shirley Robinson WMA (320 acres of mixed habitats in Todd County), and Oronoco Prairie SNA (57 acres in Olmsted County).

An innovative 2017 Minnesota Prairie Preservation Plan has been initiated as a collaborative effort by Greg Hoch in the DNR and additional conservation partners including The Nature Conservancy, Lessard-Sams Outdoor Heritage Council (LSOHC), MN Board of Water and Soil Resources, MN Prairie Chicken Society, Pheasants Forever, The Conservation Fund, and the U.S. Fish and Wildlife Service. The Section of Wildlife in the DNR restores about 625 acres of prairie annually and currently manages about 13,500 acres of restored and native prairies.

A Lesson in Networking for Prairie Bird Conservation

In 2021, pioneer Minnesota birder Bob Janssen and I had some provocative coffee break discussions about avian habitats that were the highest priority for declining species of Minnesota birdlife. We concluded that the top priority included birds of prairies and grasslands. Bob and I agreed that the Minnesota Ornithologists' Union (MOU) has done an exceptional job over eight decades, documenting the presence and status of birdlife throughout Minnesota. However, we felt there was still a huge missed opportunity for accomplishments relating to habitat conservation and preservation for Minnesota's birdlife.

There are other agencies and organizations involved with habitat conservation in Minnesota, like the DNR, The Nature Conservancy, Trust for Public Lands, Minnesota Land Trust, Pheasants Forever, and Ducks Unlimited. The MOU does not need to be in competition with these organizations, but we felt that this was an opportunity for the MOU to be partnering and advocating for habitat conservation of Minnesota's nongame birdlife—especially songbirds and other species that could be overlooked by organizations more interested in game bird conservation.

That is because the Minnesota legislature passed a .375 percent sales tax increase in 2008. Millions of dollars become available every year to be used from the new Clean Water, Lands, and Legacy Amendment sales tax. Every time anyone (including MOU members) buys a new pair of binoculars, a new camera, a car, or groceries, that purchase contributes to the conservation fund. That income is administered by a board of legislators and citizens whose members oversee the use of the Lessard-Sams Outdoor Heritage Fund.

However, the MOU has not expressed interest in how those conservation funds were to be expended. Most participation comes from hunter-related volunteers who realized the enormous opportunity this presented for wildlife conservation in Minnesota. All the decisions on use of this fund benefit habitats for Minnesota wildlife. However, this is an opportunity at the LSOHC table for MOU members to speak up to provide for the special needs of nongame birds, including their habitats. Mark Johnson is my longtime friend who administers the LSOHC program. He is doing an admirable job of administering use of the funds, but I am concerned that the MOU is missing an opportunity. They could help influence efforts for use of the funds because LSOHC funding allocations also require a modest match from private conservation organizations. MOU could help provide those smaller matches to enable major habitat conservation initiatives.

At the time, in 2021, the balance in the Minnesota Ornithologists' Union savings account was about $170,000, and that balance had remained unused and at a high level for years. We suggested contributing $25,000 to help purchase a 149-acre farm with prairie/grassland habitat in Mahnomen County that was for sale to Pheasants Forever (PF). It would become an addition to the existing DNR Rush Wildlife Management Area. This area had prairie and wetlands. Resident wildlife included prairie chickens, marbled godwits, upland sandpipers, waterfowl, and sandhill cranes.

Pheasants Forever had $400,000 available from the Lessard Sams Outdoor Heritage Council for purchase and improvement of the farm, but state law required a smaller private match from an organization like MOU to make this acquisition. Pheasants Forever needed the private match by the end of 2021, and there was only one month left in 2021 to obtain that private match and complete the acquisition.

Meanwhile, Pheasants Forever realized the need for showcasing a broader spectrum of grassland environmental benefits beyond benefitting pheasants and pheasant hunters—like climate resiliency, soil health, carbon sequestration, and expanding their support base beyond hunters to recognize benefits to nongame birdlife and prairie pollinators. This was a golden opportunity for a dramatic first-time collaboration for grassland wildlife conservation to make big news—both for the Minnesota Ornithologists' Union and for Pheasants Forever.

Eran Sandquist of PF and Bob Janssen joined the annual MOU board call on December 3, 2021, to encourage the MOU to support their first-ever land acquisition effort for prairie birdlife. I was the chair for the MOU Conservation Committee at the time, and I had also expressed my strong support for that proposal. The board approved the acquisition by a vote of thirteen to one. The MOU is to be commended for this historic, first-time commitment for land conservation that contributed to the survival of prairie birdlife as a conservation partner with Pheasants Forever. Bob played a major role in 2021 by urging the MOU to assist in helping fund a first-ever acquisition of prairie land by the MOU in partnership with Pheasants Forever. I was hopeful that the MOU would continue their involvement with PF to provide matching funds for future prairie land acquisitions.

Bob Janssen, pioneer and legend among birders, passed away in November 2023. He is remembered for his extraordinary birding skills, long-term birding records, and the books he authored. However, he also realized in his later years that making bird lists may document the decline of birds, but it does not preserve habitat for them into the future. His support for acquisition of habitat for prairie birdlife began in 2021 with his encouragement for the MOU to acquire land to add to the Rush WMA in Mahnomen County in part-

Legendary birder Bob Janssen and DNR wildlife biologist John Beech at Heron Lake, August 14, 1979, with Canada geese ready for banding.

nership with Pheasants Forever. His efforts were a success. He was also hopeful that this would be a recurring commitment for the MOU to continue to contribute into the future as a proud partner in conservation.

In addition to land conservation efforts derived from LSOHC funds, additional acquisition funds come from state lottery proceeds through the Legislative-Citizens' Commission on Minnesota Resources. The Board of Soil and Water Resources is also making a big difference in securing acquisition of thousands of acres of remaining prairie lands in the state through the Conservation Reserve Enhancement Program (CREP).

There is still an increasing, and depressing, trend for grassland acreage to be converted into row-crop production. This eliminates grazing areas, nesting sites, and breeding habitats for native wildlife. Populations of pollinators have declined up to 80 percent, and grassland birds have declined about 53 percent. Increasing land conversion eliminates grazing land that ranchers previously used for beef production, and that land would otherwise sequester carbon emissions. A decline in Conservation Reserve Program (CRP) enrollment has also negatively impacted grasslands. The CRP makes yearly payments to farmers for their land if they preserve native species, remove sensitive land from agriculture production, plant native prairie plants, and protect native wildlife. The prairie biome, as well as a conservation ethic among many farmers, is disappearing along with its unique flora and fauna.

There are a few encouraging signs for optimism. A new strategy is being advocated by agricultural planners for farmland management called precision farming whereby land use potential is plotted by each square yard/meter across an entire farm. The potential for each square yard or meter is designated for its highest and best use for producing profits and optimum crop production as well as what acres should be retired from production and used for conservation plantings. Precision farming analyses generally reveal that perhaps 20 to 30 percent of each farm acreage is best retired and converted to grassland/prairie because those poorest quality acres lose money for the farmer every year that the farmer invests in seed, fertilizer, pesticides, planting costs, and harvesting costs into those acres. If plant-

The marbled godwit nests on prairies of northwestern Minnesota, like the Rush Wildlife Management Area.

ed to grassland, those grassland acres would create a carbon sink that would help reduce the impact of global warming while concurrently providing nesting habitat for grassland birds.

For this strategy to succeed, it will be important for lending institutions to require any parties wishing to buy farmland to enroll their farmland into a precision farming contract. The National Grasslands Conservation Act is also a newly drafted piece of federal legislation modeled after the highly successful National Wetlands Conservation Act. This bill will focus on wildlife preservation, climate resiliency, habitat restoration, and preserving ranching livelihoods for generations of farmers and ranchers to come. Meanwhile, we need to continue our efforts to preserve and restore our prairie choir of grassland songbirds.

To complement the conservation efforts of Pheasants Forever, Ducks Unlimited, The Nature Conservancy, and DNR Wildlife Management Area acquisition, the Nongame Wildlife Program has approached prairie conservation with educational efforts. In 2015, I collaborated with Jim Mallman of Watchable Wildlife Inc. to fund and showcase 120 of the best wildlife viewing areas on their national website.

These educational efforts also included: publication of the *Traveler's Guide to Wildlife in Minne-*

sota (1997); a brochure on Prairie Plants of Lac qui Parle and Vicinity (1979); publication of *Birds of Minnesota State Parks* by Robert B. Janssen (2015); and a two-year program funded by the Legislative Citizens' Commission on Minnesota Resources funded by state lottery receipts, promoting nature tourism in collaboration with Explore Minnesota Tourism. The effort included emphasis on grassland and prairie sites. I also wrote seven articles relating to prairie wildlife in the DNR *Minnesota Volunteer* from 1976 through 1995, including "Prairie Wildlife in the Theater of Seasons," July-Aug 1976. The other articles highlighted the wildlife at the Lac qui Parle Wildlife Refuge and the best places to view prairie wildlife in Minnesota.

The rare regal fritillary butterfly photographed in flight at the Touch the Sky Prairie near Luverne, Minnesota.

Another big step for promoting greater understanding and opportunity to see and enjoy prairie birds was a creation of the Pine-to-Prairie Birding Trail in 2000. Field trips to northwest Minnesota in the mid-1990s and a Department of Tourism familiarization (fam) tour for midwestern and national media generated significant interest for the grassland features and prairie wildlife of northwestern Minnesota. This generated support for uniting communities along Highway 59 from Fergus Falls to the Canadian border via Roseau and Warroad. This corridor concept was consolidated into a birding trail of public lands endorsed by local communities and by organizers of the Detroit Lakes Festival of Birds.

This trail was comprised of fifty-one sites of which twenty-two had wildlife characteristic of prairies. The founders of the Pine-to-Prairie Birding Trail were U.S. Fish and Wildlife Service naturalists Betsy Beneke and Kelly Blackledge of the Tamarac National Wildlife Refuge, Cleone Stewart of the Detroit Lakes Chamber of Commerce, DNR regional nongame wildlife specialist for northwest Minnesota Katie Haws, David Bergman of Explore Minnesota Tourism, and me. Towns along the route that officially joined the birding trail project were Fergus Falls, Park Rapids, Warroad, Roseau, Thief River Falls, Detroit Lakes, and Pelican Rapids.

In 2006, I was invited to visit public wildlife areas in southern Manitoba to provide suggestions on how to promote their provincial watchable wildlife program. After touring their areas, I suggested they were doing an excellent job of accommodating nature tourism, but that they could connect their viewing sites via a birding trail as we had done in Minnesota. From 2006 through 2009 I worked with Jim Mallman in Watchable Wildlife Inc. to assist the Manitoba Wildlife, Tourism and Natural Areas program to create their new provincial birding trail.

Jim Mallman, CEO of Watchable Wildlife Inc. and an international catalyst for nature tourism.

I further recommended these sites be connected as an international birding trail between Minnesota and Manitoba. This would be the first international birding trail that I was aware of between the United States and Canada. I drafted an agreement between the State of Minnesota and the Province of Manitoba to create the new Pine-to-Prairie International Birding Trail. The agreement was formalized between the State of Minnesota and the Province of Manitoba in a ribbon-cutting ceremony at the Minnesota/Manitoba border on May 18, 2009. It extends two hundred miles north from the Minnesota border to the Interlakes region of Manitoba. It includes twenty-four sites, including the Tall Grass Prairie Preserve, Whitewater Wildlife Management Area, Hecla-Grindstone Provincial Parks, Oak Hammock Marsh Wildlife Management Area and Interpretive Center, the world-famous Narcisse Snake Dens, and the legendary Delta Marsh. The trail includes the City of Winnipeg where visitors can find a remarkable array of springtime birds at the Fort Whyte Alive nature center and its extensive network of nature paths and wetlands.

They subsequently developed an awesome Grasslands Birding Trail in southwestern Manitoba. While visiting those grasslands, I discovered those prairies still contained some of the most sought-after prairie songbirds in North America, including birds now missing from Minnesota's prairies: Baird's sparrow, chestnut-collared longspur, and Sprague's pipit.

Pine-to-Prairie International Birding trail dedication at the Manitoba/Minnesota border, May 18, 2009.

Chapter 12

Discovering the Power and Appeal of Nature Photography for Promoting Wildlife Conservation

Throughout the 1980s and 1990s, I experienced a desire to improve my photography equipment and techniques and to share my images of nature with others. Nature photography has been a wonderful investment as a hobby. It has served as an essential tool for documenting my conservation activities and the efforts of our conservation partners and staff in the Nongame Wildlife Program. On May 11, 2007, I was invited to join the Windom Dual Immersion Spanish and Open School for a nature photography workshop at the Wood Lake Nature Center in Richfield, a suburb of Minneapolis. Kevin McDonald of the Minnesota Pollution Control Agency told me his son was a participant at the Immersion School, and he invited me to the workshop. They arranged for a presentation by renowned nature photographer Dudley Edmondson. He was the author of the book *Black and Brown Faces in America's Wild Places*. The book featured interviews with people representing minority races who were highly regarded in national government and environmental organization positions. They expressed their concerns about the conspicuous lack of participation by minorities in outdoor recreation activities.

Nature photographer, author, and speaker Dudley Edmonson.

Dudley gave a presentation to forty middle school students about nature photography. He followed up by leading a photo safari for the students along the nature center's marshland boardwalk. They needed me to find local nature photographers to assist with photography coaching along the boardwalk and to locate digital cameras for the students to use on their photo safaris. This was a collaborative effort with Jim Mallman of Watchable Wildlife Inc. and staff from the DNR Nongame Wildlife Program, DNR Division of Parks and Trails, and the DNR Division of Enforcement.

Dudley gave a spell-binding presentation of photos taken on a wildlife photo expedition to Alaska. He followed up by showing beautiful photos of birds, butterflies, and flowers taken in his own backyard in Duluth. He told the students they can become photographers by discovering the beauty of nature right in their own backyards. We organized the students into pairs and gave each pair a digital camera with instructions to go on a one-hour photo safari along the wetland boardwalk at the nature center. They were each instructed to take ten photos and then give the camera to their buddy. When their hour was up, they came in for lunch. We downloaded all their photos at lunchtime so they could be shared with the whole group after lunch. Once the students were assembled, Dudley showed each selection of ten photos. He commented on the photos and complimented the students on the artistic qualities of their photos. The kids were excited to discover how they could take memorable photos as a nature photographer.

"I had an idea!" Building on my photography experiences, I collaborated with Jim Mallman, director of Watchable Wildlife Inc., to develop a new project—

Digital Photography Bridge to Nature. The project was developed using The Multiplier Effect. In other words, if you have an important conservation message, don't attempt to teach the students. Teach the teachers.

This was a **Hands-On** project that would be targeted at grades three through nine at schools, state parks, nature centers, and national wildlife refuges throughout Minnesota. I applied to the Legislative Citizens' Commission on Minnesota Resources (LCCMR) for an Environment and Natural Resources Trust Fund appropriation which is derived from state lottery proceeds. This cooperative project involved the Minnesota DNR, Watchable Wildlife Inc., U.S. Fish and Wildlife Service, Minnesota Master Naturalist Program, Minnesota Pollution Control Agency, Minnesota Extension Service, White Earth Indian Band, and Minnesota Nature Photography Club.

My application to the LCCMR for $160,000 was successful. I hired two statewide project coordinators and eight experienced teachers and nature photographers to deliver the workshops in collaboration with local natural resource managers, biologists, nature photographers, and conservationists. Jan Welsh, Project WILD program coordinator, managed the Digital Bridge program. Steve Maanum from Park Rapids was the outstate coordinator, and Mary Spivey was the metro region coordinator for the project for fifteen workshop facilitators.

Our goal was to deliver eighty workshops to one thousand teachers over a two-year period. I purchased five hundred Nikon Coolpix S8100 digital cameras at a discount from the National Camera Exchange. I am grateful to the National Camera Exchange in Golden Valley for their involvement and support for helping to provide refurbished high-quality cameras for this project. We also benefited from a $20,000 estate donation to the Nongame Wildlife Program. Jan Welsh and I created thirty learning trunks for project facilitators, including Nikon digital cameras for each learning trunk, memory card readers, and wildlife nature guides. These trunks were made available to teachers who had taken Digital Bridge training. They could check out the trunks for a week at a time.

I wanted to invite Minnesota's most famous nature photographer, Jim Brandenburg, to deliver the keynote address at our first teacher workshop. However, he was on a photo assignment for National Geographic in Asia. I kept checking with his wife Judy for about nine months until he returned to Minnesota. When I finally caught up with him, he agreed to provide the keynote address at his hometown of Luverne, Minnesota, on July 10, 2010.

We invited sixty-five teachers from grades three through nine to attend the workshop. Jim gave an inspiring talk about how as a child he was one of the smallest children in his class; he did not excel in sports, and his grades were poor. He consistently got Fs in English classes, but now he writes books. His life was transformed when he purchased a three-dollar camera as a child in Luverne. He took a closeup photo of a red fox on a local prairie that he attracted by imitating the squeaking sound of a field mouse in distress. That photo and his new hobby of photography changed his life. It gave him a sense of self-esteem, a purpose, and a vision for sharing the beauty of nature.

After Jim's presentation, the teachers had a classroom session on photo techniques. Then Jim took the teachers to the Touch the Sky Prairie near Luverne. He helped purchase that prairie in cooperation with the U.S. Fish and Wildlife Service. The teachers spent the afternoon on the prairie photographing regal fritillary butterflies, bobolinks, and rare prairie white-fringed orchids with Jim. That day on the prairie was an inspiring experience for the teachers and for Jim. He shared the joy and beauty of the prairie with them so they could inspire the next generation of students about Minnesota's prairies.

The Digital Photography Bridge to Nature project massively exceeded our hopes. We got additional funding for a third year of workshops with DNR funding from the Critical Habitat Matching Fund conservation license plate sales. Over three years, we presented 114 teacher workshops to 1,560 teachers. Each teacher participant subsequently provided digital bridge training sessions and photo safari experiences to an average of sixty students, so this program is estimated to have reached about 93,600 Minnesota children. Hopefully this approach to conservation stimulated a lifetime interest in wildlife conservation in children who learned to discover wildlife through the lens of a digital camera.

Perhaps the most inspiring revelation in the Digital Photography Bridge to Nature Program was the amazing transformation that occurred when a good quality digital camera was placed in the hands of a youth on a photo safari in a natural habitat area. They slowed down. They became acutely aware of nature and the myriad creatures around them—bugs, but-

The author and Jim Brandenburg on Touch-the-Sky Prairie.

terflies, birds, animal tracks, wildflowers, trees, leaves, colors, and patterns.

The second revelation occurred when students returned to their classrooms. The participants discovered the joy of sharing their discoveries and photos with others. They learned how to use creative photo apps to enhance and manipulate their digital photos. They also learned how to create photo prints, develop educational presentations, tell stories about wildlife and nature, and create their own photo books. For many students, I believe it appeared to be the beginning of a lifelong passion for both nature and photography.

The author teaching photography techniques to students at a Digital Bridge youth workshop in Itasca State Park. DNR photo by Deb Rose

There was another dimension to this phenomenon. This is a hobby that students can enjoy and excel in even if they do not excel in sports. They can learn how to excel in nature photography as a hobby or even as a profession, like Jim Brandenburg did. It is a potential hobby that students with mobility impairments can excel in by having the patience and skills to photograph wildlife from blinds, accessible nature trails, or even in their own backyards. The teachers reached through this program are estimated to have introduced over ninety thousand students to the joy of nature photography on their nature photo safaris.

The Digital Photography Bridge to Nature project reached 1,560 teachers at 114 workshops throughout Minnesota.

Expanding the Digital Photography Bridge to Nature Program to Latin America

A schoolteacher learning photography skills at a Digital Bridge workshop in the Bahamas at a Birds Caribbean conference. presented by our Digital Bridge team after we were invited to present our program for teachers from throughout Caribbean countries in the Bahamas at the international Birds Caribbean conference in July, 2011.

Schoolteachers learning photography skills at the Birds Caribbean conference in the Bahamas, July, 2011.

Some of Minnesota's most important nesting birds are neotropical migrants that winter in Latin America. Examples of prairie and grassland species are the upland sandpiper, dickcissel, and bobolink. Efforts to help those species have been explained previously and were based on my twenty-eight birding trips to Costa Rica. I was aware that there were also wetland and forest bird species that migrate to and winter in the northwestern estuaries, wetlands and forests of Costa Rica. Because of the success that had occurred with the Digital Photography Bridge to Nature Program, I developed a photographic approach to generating conservation interest among youths in a northwestern Costa Rican community through an international program sponsored by the Association of Fish and Wildlife Agencies (AFWA) that was called Southern Wings. The program was implemented to benefit wintering habitats in Latin America for neotropical migrant birds that nest in Minnesota.

I felt that our Minnesota efforts for promoting conservation of neotropical migrant birds (AFWA) that wintered in Latin America were lacking and needed to be addressed. The Minnesota DNR is a member of AFWA. When I worked in the Section of Wildlife, I had become aware of a collaborative AFWA funding effort by the Minnesota DNR Section of Wildlife to fund habitat conservation projects to benefit migratory waterfowl in the prairie pothole provinces of Canada. This resulted in a "Connect the Dots" moment for me. I knew the Section of Wildlife had already created the legal legislative precedent for funding international migratory bird conservation efforts by a state agency through providing funding to Ducks Unlimited. That money was forwarded to prairie pothole provinces in Canada to benefit waterfowl populations through wetland management. This activity had been practiced for several decades.

If the Minnesota DNR could provide funding to help ducks in Canada, why couldn't they help migrant warblers in Latin America? I saw an opportunity to help preserve warblers, shorebirds, great blue herons, ospreys, and peregrine falcons that wintered in Latin America. I drafted a legislative proposal for consideration. It was approved by the DNR and approved by the Minnesota legislature.

Meanwhile, AFWA created an international effort called Southern Wings for collaboration between state wildlife agencies and conservation entities in Latin America for conservation of nongame neotropical migrant birds. Ethelle and I had led twenty-eight birding tours to Costa Rica since 1987. I had developed a database and map of three thousand neotropical bird sightings for migrant species that wintered in Costa Rica including the Guanacaste province where many of those species wintered.

I collaborated with Dr. Daniel H. Janzen for a conservation project to designate and protect Costa Rica's first Bird Conservation Area in the mangrove forests and adjacent tropical forests near the town of Cuajiniquil. The project was administered through the DNR with a $10,000 contract with the Guanacaste Dry Forest Conservation Fund which is a 501c3 nonprofit. The fund had no overhead, and all funds were used for operational expenditures. The money was used for acquiring five pairs of binoculars and ten Canon SX50 cameras. Those were the world's first compact digital cameras with fifty power magnification.

The local team that spearheaded this effort included: Dr. Janzen (from the faculty of the University of Pennsylvania); Dr. Frank Joyce (Director of Tropical Biology and Conservation Programs, University of California); and Maria Marta Chavarria (Research Director of Guanacaste National Park). They recruited local youths from eleven through fourteen years old from Cuajiniquil to identify and document the birdlife in their local national park.

On December 28, 2015, a dozen experienced birders carried out the Christmas Bird Count for Santa Rosa National Park, and they were joined by an enthusiastic group of apprentice youths who began referring to themselves as Los Trogones (the Trogons). They tallied 185 bird species including 45 neotropical migrants.

A special priority for me included birds that nest in Minnesota, including waterbirds like the spotted sandpiper, blue-winged teal, great blue heron, and great egret. Forest songbirds included the great crested flycatcher, yellow-throated vireo, summer tanager, and ruby-throated hummingbird. Other neotropical migrants wintering in northwestern Costa Rica include the northern waterthrush, prothonotary warbler, yellow warbler, mourning warbler, Tennessee warbler, black- and-white warbler, American redstart, worm-eating warbler, Connecticut warbler, blackburnian warbler, wood thrush, mourning dove, red-eyed vireo, acadian flycatcher, and Baltimore oriole. Raptors included the osprey and broad-winged hawk. In other words, this was an important wintering habitat for birds of interest to Minnesota bird-lovers.

One of the most important and unique components of this effort was incorporation of support for bird conservation into the local community. Both local citizens and youths could see the multiple benefits of the national park both as habitat for birds and as a future employer for local youths who may eventually work as biologists, park rangers, birding guides, and tourism agents.

Frank Joyce and Maria Marta acquainted the youths with local birdlife by taking them afield in 2014 and 2015 on their Christmas bird counts and teaching them how to use the new binoculars and Canon digital cameras. They tallied eighty-eight bird species on two Christmas bird counts and designated a five-hundred-hectare area as their new Guanacaste Conservation Area. After their local expeditions on land, mangrove swamps, and adjacent dry forests, they would meet at a local member's home and review their bird lists and photographs. The binoculars and cameras were distributed to the youths at the beginning of each outing and returned to the national park staff when they completed each field trip.

Los Trogones in action on a bird survey expedition with new binoculars and cameras in Costa Rica, May 2015.

Two "Trogones" scanning for birds in the mangrove forests of Cuajiniquil, Costa Rica.

Southern Wings is a Success

The concept for Southern Wings is a success. The youths who began birding as part of a Costa Rican Southern Wings group in 2014-2015 have remained active. They are now recruiting fledgling Trogones to join them on their outings. The binoculars and cameras have held up well. Southern Wings has been an excellent long-term investment in this neotropical migrant conservation project that benefits midwestern birdlife.

Over my forty-plus years of nature photography experiences, I created an image collection of thousands of photos of birds, mammals, reptiles, amphibians, butterflies, moths, wildflowers, and other invertebrates. I used many of those photos in the five books I wrote for the DNR Nongame Wildlife Program. Those images have documented the beauty of Minnesota's wildlife and the activities and accomplishments of the nongame staff and conservation partners of the DNR Nongame Wildlife Program.

The author and his wife Ethelle with their enthusiastic group of Trogones who explored the mangrove forests of Cuajiniquil in 2015.

My reason for highlighting nature photography in this chapter is that it provides an extremely powerful opportunity—and tool—for biologists, conservationists, and nature lovers to inspire individuals, from children to senior citizens, with the beauty and value of wildlife, wildflowers, and natural ecosystems. Whether photos are taken of swallow-tailed butterflies in one's backyard or loons in northern Minnesota, they can inspire us with the beauty of wildlife and the importance of preserving the world's diverse wildlife populations and their habitats.

Chapter 13

Reptiles and Amphibians of Minnesota

Over the course of my career I found it was easy to generate interest in many wildlife species like bluebirds, swans, loons, butterflies, frogs, and turtles. However, it was more challenging to create citizen interest and appreciation for snakes. There is an innate fear many people have for snakes–especially if they are venomous. Many people hate snakes even if they are not venomous. Sometimes parents teach their children to fear snakes. This creates a huge challenge for conservationists who are trying to advocate the ecological value and benefits of species, like the timber rattlesnake.

This is a huge misunderstanding. It has been exaggerated by far too many movies and television westerns. One of the greatest hurdles to achieving conservation of Minnesota's reptiles, including snakes, is to dispel misleading folklore and advocate the positive ecological role that snakes, including timber rattlesnakes, play as an important component of biodiversity in Minnesota.

That is one of the leading challenges and opportunities for the Nongame Wildlife Program. It poses an opportunity for the DNR to advocate for conservation of reptiles and amphibians in Minnesota, including timber rattlesnakes. Reptiles and amphibians comprise an important component of Minnesota's biodiversity and are typically not a threat to our health and safety in the outdoors.

Adding to the threats for rattlesnake survival are news accounts of people being bitten by rattlesnakes. The threat is overblown. Dr. Dan Keyler of the Hennepin County Medical Center (Poison Control Center) objectively documented fifteen rattlesnake bites in Minnesota over the ten-year period from 1982 through 1992. Only five bites occurred as natural bites in the wild. The other ten bites were the result of human ignorance, inebriation, or foolishness when rattlesnakes were mishandled by amateur herpetologists with rattlesnakes in their possession or by young men teasing or harassing the snakes. Apparently playing with rattlesnakes is a guy thing.

Jaime Edwards was aware of three rattlesnake bites in southeastern Minnesota between 2000 and 2023. Near Lake City a photographer slipped and fell while attempting to photograph a rattlesnake and was bitten in the hand. It was a dry bite, so no venom was injected. A farmer in Houston County was bitten on the leg while opening the door to his barn. He required hospital treatment. Another person was bitten when he ran over a rattlesnake and got out of his car to check under the car for the snake. He was bitten on the leg and required hospital treatment.

Minnesota's Reptiles and Amphibians—a Conservation Opportunity

Frogs, toads, lizards, salamanders, turtles, and snakes are present from lakes and wetlands throughout the state to the upland bluff country of southeastern Minnesota. These creatures capture the attention of children who can develop a lifelong appreciation for our cold-blooded fauna. They comprise wildlife species and populations that are increasingly threatened by habitat loss, chemical pollution, and human exploitation.

There is a need to produce publications that educate the public about the natural history, survival threats, and conservation of these wildlife species. The only publication about reptiles and amphibians of Minnesota previously available to Minnesotans was *Reptiles and Amphibians of Minnesota* by Dr. Walter J. Breckenridge, published by the University of Minnesota Press in 1944. Conservation and management for reptiles and amphibians was a low conservation priority for the next several decades. The amount of information available about reptiles and amphibians in Minnesota increased dramatically after the publication of *Amphibians and Reptiles Native to Minnesota* in 1994 by Barney Oldfield and John Moriarty. I arranged for donations to the Nongame Wildlife checkoff to fund publication of the book.

Barney Oldfield moved to New Mexico after the 1994 book was published, but John Moriarty felt it was important to bring the former publication up to date after twenty years to include new information resulting from herpetological research and surveys by Department of Natural Resources staff and amateur herpetologists. John is an avid herpetologist, a member of the Minnesota Herpetological Society, and he served as natural resource manager for Ramsey County Parks. He then took a position as senior wildlife manager for the Three Rivers Park District and retired from his remarkable career there in October of 2024.

The Nongame Wildlife Program helped produce two major books on reptiles and amphibians of Minnesota and initiated significant management programs for protection, restoration, and management of timber rattlesnakes. John began discussions with DNR herpetologist Carol Hall and me about the need to revise the 1994 book. Carol had previously worked for the U.S. Fish and Wildlife Service and the Minnesota chapter of The Nature Conservancy. I enthusiastically endorsed their idea and agreed to provide the support needed to move the book through the DNR administrative process with funding from the Nongame Wildlife Fund. I agreed to manage the contracts with the University of Minnesota and have the DNR publish the book. I also wrote a foreword for the book. The introductory paragraph that I wrote reflects my enthusiasm for the opportunity to promote an interest in reptiles and amphibians of Minnesota:

"Frogs, toads, turtles, and snakes! What better way to introduce children to nature than with the wonderful array of wildlife that can be discovered literally in your own backyard, including reptiles and amphibians. For many people, a childhood interest in reptiles and amphibians grows into a lifelong interest in and concern for all nature."

Amphibians and Reptiles in Minnesota by John J. Moriarty and Carol D. Hall was published in 2014, twenty years after the first edition, *Amphibians and Reptiles Native to Minnesota* by Oldfield and Moriarty, in 1994. During that period the staff of the DNR Minnesota Biological Survey, members of the Minnesota Herpetological Society, and private herpetologists, collected an enormous amount of data on the natural history and distribution of the state's reptiles and amphibians. There were two new salamanders discovered (spotted salamander and four-toed salamander), one new turtle (eastern musk turtle) was found in the state, and one introduced species (pond slider) was documented. Taxonomic or common name changes also occurred for about 40 percent of the state's reptiles and amphibians during that twenty-year period.

Minnesota DNR Nongame Wildlife Program staff, both past and present, contributed distributional records and natural history information for the book, including Richard Baker, Jaime Edwards, Joan Galli, Lisa Gelvin-Innvaer, Maya Hamady, Erica Hoaglund, Krista Larson, Pam Perry, Ed Quinn, John Schladweiler, and Konrad Schmidt. Minnesota Biological Survey staff also submitted many distributional records, including Jeff LeClere, Liz Harper, Gerda Nordquist, Kelly Lynch Pharis, and Christi Spak.

The following account for the timber rattlesnake is a graphic example of how far our perceptions have come regarding a native species that was vilified, killed, and bountied by the thousands until 1989. Attitudes about snakes in general and rattlesnakes in particular have changed for the better, albeit very slowly. We have come to recognize the role that rattlesnakes play in the environment and the need for stewardship, legal protection, and management of rattlesnakes as an integral part of our Minnesota fauna.

Timber Rattlesnake

Among hundreds of nongame wildlife species in Minnesota, the most maligned, misunderstood, and persecuted creature is undoubtedly the timber rattlesnake. For those reasons, the timber rattlesnake would qualify as a **High-Profile** species—but for the wrong reasons. Just the word rattlesnake usually evokes feelings ranging from fear to animosity. The historic legacy of rattlesnakes in Minnesota is summarized by one word: bounties. Bounties were paid for killing rattlesnakes from 1909 until 1989. Bounties were paid in eight southeastern counties where rattlesnakes occurred on rocky blufflands, forests, and farmlands. In Houston County alone, 28,685 bounties were paid from 1967 through 1982.

Over 5,000 bounties were paid in Houston County in 1970, but in 1987 only 191 rattlesnake bounties were paid. Killing rattlesnakes was further encouraged by payment of bounties for not only gravid (pregnant) females, but bounties were also paid for unborn rattlesnakes that were removed

Adult timber rattlesnake. Photo by Jaime Edwards

from dead females. The cumulative effect of bounties also took a dramatic toll on Minnesota's rattlesnake population through the long-term destruction of rattlesnake blufftop den sites.

There are seventeen snake species known in Minnesota. Southeastern Minnesota has the highest number of species. The timber rattlesnake is the only venomous pit viper known in the state since there are no recent records for the massasauga. Timber rattlesnakes have variable patterns of dark chevron markings along a background coloration that may range from reddish, tan, or brown to gray. They have a broad head, eyes with vertically elliptical pupils, and facial (loreal) pits on each side of the face that serve as heat-sensing organs for locating prey at night. As their name implies, rattlesnakes have rattles at the tip of the tail. A new rattle is added each time the snake sheds its skin, but the number of rattles does not tell the age of the snake as the oldest rattles may break off with age. Rattlesnakes may be three to four feet long.

A timber rattlesnake showing the banded scale pattern, vertical pupils, loreal "heat- sensing" pits, and rattles. Photo by Jaime Edwards.

Rattlesnakes hunt mainly at night by waiting for small rodents, shrews, small rabbits, or other mammals to pass nearby. As prey approaches, the snake detects its body heat with its loreal pits. When close enough, it strikes, inserts venom, releases the animal, follows the animal's scent trail, waits for the prey to die, and then swallows it. Rattlesnakes may live up to thirty-five years. A female may not become pregnant until four to seven years old. Then she may only become pregnant every three to four years, so a female may only produce three to five litters of live young, ranging from three to fourteen young, during its lifetime. Courtship and mating usually occurs from July through September.

After mating, females store sperm in their bodies, and the eggs are fertilized the following spring. It was previously thought that gravid females do not feed, but DNR Nongame Wildlife Program regional specialist Jaime Edwards documented from X-rays that gravid females may also consume prey during summer months before the birth of their young, which are born from August through September.

Historically, timber rattlesnakes inhabited eight counties of southeastern Minnesota where they were at the northwestern limit of the species' range in the eastern United States. They have disappeared from Washington and Dakota Counties and are now found in Fillmore, Goodhue, Houston, Olmsted, Wabasha, and Winona Counties. In 2009, a total of eighty-five rattlesnake den sites were recorded for those counties. Previous den sites have been lost due to killing, disturbance, den site destruction, habitat change, and homesite development.

Even with the end of bounty payments, rattlesnakes have declined because of other environmental factors. Rattlesnakes need the open habitat of rocky outcrops surrounded by bluffland goat prairies. However, a lack of natural fires or prescribed burning in those habitats has allowed brush, trees, and exotic buckthorn to mature and shade those habitats which has reduced the amount of open grassland on bluff prairies. That compromises the quality of snake habitat and denning sites.

Gravid (pregnant) females need the warmth of the sun provided by the open landscape of bluff prairies for normal growth of their unborn young during the summer before they give birth in fall. The loss of open bluff prairies impairs the long-term

Examples of a rocky outcrop necessary for survival of timber rattlesnakes. Photo by Jaime Edwards

habitat necessary for the rattlesnake population. Rattlesnakes are also subject to being run over when crossing highways or while sunning themselves on highways. Some people intentionally swerve onto the snakes to kill them. Other rattlesnakes are killed by panicked people who encounter them near their homes, yards, or farmsteads.

Another loss of rattlesnakes has occurred in recent times because some people hunted for den sites to kill the snakes, or collectors searched for rattlesnake dens to capture them for sale in the illegal pet trade. A more recent threat to rattlesnakes has been the demand for rural homesites with views overlooking the scenic bluff country. Those home sites are typically built on edges of bluffs, which are the types of habitat needed by rattlesnakes for dens. This sets up a classic and predictable conflict with rattlesnakes and the additional loss of snake denning habitat. Land use zoning changes are needed to require a residential setback of at least two hundred feet from bluff edges.

These multiple issues resulted in a gathering of rattlesnake experts and biologists who decided that a ten-year Timber Rattlesnake Recovery Plan should be developed by the Minnesota Department of Natural Resources. The recovery team included nineteen herpetological experts from Minnesota, Wisconsin, and New York. Included were: Richard Baker, Faith Balch, Bonita Eliason, and Jane Norris from the St. Paul office of the Nongame Wildlife Research Program and the Division of Ecological Resources; Ed Quinn, head of the Division of State Parks and Trails Natural Resources Program; Shawn Fritcher, DNR Resource Specialist with Minnesota Parks and Trails; Carol Hall, staff herpetologist for the County Biological Survey; Jaime Edwards, DNR regional nongame wildlife specialist for southeastern Minnesota; and Barb Perry, who served as Jaime Edwards' nongame field technician and assistant for rattlesnake surveys and habitat management activities. This effort resulted in a comprehensive strategy to help Minnesota's timber rattlesnakes recover.

The forty-seven-page plan was finalized in April of 2009. It outlined activities and goals for the next ten years. The plan reviewed the history of timber rattlesnakes in Minnesota and their life history, habitats, and threats to their survival. The plan set recovery goals for population size, habitat preservation and recovery, and public outreach. The plan also set goals for population monitoring, habitat monitoring, and photo monitoring.

Jaime Edwards joined Minnesota's Nongame Wildlife Program in 2000 as the DNR southeastern regional nongame wildlife specialist after previously working for the Nongame Wildlife Program in the Iowa Department of Natural Resources. She was the perfect person for that job. She was an outstanding and energetic field wildlife biologist with an intense sense of dedication for her work to benefit not only rattlesnakes but other reptiles like the wood turtle. She had the athletic skills for traversing southeastern Minnesota's rocky outcrops, hilly goat prairies, and hillside woodlands inhabited by timber rattlesnakes.

Jaime created impressive rapport with local farmers, landowners, and law enforcement officers by helping them understand and appreciate the ecological significance of timber rattlesnakes. She teamed up with wildlife technician Barb Perry. They became the dynamic duo for rattlesnake conservation and management in the southeastern bluff lands of Minnesota. They made a big difference in implementing recommendations of the Timber Rattlesnake Recovery Plan.

Jaime had an impressive grasp of the publics who needed to be involved in conservation, management, and educational outreach efforts, including conservation officers, local law enforcement agencies, emergency responders, DNR state park and trail managers and naturalists, media contacts for newspapers, radio and TV, DNR wildlife managers, local herpetologists, and school teachers. She defused animosity toward rattlesnakes into curiosity and appreciation for rattlesnakes and the habitats upon which they depend.

During her tenure as the southeastern region nongame wildlife specialist Jaime teamed up with Project WILD coordinator Jan Welsh to produce two Rattlesnake Learning Trunks which were made available to school teachers, nature centers, and state park naturalists to teach adults and school children about rattlesnakes. One other strength of Jaime was that she had the unique ability to "connect the dots" related to rattlesnake conservation. She realized that good rattlesnake habitat was also good wild turkey habitat. She developed a lasting partnership with the Minnesota Wild Turkey Federation for habitat management that was co-funded by the Nongame Wildlife Program and the Wild Turkey Federation. It was the proverbial win-win solution that benefited advocates for rattlesnake conservation and wild turkey management.

The other example of connecting the dots was that Jaime realized good bluff prairie habitat for timber rattlesnakes also benefited state-listed Leonard's skippers, regal fritillary butterflies, and the federally listed rusty-patch bumblebee. This connection brought in more project partners and state, federal, and private funding opportunities including participation by Audubon Minnesota, Trust for Public Lands, and the Minnesota Land Trust. Jaime Edwards continues to provide rattlesnake conservation initiatives as DNR manager of the Whitewater Wildlife Management Area.

Rattlesnake conservation efforts have continued with Shawn Fritcher and Ed Quinn of DNR State Parks providing guidance and management for rattlesnake conservation on state park lands. There are seven state parks in southeast Minnesota that have timber rattlesnakes present. They have carried out an impressive program of comprehensive rattlesnake management on state parks over the past twenty years that has included use of remote cameras and trail cameras surveys for monitoring use by rattlesnakes. They keep track of five to six rattlesnake dens and carry out habitat management on bluff prairies, actual or potential wintering hibernacula, basking areas, and habitats used by snakes as they travel between summer and fall denning areas. Their habitat management has included cutting woody vegetation and girdling trees on bluff prairies, brush removal of shrubs, browsing by goats to control invasive shrubs, and prescribed burning where appropriate.

Timber Rattlesnakes—the Next Chapter...

The next chapter in the story of timber rattlesnakes in Minnesota is still being written. It requires continuing attention and funding for meeting their specific seasonal habitat management needs that will likely require prescribed burning, browsing by goats, and herbicides as necessary. It requires a commitment to long-term monitoring, protection of den sites, intensive protection from poaching, a commitment to assisting private landowners with opportunities for enhancing rattlesnake habitat on private lands, and creative educational efforts to help children living within rattlesnake country to understand and appreciate the beneficial role that rattlesnakes play in the environment instead of fearing or hating them. Perhaps rattlesnakes could also be reintroduced to former habitats or potential denning sites could be restored or created.

Chapter 14

Wood Turtle

I have been fascinated by turtles since childhood when I discovered snapping turtles living in Minerva Creek on our Iowa farm. I have since encountered memorable turtles on my international wildlife travels: there was Lonesome George (the last Galapagos tortoise of his kind), leatherback turtles nesting on beaches in Costa Rica and Trinidad (the largest turtles in the world), and leopard tortoises in the savannas of Kenya. There were also four-spotted river turtles basking along the Napo River in Ecuador as colorful butterflies sipped salty turtle tears from the corners of their eyes.

When I assumed the role of Nongame Wildlife Program supervisor with the Minnesota DNR, I was responsible for initiatives to benefit native turtle species. There were Blanding's turtles and wood turtles especially in need of conservation action, and there were other species where inadequate laws still allowed trapping and harvest with no bag limits. Exportation of Minnesota's turtles to international Asian markets was unregulated, and most of those Minnesota turtles were likely destined for use as food. Turtles had fallen through the cracks of Minnesota's conservation laws.

There is an irony regarding turtles as a conservation priority. Most turtles have a hard shell that protects them from predators. However, their shell offers no protection against mortality caused by humans or a lack of laws necessary to protect them. Minnesota's iconic turtle species like the wood turtle have become threatened internationally and locally by illegal exploitation for the pet trade as well as by land development and agricultural practices that destroy their nests and nesting habitats.

The wood turtle needs research, surveys, population assessment, and conservation actions to recover from a significant decline in their numbers over the past forty years. It falls into the Four-H category as a holistic species that is historically an important but poorly known component of rivers and riparian forest communities in northeast and southeast Minnesota.

Wood turtles are one of the least known and rarest of Minnesota's eleven turtle species. Photo by Gaea Crozier

Meet the Wood Turtle

A medium-sized turtle smaller than snapping turtles, a wood turtle measures from five to eight inches along the top of the carapace (dorsal shell). The brownish carapace is comprised of pyramidal dome-shaped shell components called scutes highlighted by annual growth rings—like the growth rings in the cross-section of a tree trunk. The plastron (ventral shell) of a wood turtle is bright yellow with irregular black splotches and annual growth rings on each scute that can be used to determine the age of younger turtles.

Wood turtles inhabit medium-sized, fast-flowing streams or rivers along forested habitats of eastern Minnesota. They have been documented in sixteen counties of eastern Minnesota, but they are rare or uncommon in most watersheds other than on the St. Louis River in northeast Minnesota and several watersheds of southeastern Minnesota. They prefer fast-flowing rivers with sandy or gravelly bottoms and clean water. They thrive in rivers adjacent to hardwood or boreal forest habitats that have occasional heavy rainfall events that create sandy embankments or cut banks. These turtles are not found along larger rivers. However, Jaime Edwards and Barb Perry found that wood turtles did use smaller side channels of larger rivers, especially hatchlings that may find it easier to navigate the slower currents of the side channels.

Wood turtles overwinter in cut bank cavities, log jams, and other protected streamside habitats. They emerge in spring where the females seek nesting sites on sandy points, cut banks, or sandbars. Wood turtles mate in spring and lay eggs from May to June. From four to twelve eggs are usually laid in holes dug into sandbars, riverbanks, and in corn or soybean fields with sandy or gravelly soils near rivers. Nesting sites chosen by gravid females may include locations subject to human disturbance like gravel pits, cut banks along rivers, sand mines, highway shoulders, roads between their river habitat and their chosen upland nesting site, and agricultural fields adjacent to rivers in southeastern Minnesota. Farm equipment may destroy turtle nests, nesting turtles, and hatchlings.

When wood turtles nest on sand bars along the river, those sites may also be appealing to canoeists for shore lunches. If canoeists leave food scraps or garbage on the beach, it can attract raccoons, skunks, foxes, or opossums where they could discover and destroy the turtle nests. In northeastern Minnesota, badgers are also a predator of turtle nests. Many wood turtle nests do not last more than several days because of depredation by mammalian predators.

It takes fifty-eight to seventy-one days for the eggs to develop before hatching from August to September. The hatchlings then scurry for the river. These travels may require a perilous trip for the hatchlings as they attempt crossing railroads or highways where they can be killed by traffic. They may also be eaten by raptors or snapping turtles after arriving in the river. In southeastern Minnesota, they sometimes nest in corn or soybean fields where nests or hatchlings can be crushed by tractors or farm equipment. In some areas of southeastern Minnesota nearly half of the turtle nests in crop fields are destroyed by farm equipment. Wood turtles do not nest annually, so they are vulnerable to long-term declines in reproductive success.

Wood turtles forage in forests along rivers throughout the summer for raspberries, blackberries, strawberries, insects, mushrooms, earthworms, succulent plants, dandelions, leaves, and mollusks. They may be seen basking on logs along rivers, but they spend most of their summer months foraging in forests and scattered grasslands within about a quarter mile of the nearest river. Researcher Ron Moen and his team used GPS telemetry to learn that the females ranged farther from water than the males.

Wood turtles do not reach sexual maturity until they are twelve to fifteen years old. They only lay eggs once a year, and they may not reproduce every year. They may live for fifty-years or more, but their numbers have declined significantly in the past forty years. The wood turtle became protected as a state threatened species in 1984, but they still have many challenges to their survival, including turtle poachers determined to sell them illegally for the pet trade.

Early efforts to assess the distribution and abundance of wood turtles were carried out by turtle researcher Michael A. Ewert of Indiana University in 1984 and 1985 in northeastern Minnesota with funding from the DNR Nongame Wildlife Program. Michael Ewert estimated a population of forty-four-wood turtles in 1969, and herpetologist Barney Oldfield found only six turtles with twenty-three hours of survey effort in 1988. Linda Dahl of Lewiston, Minnesota, subsequently found one wood turtle after spending one hundred hours of survey effort in 1996. This was a significant call to action to mobilize an effort for conservation and recovery of the wood turtle.

How Can We Apply What We Have Learned from Research and Surveys to Implement Restoration Strategies?

The wood turtle was identified as a state-threatened species in Minnesota and designated as a species in need of a statewide management plan in Minnesota's 2015 to 2025 Wildlife Action Plan. A planning team of biologists with wood turtle expertise was selected to develop a ten-year plan which was published in 2020. The plan identified strategies to start moving this species toward recovery.

The wood turtle planning team included: Rich Baker, Gaea Crozier, Carol Hall, Krista Larson, and Jeff LeClere (MNDNR); Mike Majeski, Jimmy Marty, and Jason Naber (Emmons and Olivier Resources, Inc.; Tricia Markle and Seth Stapleton (Minnesota Zoo); John Moriarty (Three Rivers Park District); and Tim Lewis (University of St. Thomas).The Northeast Working Group included: Gaea Crozier (MNDNR); Dan Ryan (U.S. Forest Service); Jeff Hines (MNDNR); Mike Schrage (Fond du Lac Resource Management Division); and Jason Naber (EOR). The Southeast Working Group included: Carol Hall, Barb Perry, Krista Larson, Russell Smith, Jeff LeClere, Michael Worland (MNDNR); and Seth Stapleton, Tricia Markle (Minnesota Zoo).

The planning team identified five issues that needed to be addressed in their recovery plans: 1) habitat, 2) adult mortality, removal, and sub-lethal impacts, 3) juvenile recruitment, 4) knowledge gaps, and 5) partnerships.

An implementation plan summarizing this information was developed collaboratively by the planning team and by northeastern and southeastern regional work groups. There were seven steps identified for implementing their plan:

1 Clearly delineate the seasonal habitats needed throughout the year and the acreages necessary to accommodate their nesting habitats, travel corridors, wintering sites, and to sustain a viable breeding population.

2 Identify the natural foods necessary for sustaining a population and determine if there are berry-producing plants that could be planted along rivers to provide a summer food source for wood turtles.

3 Identify the amount of habitat that must be sustained and managed along riparian corridors to protect corridors for long-term survival of the turtle populations and determine if sandy cutbanks, sandy points, or streamside mounds could be created to provide safe nesting sites that would not require crossing roads or railways for nesting.

4 Identify specific soil types, topography, and land use of the nesting sites necessary for successful reproduction.

5 Identify the seasonal hazards to survival including predation of adults, eggs, and hatchlings.

6 Identify conservation partners for northeastern Minnesota: United States Forest Service, Natural Resources Research Institute of the University of Minnesota, The Nature Conservancy, Minnesota Herpetological Society, Indiana University, West Virginia University, Fond du Lac Band of Lake Superior Chippewa, Mark Nelson, Richard Buech, Ron Moen, Donald Brown, Maya Hamady, Gaea Crozier, Maria Berkeland, Linda Dahl, Michael Ewert, and Dr. Stanley H. Anderson.

7 Identify conservation partners for southeastern Minnesota: Chris Smith of the Minnesota Department of Transportation, Barney Oldfield, John Moriarty, Bonnie Brooks Erpelding, Carol Hall, Tricia Markle (Minnesota Zoo Wildlife Conservation Specialist), and Seth Stapleton (Minnesota Zoo Director of Conservation).

Researchers needed to identify strategies for reducing hazards to survival including mammalian predation, highway mortality associated with crossing roads, farm equipment mortality to adults and turtle nests in agricultural fields, human-related problems like poaching for the pet trade, and in southeastern Minnesota—garbage strewn on sand bars by canoeists who leave food scraps that attract mammals to turtle nesting sites. It was also necessary to explore the feasibility of head-starting to increase the survival odds for hatchling turtles.

Gaea Crozier, the DNR Nongame Wildlife Program regional specialist for northeast Minnesota, has participated in two competitive state wildlife grants from the U.S. Fish and Wildlife Service and is working with the Departments of Natural Resources in Wisconsin, Michigan, and Iowa to identify threats to wood turtles in the Upper Midwest and to evaluate the effectiveness of different conservation techniques.

Gaea worked with Dr. Ron Moen at the University of Minnesota Duluth and Donald Brown. Graduate students Maddy Cochrane, Maria Berkland, and Cole Weigartz have been part of the research project. Based on the University of Minnesota's Natural Resources Research Institute (NRRI), they have used field surveys, trail cameras, and telemetry of adults and hatchlings for finding long-term strategies to reduce mortality. Some hatchlings have been equipped with microchips to document their survival. These strategies have included: 1) creation of flood-safe nesting habitats; 2) protection of nests from predators with fencing exclosures; 3) installation of barrier fencing to prevent turtles from crossing roads; and 4) enhancement of foraging habitat. It was surprising when researchers discovered that badgers were a significant predator of turtle nests.

Additional conservation actions were taken by the Minnesota Herpetological Society: 1) Put up fencing to keep them off roads; 2) Create alternative nesting habitat sites; 3) Create flood-safe nesting habitat; and 4) Install electrified predator-proof (and badger-proof) nesting structures powered by solar panel collectors.

Since 1998, the Nongame Wildlife Program has been monitoring wood turtles along southeastern Minnesota streams to determine population size and age, range, and habitat use. They partnered with the Minnesota Biological Survey and the Minnesota Zoo to do telemetry work. They are monitoring adult and juvenile turtles to determine habitat preferences and movements of head-started wood turtle hatchlings.

In southeastern Minnesota, adult females may lay eggs in agricultural fields and farm tractor tires can crush turtle nests. There is a high frequency of depredation on eggs by skunks, raccoons, foxes, and opossums within a few days of when the eggs are laid. Few eggs survive. One additional hazard observed by Jaime Edwards and Barb Perry was that turtle nests sometimes also failed due to fly parasitism. Another observation was that hatchlings used different habitats than the adults, preferring willow thickets, so that is an important habitat to be preserved.

About 90 percent of the eggs laid by wood turtles are destroyed by predators in the first several days after they are laid. When wood turtles hatch, they are so small that they become bite-sized snacks for mammals, raptors, and large fish.

Key personnel who have contributed to the survival of wood turtles in southeastern Minnesota have included Bonnie Brooks Erpelding, Jaime Edwards, Barb Perry, Krista Larson, Ed Quinn, Chris Smith of the Minnesota Department of Transportation (DOT), Tricia Markle (Wildlife Conservation Specialist from the Minnesota Zoo), and Seth Stapleton (Director of Conservation at the Minnesota Zoo). Another essential partner in this recovery effort has been wildlife biologist and avid herpetologist Christopher Smith of the MN DOT. He helped plan and install fencing along highways where female wood turtles were being killed while attempting to cross en route to their nesting sites.

Head-Starting Wood Turtles

My introduction to wood turtles came in 2004 when DNR regional nongame biologist Jaime Edwards and wildlife technician Barb Perry invited me to visit them to learn about their wood turtle radiotelemetry research in southeast Minnesota. They were helping local farmers learn about wood turtles and how they could avoid or reduce disturbance or injury to turtles nesting in agricultural fields adjacent to wood turtle streams.

DNR nongame biologist Jaime Edwards and wildlife technician Barb Perry with wood turtles outfitted with radios in 2003 and 2004.

Head-Starting Becomes a New Strategy for Helping Wood Turtles

Head-starting is a strategy involving collecting turtle eggs when they are laid, hatching and rearing them in captivity, and providing them with supplemental feeding in captivity for a year. By then they have become much larger than they would have been in the wild, making them less vulnerable to predation. In late summer of the following year, they are released into their original river habitat.

Jaime Edwards and Barb Perry of the Nongame Wildlife Program began using head-starting to help survival of wood turtles in southeastern Minnesota in 2003 and 2004. They collected eggs and hatched twelve turtles in 2002 and twenty-three turtles in 2003. They kept the hatchlings in captivity from late summer when they hatched until they released them about ten months later in early summer of the following year.

One of the most fascinating discoveries in this project was that four head-started turtles released in 2003 and 2004 by Jaime and Barb survived and were recaptured in 2017 and 2018, including three males and one female. The female was outfitted with a GPS transmitter, and her nest was located. Her eggs were collected, and the offspring were head-started to become the second generation of head-started wood turtles. This was a marvelous validation that head-starting was an important strategy giving wood turtles a desperately needed survival edge.

Minnesota Zoo conservation biologist Dr. Tricia Markle began a collaborative project in 2017 with Krista Larson, herpetologist and research biologist for the DNR Nongame Wildlife Program, with a grant from the Legislative-Citizen Commission on Minnesota Resources (LCCMR). The funding would be used to study the life history, survival, and reproductive patterns of the wood turtle. Krista Larson and Dr. Markle have been using radiotelemetry and GPS data loggers to track the movements of the turtles to identify their preferred habitats and nesting sites.

Female wood turtle with a radio transmitter entering a soybean field to lay its eggs.

Wood turtle hatching. Photo by Tricia Markle

They have head-started 130 yearling wood turtles and released them back to their native streams from 2017 through 2023. Their efforts for locating turtle nests were so successful that Krista and Tricia collected another 105 eggs that they hatched in captivity. The Minnesota Zoo, however, did not have the laboratory capacity to head-start all 105 of those additional turtles for the following year, but they kept those turtles in captivity through their first

A solar GPS transmitter and antenna fastened to the back of a female turtle so it can be located while nesting and the eggs can be collected. Photo by Tricia Markle

Tricia Markle with a head-started turtle ready for release. Photo by Tricia Markle

summer, fed them well, and released them in the fall after they had grown significantly from their enhanced diets. They would still have a better chance of survival because of their larger size after even one season of supplemental feeding.

A total of twenty-three more one-year-old, head-started wood turtles were released at three sites in southeast Minnesota in the summer of 2024, and another thirty hatchlings from 2024 were head-started for release in the summer of 2025. Dr. Markle continues to track twenty to twenty-five wood turtles to learn more about their habitat use, nesting sites, and other threats to their survival.

Other strategies have also been necessary to protect wood turtles. Hardware cloth screens are placed over wood turtle nests after locating them with the use of telemetry. This protects the eggs from depredation. Shorelines can also be provided with electric fencing to keep mammalian predators from either digging up turtle nests or devouring the hatchling turtles.

Krista Larson and Carol Hall saving eggs from destruction in a cornfield so they can be head-started. Photo by Tricia Markle

Krista Larson with a head-started turtle ready for release. Photo by Krista Larson

Krista Larson encountered an unusual challenge during the 2017 wood turtle nesting season. It was an extremely dry summer for croplands adjacent to the river. When turtles emerged from the river at night to lay their eggs in nearby fields, the soil was very dry, and the turtles were unable to dig into the hardened soil to create a nesting hole. Krista watched them attempt to dig a hole for their eggs, but they would finally give up, lay exhausted, and eventually return to the river without laying their eggs.

The next night, Krista devised a plan for the expectant mother turtles. She showed up with her telemetry gear and a large spray bottle of water. Each time she located a turtle ready to lay eggs, she sprayed its butt and the soil below its tail to soften up the soil so she could dig a hole and lay her eggs—at three in the morning. It worked. I think that qualifies Krista as the god-mother for those hatchling turtles. Hats off to Jaime, Barb, Krista, Carol, and Tricia for their years of service for the conservation of wood turtles in southeastern Minnesota.

Turtle Legislation—at Last!

It has been difficult to generate legislative interest or concern for protecting Minnesota's turtle populations over the past thirty-five-plus years. State laws for protecting or managing turtles were grossly lenient or lacking. In 2021 alone, over ten thousand western painted turtles were trapped in Minnesota's lakes by nineteen licensed turtle trappers and sold—mostly to oriental markets to end up in a soup bowl. Western painted turtles are much more beautiful when basking in the sun on a Minnesota lake than boiling in a soup bowl.

In 2024, turtles like the western painted turtle were finally protected by the Minnesota legislature from turtle trappers. Thanks to long-term lobbying efforts by members of the Minnesota Herpetological Society like conservation chair Christopher Smith and herpetologist John Moriarty, DNR assistant commissioner Bob Meier, Collette Adkins of the Center for Biological Diversity, and past and present DNR staff, efforts to achieve more protective legislation passed in 2023 and became effective on January 1, 2024. It took over thirty-five years of legislative advocacy since John Schladweiler in the DNR Nongame Wildlife Program was first assigned to prepare recommendations for tightening Minnesota's laws relating to reptiles and amphibians. Those recommendations languished for many years waiting for support from legislators and conservationists to bring these laws to fruition. In 2023, it finally happened.

It has taken decades for society to evolve to the point of becoming more concerned about the need for conservation of our state's biodiversity beyond game species and conspicuous vertebrates like birds and mammals. Reptiles, amphibians, and thousands of invertebrates like butterflies, moths, bees, dragonflies, mollusks, and other invertebrates that comprise Minnesota's ecologically valuable web of life are finally receiving the long overdue attention that they richly deserve.

A Western painted turtle.

Chapter 15

Uncommon Terns— "A Conservation Challenge"

Common tern hovering over Interstate Island.

The common tern is a little-known but incredibly beautiful and graceful waterbird found on only a handful of islands in the state. Ironically, it has become uncommon. In flight it assumes angelic postures as it hovers to locate minnows that serve as prey. However, there is nothing angelic about these terns when they dive at tern researchers visiting their colony to monitor their nesting success. A common tern colony is a hard hat zone where hard hats prevent blood loss on the researchers' heads. This is a story spanning forty-five years of networking and collaborative efforts to protect and manage Minnesota's common terns.

In the nongame wildlife 4-H Priority spectrum, the common tern qualifies in the Holistic category because it is rarely seen except on Minnesota's larger lakes like Lake of the Woods, Leech Lake, Mille Lacs Lake, and in the Duluth Harbor of Lake Superior. It could easily be confused with the similar Forster's tern which inhabits smaller lakes and prairie marshes. When I was hired to begin the Nongame Wildlife Program, I created a volunteer survey to inventory Minnesota's colonial waterbird nesting sites. Colonial waterbirds include herons, night-herons, egrets, grebes, gulls, terns, pelicans, and cormorants. A total of 191 colonies were reported, including six common tern colonies. These species were a high priority as well as a holistic priority because those nesting sites were vulnerable to disturbance by humans, free-ranging dogs, avian and mammal predation, and unpredictable fluctuations in lake water levels.

In 1978, ten common tern colonies were reported at sites in Lake of the Woods, Gull Island in Leech Lake, and Spirit and Hennepin Islands in Mille Lacs Lake. Each colony had five hundred to one thousand pairs. Two sites were of special interest to me--Pine and Curry Islands in Lake of the Woods and Hearding Island in Duluth Harbor.

Early in 1980, I heard from DNR wildlife manager Larry Bernhoft that piping plovers and common terns were nesting on Pine and Curry Islands. I wanted to view this site, so I arranged a visit with Larry to explore the island. I needed an expert on piping plovers to accompany us, so I invited tern expert Ann Lambert from the Point Pelee Bird Observatory in Ontario. We visited the islands on June 12, 1980, and we were very impressed. We encountered a successful common tern colony on the beach at the western end of the island. There were several piping plover nests on the periphery of the tern colony. Piping plovers also nested at the northeastern end of the island.

I felt there was adequate justification for designation of the islands as a DNR Scientific and Natural Area for their value as important nesting habitat for both species. The land was privately owned, but the owner wished to do a land exchange for state-owned land in Lake of the Woods County. At this point, the DNR Scientific and Natural Areas program took over negotiations for the islands. On April 12, 1983, Pine and Curry Islands were designated as a DNR Scientific and Natural Area. This important area was preserved with no nongame program expenditures necessary for land acquisition.

Not long after this happened, Larry Bernhoft passed away from cancer. His passion for all wildlife, including nongame, is sincerely remembered and appreciated because it was still an era in which game species were a priority for the DNR. Meanwhile, DNR wildlife manager LeRoy Angel from Duluth contacted me about the potential for forty-acre Hearding Island in Duluth Harbor to serve as habitat for piping plovers and common terns.

Hearding Island was created from dredged spoils excavated from Duluth harbor in the 1930s. Common terns nested there from 1946 through 1955. We designated the island as a DNR Wildlife Management (WMA) on July 8, 1978, and LeRoy cleared southern portions of the island to attract nesting piping plovers and common terns. However, the island was too close to Park Point. Kids from Park Point spent a lot of time living out Tom Sawyer and Huckleberry Finn adventures on the island. They disrupted any potential for attracting nesting terns or plovers.

In 1980, the statewide common tern population was estimated at two thousand pairs. It was time for plan B in Duluth harbor. Sites previously used in the harbor by common terns were Sky Harbor, Minnesota Point, and the Port Terminal. Those sites were being developed, and they were no longer available for use by terns. However, there was a seven-acre dredge spoil island, Interstate Island, that was still in the public domain. It was available for designation as a DNR WMA, and it was not near any residential areas where human disturbance would be a problem. However, the Minnesota/Wisconsin boundary bisected the island so we needed to work out details with the Wisconsin DNR to cooperatively designate and manage the island.

I hired DNR wildlife research specialist Jack Mooty from Grand Rapids in 1981 as the DNR's first northeastern regional nongame wildlife specialist. He began efforts to have Interstate Island cooperatively designated as a DNR Wildlife Management Area with Wisconsin DNR area wildlife manager Fred Strand. That collaborative effort continued for over forty years. They formed a great partnership and began monitoring and managing nesting activity on the island. Wildlife researcher Don Goodermote, shown above, also helped with surveys on the island.

Interstate Island WMA was officially designated on April 13, 1983. Jack and Fred began working to protect and manage the nesting terns. Common terns had continuing depredation problems caused by foxes, mink, great horned owls, stray dogs, Franklin's ground squirrels, peregrine falcons, short-tailed weasels, and storm damage. However, common tern nest counts from 1983 through 1985 declined from 198 to 140.

In 1987, the St. Louis River estuary was designated as an Area of Concern under the Great Lakes Water Quality Agreement, but the tern nest counts dropped to eighty-one nesting pairs in 1989. There have been additional efforts to protect and manage common terns at two other sites in Minnesota provided by Steve Mortenson and the Leech Lake Band of Ojibwe and by

Fred Strand, Jack Mooty, and Don Goodermote (left to right) on Interstate Island, 1993.

the National Park Service and U.S. Fish and Wildlife Service for the historical tern colonies on Spirit and Hennepin Islands in Mille Lacs Lake. The relevance of Pine and Curry Island in Lake of the Woods has diminished dramatically for piping plovers and common terns. There was only one nest of piping plovers at nearby Morris Point in 2022, and that nest was flooded by high water. High water conditions also flooded the shoreline on Pine and Curry Island in 2022, and there was no nesting by common terns or plovers. There was one successful nest that fledged four piping plovers in 2023.

Katie Haws and Bruce Lenning surveying common terns and piping plovers on Pine and Curry Island.

The DNR's Angle Island Wildlife Management Area is one of Minnesota's last important common tern nesting areas in Lake of the Woods. It is a three-acre rocky island about seven and a half miles from the nearest public water access. DNR regional nongame wildlife specialist Katie Haws proposed protection of Angle Island in Lake of the Woods as a DNR Wildlife Management Area (WMA), and it was designated as a WMA on March 1, 1992. It is so remote that it is only checked once annually by making nest counts from boats to determine the extent of nesting by common terns. It also provides nesting habitat for ring-billed gulls, herring gulls, and double-crested cormorants. It is not possible to survey the tern nesting site by entering the colony because landing on the rocky island would flush terns from their nests long enough to expose their eggs and chicks to immediate depredation by gulls.

In 2023, terns did not nest on Angle Island, but about 175 pairs did nest on nearby Crowduck Island and produced one hundred young. Amy Westmark, the current DNR regional nongame wildlife biologist in northwest Minnesota, is in charge of monitoring common terns in Lake of the Woods.

Ensuring the long-term survival of common terns is a continuing challenge. By 1989, Jack and Fred had completed habitat management work on Interstate Island, protecting the terns by installing string grids throughout the desired nesting area to deter nesting by ring-billed gulls. Terns are agile enough to helicopter down to their nests in areas with parallel string grids about three feet apart and three feet above the ground. Gulls are not agile enough to drop vertically to land within the tern nesting area. The terns responded by successfully nesting there for the first time in several years. By 1990, the only common tern nesting in Duluth harbor was on Interstate Island.

From 1989 through 2018 there was an annual average of 180 nests recorded. However, there have been continuing problems with ring-billed and herring gull predation, sporadic problems with great horned owls, and egg depredation by Franklin's ground squirrels, peregrine falcons, and even short-tailed weasels.

The Legislative Citizens' Commission on Minnesota Resources (LCCMR) approved a contract with the Natural Resources Research Institute of the University of Minnesota for monitoring common tern colonies in Minnesota beginning in 2024.

The intervening years have provided an opportunity for a classic case study in the evolution of wildlife conservation for common terns: annual nest counts, long-term banding of tern chicks, weekly spring and summer visits to the nesting colony, management of string grids in the prime nesting areas, providing wooden nesting shelters for tern chicks, peripheral fencing to keep out ring-billed gulls, targeted predator control of some ring-billed gulls and mammalian predators, use of geolocators to determine migratory traditions, and a Great Lakes Restoration Initiative funding grant in 2020 from the Environmental Protection Agency.

Common tern nesting area on Interstate Island with string grids to prevent depredation by ring-billed gulls.

Common tern chicks begging for food.

To keep up with the evolving management and research activities on Interstate Island, I made numerous trips over the years to join Jack Mooty, Maya Hamady, Gaea Crozier, Fred Strand, Annie Bracey, and Alexis Grinde at Interstate Island to keep up on progress with tern conservation. It was impressive to see the results of banding, use of geolocators, use of the string-grid lines, fencing, targeted predator control, and enhancement of the island for tern nesting.

I assisted in recent years by photographing their banding and management efforts. I donated my photos to the University of Minnesota Natural Resources

Research Institute, Minnesota DNR, and Wisconsin DNR. Fred Strand and Sumner Matteson of the Wisconsin DNR were able to use the photos for publication in their research reports and at conference presentations. On one occasion I photographed terns carrying minnows of different species to their chicks. The photos were later analyzed by DNR Biological Survey staff to make an inventory of the minnow species taken by terns for feeding their young.

The backbone of this effort has involved the long-term dedication and collaboration of many dedicated wildlife researchers and wildlife managers—LeRoy Angel, Fred Strand, Annie Bracey, Alexis Grinde, Jack Mooty, Maya Hamady, Gaea Crozier, Don Goodermote, Sumner Matteson, Bill Penning, Rich Staffon, and Martha Minchak.

Common tern carrying a minnow to feed its chicks.

Researchers and biologists Gaea Crozier and Fred Strand at Interstate Island.

Tern chick being fed a minnow.

Author taking tern photos at Interstate Island.

Dr. Annie Bracey, common tern researcher from NRRI with a tern chick ready for banding.

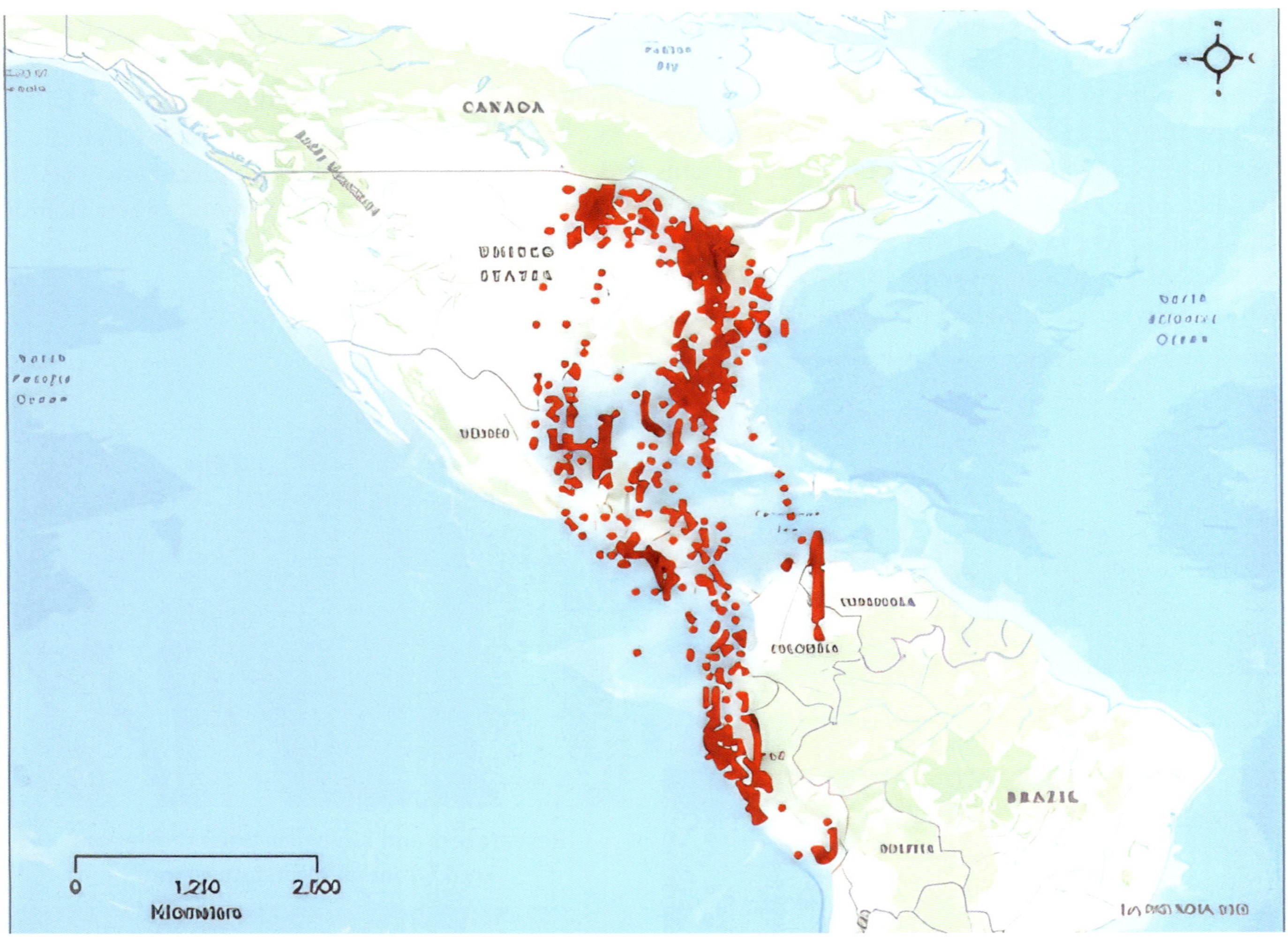

Migration route of common terns during the non-breeding season based on solar geolocation tracking devices placed on adults breeding on two nesting colonies in Lake Superior (Interstate Island in the Duluth-Superior Harbor and Ashland Island in Ashland, WI). Courtesy of Dr. Annie Bracey, NRRI

Intensive management and protection of common terns in the Great Lakes region has not sustained tern numbers. The number of breeding pairs has declined by 18 percent between 1976 and 2009. There was a need to learn more about the international migratory patterns of common terns to determine if there were other mortality factors affecting population trends. Minnesota's tern researchers collaborated with researchers from Manitoba to the Atlantic coast on a study involving geolocators to monitor migratory movements.

Geolocators revealed that female terns departed in the fall on August 9, and males departed on August 24. The terns flew southeast through Florida and Cuba, then through Central America to South America, including the northwestern Caribbean coast of Venezuela and then southward to the Pacific coasts of Ecuador and Peru. Most terns wintered along the coast of Peru. Females arrived on their wintering grounds about November 2, and males arrived approximately November 20. The terns spent an average of eighty-eight days migrating during the fall.

Common terns have a survival advantage wintering along the Peruvian coast because cold waters of the Humboldt current usually pass northward along the Pacific coast. The Humboldt current is rich with marine life, including anchovies. They are small fish that comprise an important food source for terns. After wintering for about 150 days, common terns begin a westerly springtime migration route different from the fall migratory route. Terns traveled along the Pacific coast of Peru and Ecuador through Central America and the Yucatan Peninsula. They pass along the Gulf Coast of northern Mexico and Texas and then northward to Minnesota.

The springtime migration was quicker and averaged only thirty-two days. In spring, males arrive about a week earlier than females, averaging May 12. Females arrive about May 19. Additional research conducted at the Lake Superior colonies documented another issue. There was a local mercury exposure to chicks in the Duluth harbor area. Chicks that were fed more fish from the river had higher mercury concentrations than those that foraged primarily in the open waters of Lake Superior, underscoring the local significance of local contamination. Researchers continue to study mercury exposure to terns and are attempting to identify sources of contamination and patterns of food web transfer.

Tern researchers were awarded funding from the Legislative Citizens' Commission on Minnesota Resources (LCCMR) which began in July 2023. That funding is derived from state lottery proceeds. It continued through 2025 and will assess the status of common tern populations in Minnesota. The project will focus on facilitating monitoring efforts and identifying projects that will enhance site quality for nesting terns. This project will bring together partners across the state to determine whether recovery goals are being met, to identify factors that may be limiting nesting success, to develop standardized monitoring protocols and create an online data management system to facilitate the long-term monitoring and management goals for the terns.

In 2017-2018, Dr. Bracey and her research staff put global positioning system (GPS) tags on nineteen birds from Interstate Island and Ashland, Wisconsin. Then, in 2019 and 2020, they incorporated a third tracking technology to the common tern research with nanotags that allowed tracking sixteen adults and forty-three juveniles via the international Motus wildlife tracking system to document tern migratory movements.

These triple-tracking efforts help identify locations outside their breeding colonies that could be critically important to their survival and assess management options for both adult terns and for young-of-the year terns migrating for the first time. Identifying these locations will allow biologists to identify potential migration bottlenecks, migratory stopover habitats, and evaluate conservation options in key stopover and wintering locations. Analysis of the international migration patterns and wintering sites of common terns will reveal significant conservation implications and options.

Climate change could change the availability and composition of minnow species in their diet. Rising water levels could impact areas used for nesting and foraging on both summer nesting sites and wintering grounds. The unpredictable effects of El Niño along the Humboldt current could also have sporadic impacts on tern survival by reducing the availability of the fish they depend on. Climate change is a quite cosmic and difficult problem to address.

However, there is a more immediate and tangible opportunity to improve the nesting habitat and reproductive success for terns on Interstate Island. This six-acre dredge spoil island in the Duluth-Superior Harbor began disappearing under dramatically rising water levels in 2015. The Minnesota Land Trust has since managed this project for the Minnesota and Wisconsin Departments of Natural Resources. EPA's federal partners include the U.S. Fish and Wildlife Service and the U.S. Army Corps of Engineers.

The habitat work cost roughly three million dollars, with $840,000 coming from Great Lakes Restoration Initiative (GLRI) funding. The GLRI was launched in 2010 as a non-regulatory program to accelerate efforts to protect and restore the Great Lakes as the largest system of fresh surface water in the world.

What a wonderful example of interagency networking and collaboration on behalf of the terns. The coordinator for restoration projects in the estuary is Melissa Sjolund. Interstate Island and its common tern colony also found a champion in the Minnesota Land Trust in Gini Breidenbach, restoration program manager. Breidenbach and Minnesota Land Trust's involvement was critical to launching this project by bringing much needed organizing capacity and restoration management expertise to the initiative. Breidenbach commented: "Minnesota Land Trust was the missing piece in getting this project done. We finally had the capacity to write grant proposals, secure funding, bring together the strategic partners to design the project, work through the permitting processes in both Minnesota and Wisconsin, and manage the construction process—it was no small feat!"

There are changing threats every year for the common tern, but I am optimistic because of the dedicated efforts that have emerged from this collaborative conservation effort. That networking effort included University of Minnesota NRRI researchers Annie Bracey and Alexis Grinde, and initial support provided by the graduate research of Bill Penning and the DNR Nongame Wildlife Program staff over the years, including Jack Mooty, Maya Hamady, Gaea Crozier, LeRoy Angel and Martha Minchak in the Section of Wildlife, and Fred Strand and Sumner Matteson of the Wisconsin DNR. What a great team!

Chapter 16

Pelican Etiquette— Watch Where You Aim Baby Pelicans

American white pelican in flight.

The American white pelican is one of the most impressive and graceful birds in flight that I had ever observed. In the fall of 1975, I experienced a totally inspiring encounter with white pelicans. A storm was brewing over the south end of Lac qui Parle Lake. The sky had turned dark bluish-gray when I spotted a formation of white pelicans circling above, apparently exercising in preparation for their upcoming migration to wintering grounds along the Texas Gulf Coast. As they circled and soared above in single file, they demonstrated extraordinary grace and beauty in flight. Their bright white plumage glowed like a string of pearls against the dark skies above.

In contrast to my awe of viewing pelicans in flight at a distance, they create a quite different impression up close. The pelican colony on Marsh Lake was within the Lac qui Parle Wildlife Management Area when I was hired as assistant manager in the spring of 1974. In July of 1975, I volunteered to assist St. Cloud University professor Dr. Al Grewe and his volunteers with banding pelican chicks on a nesting island in Marsh Lake.

That was where I got my close-up introduction to the American white pelican. My first visit to a pelican nesting island was a step back into a prehistoric era of sounds, smells, and sights associated with waterbird colonies. The ground was spongy from the long-term accumulation of pelican and cormorant guano. The smells were an overwhelming blend of pelican poop, partially digested fish, and decomposing pelican chicks that had not survived. Naked and downy pelican chicks resembled baby sparrows—weighing a couple pounds. They waddled across the island in gangs of several dozen chicks like a group of Minions©. Our job was to surround each cluster of chicks, kneel, grab each chick, and clinch a federal bird band onto its leg with a pair of pliers. We passed each banded chick behind us and kept banding until we had banded the entire group of chicks.

That day I got a quick education in pelican wrangling. When you pick up a pelican chick, it has a very effective double-barreled defense. It barfs its most recent meal—perhaps a partially digested bullhead or salamander—and then it poops. You must pick up a pelican chick sideways, or you will regret it. I returned home from my Marsh Lake adventure that day smelling like a pelican colony.

Al Grewe began banding pelicans in 1972. Thanks to the dedicated efforts of Dr. Grewe, Jeff DiMatteo, and many dozens of volunteers, Marsh Lake has the best long-term banding totals for American white pelican nest records in North America.

American white pelicans became extirpated from Minnesota when they disappeared as a nesting species in 1904. This is an amazing restoration story because, like sandhill cranes, they recovered on their own over the past one hundred years. Pelicans nested in western Minnesota in presettlement times. However, early settlers killed pelicans in their nesting colonies because they ate fish. There were sporadic reports of summering or migrating white pelicans throughout the 1900s, but they did not occur again as a nesting species until about seventy pairs were discovered nesting in Marsh Lake on the island where we banded pelicans in 1975.

An American white pelican chick begging for food.

Anglers need to realize that pelican diets are comprised primarily of rough fish, smaller panfish of little significance to anglers, salamanders, and other aquatic creatures. They do not dive for aquatic prey, like walleyes, in deeper water. They tip downward with their bills so they primarily take prey within several feet of the surface. Walleye and bass are not a significant component of their diet.

With my appointment as supervisor for the Nongame Wildlife Program, the responsibility for watching over pelicans became part of my job. I was encouraged to see the continuing increase in their numbers, but I was disappointed to sense the outdated and parochial attitudes many people had about pelicans, especially some fishermen. They perceived pelicans as competing with them for game fish like bass and walleyes. There were even federal biologists who suggested that we might have to start controlling pelicans. Those people apparently did not need facts. They just needed opinions. I could see that one of my responsibilities was to provide positive information to the public about the life history and food habits of white pelicans.

A survey in 1983 showed that the Marsh Lake pelican colony had split. The main colony on the island decreased from the 1000 nests counted in 1982. A larger new colony formed on a peninsula in Marsh Lake northeast of the island. It contained over 1200 nests. There was also a colony in Lake of the Woods on Crowduck Island that contained about 50 nests, so the statewide count grew to about 1500 nesting pairs.

In the 1980s, most Minnesotans did not realize the state had pelicans, so they contacted the DNR whenever there was a pelican sighting. One time my secretary got a call from a DNR conservation officer in Worthington who had found six dead pelicans. He wanted to know what I wanted to do with them. My secretary gave me his phone number. When I returned the call, a man answered. I said, "Hello, I'm calling about your six dead pelicans." There was a prolonged silence. I repeated, "Hello, I'm calling about the six dead pelicans you reported." After another silence, the man said, "I'm sorry, I have no idea what you're talking about. This is a gynecology lab." He hung up. I asked my secretary about the note she had left. Uffda! She had failed to write the 507 area code for Worthington with the phone number, so I had called a Twin Cities number for a gynecology lab.

The American white pelican became a special concern species in Minnesota in 1984. It has been designated a Species in Greatest Conservation Need (SGCN) by the Minnesota Department of Natural Resources, and it is designated a Stewardship Species by Audubon Minnesota.

The American white pelican typically lays two eggs in a clutch and usually fledges one chick per nest. The older and larger chick usually kills its nest mate. This is called siblicide. Nevertheless, the American

A migrating "kettle of pelicans" circling above the DNR parking lot in St. Paul, Minnesota, September 2, 2004.

white pelican has staged a remarkable recovery. Since 1967, pelican numbers in Minnesota have increased by about 13 percent per year. Pelicans have expanded the number of nesting sites on Marsh Lake to four islands and one peninsula. They have also colonized islands in Minnesota Lake, Pigeon Lake, Leech Lake, Lake of the Woods, and Lake Pepin on the Mississippi River.

White pelicans normally fly in V-shaped formations in which they derive extra lift from the wingtip of the pelican ahead of them. In migration, they can also take advantage of heat rising as thermals above grasslands, and even urban asphalt parking lots, as they migrate. They circle and soar upward within the column of rising warm air to a higher elevation until the upward lift from the thermal subsides at cooler elevations. Then they set their wings to glide downward in the direction of their migration to save energy in flight. Then they find another thermal over a grassland or urbanized site covered by asphalt or concrete heated by the sun to continue their migration. On September 2, 2004, I even observed a kettle of pelicans migrating south, circling above the Minnesota Department of Natural Resources asphalt parking lot at 500 Lafayette Road in St. Paul.

They were responding to the phenomenon of hot air rising from the DNR asphalt parking lot which created a thermal updraft. Thermals are an important aid for migrating American white pelicans to save energy as well as for migrating raptors.

Our Nongame Wildlife Program emphasis on American white pelicans, as well as common loons, changed dramatically on Earth Day in 2010 when the Deepwater Horizon oil spill occurred. Unfortunately, there were still Minnesota migrant birds, including common loons and American white pelicans, in the Gulf of Mexico at the time of the spill.

Minnesota Senator Amy Klobuchar called a meeting of state conservationists to assess the extent of the damage from the oil spill on Minnesota wildlife. We conducted a review of bird species wintering in the Gulf and decided the common loon and the American white pelican were the species most likely impacted and the species for which we had the best long-term population data.

This project needed to determine if there were detrimental consequences resulting from the Gulf oil spill causing population declines or threats to Minnesota-origin American white pelicans and common loons. The activities proposed were intended to provide valid data critical to accessing any remediation funds that could become available from the Natural Resource Damage Assessment (NRDAR) process.

Dr. Francie Cuthbert of the University of Minnesota was contracted to survey sixteen Minnesota pelican nesting sites and check an additional twelve locations with summering pelicans that could become nesting sites. A final report documented the survey results and compared the counts with those previously done in 2004 and 2010.

Our Lac qui Parle pelican research crew in action.

Dr. Mark E. Clark and Dr. Jeff DiMatteo of North Dakota State University were contracted to carry out a study of potential contamination of pelican eggs and bill knobs by BP contaminants, and Dr. Mark Martell and Kristin Hall of Audubon Minnesota were contracted to study the migration ecology and wintering areas of pelicans wintering in the Gulf. Lac qui Parle Wildlife Management Area assistant manager John Wallenberg helped the pelican research crew. Dr. Christopher Perkins of the University of Connecticut Center for Environmental Sciences and Engineering was contracted to do the contaminant analysis. They were involved with comparable studies on the environmental contamination resulting from the Deepwater Horizon oil spill and I wanted the results from Minnesota to be comparable with those analyses.

I knew that bill knobs grew on the bills of white pelicans on their wintering sites in the Gulf of Mexico. It was likely that British Petroleum contaminants could be found in the bill knobs when they were shed in the Marsh Lake colony after nesting. This was the first time that pelican bill knobs had ever been analyzed for environmental contaminants. There were thirty-seven bill knobs found in the Marsh Lake colony. Twenty-nine of the thirty-seven-bill knobs had nine PAH oil contaminants: naphthalene, acenaphthylene, flourene, anthracene, phenanthrene, fluoranthene, pyrene, crysene, and benzo(a)anthracene. There were seventeen of thirty-seven bill knobs containing DOSS (dioctyl sodium sulfosuccinate) contaminants. Those were the dispersants spread in the Gulf after the oil spill supposedly to mitigate the effects of the oil pollutants, but they were also environmental contaminants.

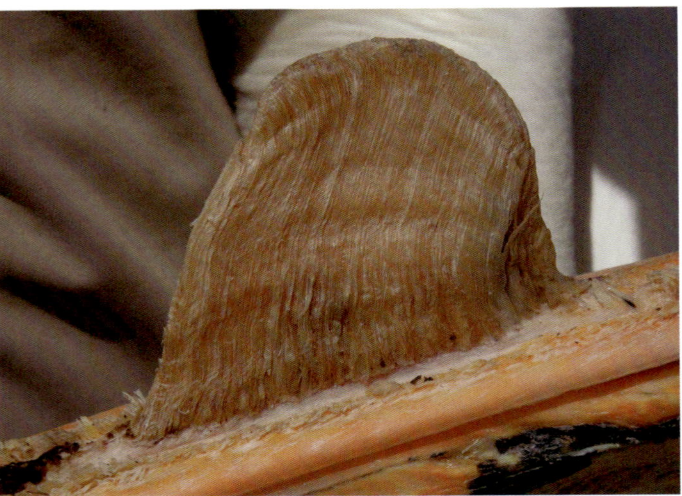

Example of a pelican bill knob that was analyzed for environmental contamination.

Pelican in flight showing radio transmitter and wing tag.

The migration data collected from banding records of Minnesota pelicans and data gathered from telemetry work conducted by Audubon Minnesota showed that the pelicans wintered farther offshore where less petroleum contamination would have occurred. Few dead white pelicans were found in the Gulf of Mexico during oil spill mortality surveys. It was felt that the impact of the oil spill was significantly less for white pelicans than research revealed for Minnesota loons.

American white pelicans have demonstrated their resilience over the past century and have staged a remarkable recovery back to the skies and lakes of Minnesota. The Department of Natural Resources, University of Minnesota, and NRRI carried out nesting surveys of white pelicans in 2004, 2011, 2015, and 2020-2021. In 2015, the population estimates were 31,220 to 45,012 adults, but that estimate did not include nonbreeding birds.

The 2020 surveys were conducted by researchers at the University of Minnesota-Twin Cities campus, and the 2021 surveys were conducted by researchers in the Avian Ecology Lab at the Natural Resources Research Institute (NRRI), Duluth, MN. Pelicans were found nesting at eleven sites, including Egret Island (ten pairs), Marsh Lake (8,930 pairs at three sites), Leech Lake (1,476 pairs), and Lake of the Woods (991 pairs at three sites) but several other sites were not accessible or available for counting. For surveys conducted in 2020 and 2021, the monitoring data from priority sites indicated an estimate of 11,847 pairs of nesting American white pelicans. This was similar to the estimate from the 2015 census of 16,501, noting that in 2020 numbers of nesting pairs were not estimated at all priority sites.

The latest monitoring approach was not adequate for estimating the state's total breeding population size, or long-term changes in productivity, trends, or changes in distribution over time. Changes are anticipated to add the use of drones in the future to facilitate more comprehensive counts on sites not accessible for on-the-ground site visits. Considering increases in Minnesota's pelican populations over the past fifty years, I feel that the American white pelican population is secure since no significant losses were apparent from the Deepwater Horizon oil spill.

The U.S. Fish and Wildlife Service decided that the impact of the Deepwater Horizon oil spill on American white pelicans from Minnesota did not merit use of NRDAR funds for restoration. It was the right decision. Minnesota's pelicans are doing just fine.

Chapter 17

Common Loon—Our State Bird Is a Great State Bird, but It Needs Your Help

A loon incubating its eggs on Big Mantrap Lake, Minnesota.

Over the past forty-seven years the common loon has been a focal point for the Nongame Wildlife Program staff, private citizens, wildlife researchers, loon lovers, lake associations, U.S. Geological Survey researchers, the National Loon Center, and me. All these publics are dedicated to the cause of surveying, protecting, and ensuring the protection and long-term survival of Minnesota's common loons. It would be a tragedy for loons to decline in Minnesota due to global warming or other losses caused by pollution, lead poisoning, or excessive shoreline development. We all share in the challenges and opportunities for helping to preserve our state bird.

I assisted with capturing loons on Whitefish Lake in central Minnesota in the summer of 2013 as part of our DNR research on the impact of the Deepwater Horizon oil spill on Minnesota loons. We searched for them from about nine p.m. until three a.m. with the research crew led by Kevin Kenow of the U.S. Geological Survey.

I have enjoyed the sight and sound of loons many times on Minnesota's northern lakes while fishing or photographing them on family outings at Eagle Lake, near Crosslake. However, I didn't realize the magic experience of hearing loons in the middle of a starlit night. It was two a.m. The stars sparkled like diamonds, and the night sky was highlighted by falling stars. The lake was eerily silent as our loon capture crew floated, quietly seeking our next loon. There were no motorboats, anglers, or anyone else on the lake. Then a loon began its tremolo call which echoed across the lake. The call had a resonant and profound three-dimensional quality. I had heard loons many times during daytime hours, but in this setting the loon's call could only be described as one of the most enchanting and captivating experiences I have ever had.

Regional DNR Nongame Wildlife Program Specialist Pam Perry posting a loon nesting area sign.

The sight of common loons accompanied by their chicks on a northern Minnesota lake, the haunting call of loons on a moonlit night, and the lifelong memories they create among anglers, photographers, and outdoor enthusiasts make them a most enchanting bird. It is quite appropriate that it is Minnesota's state bird. They demonstrate a powerful family bond as they care for, defend, and feed their chicks in a manner that visitors on our northern lakes can appreciate and remember for many years.

Many Minnesotans can recall a magic moment when they observed loons up-close and personal. I had such a moment in 2009. Ethelle, our son Craig, and I spent a week every summer at Eagle Lake Lodge, near Crosslake. Each morning, I arose at sunrise, took a sport boat, and circled the lake to photograph loons and other wildlife. On July 19, 2009, I encountered a pair of loons with a downy chick. I maneuvered my boat so that the rising sun was at my back. I slowly approached the loons using my quiet electric trolling motor. The loons were diving to capture small fish to feed their chick. To put the loons at ease, I began making soft, low whoot calls like loons make when calling to each other to reassure their family that all is well.

Loon parents feeding their chick a green sunfish on Eagle Lake, July 19, 2009.

One of the loons surfaced with a small green sunfish. The chick quickly approached and grasped the sunfish as the other parent moved nearby to watch the feeding ritual. I took a photo just as the sunfish was passed to the chick. It was a magic moment that characterized the wonderful parental bond for which loons are so well known. The photo appeared on fifty thousand Nongame Wildlife Program posters in 2011 to encourage Minnesota taxpayers to donate to the Nongame Wildlife Checkoff on their state tax forms.

The Nongame Wildlife Program has provided many initiatives over the years for citizens and DNR staff to survey loons across their breeding range. In 1979 and 1980, I initiated a volunteer loon observation program to assess the distribution of nesting loons in Minnesota, determine their nesting success, and find out what kind of survival threats existed for loons. I got reports of loons nesting in forty counties and estimated Minnesota's population at 10,700 loons that were producing about four thousand chicks annually.

The most important long-term strategy for loon surveys was developed in 1993: the Minnesota Loon Monitoring Program. The project involved the random selection of six groups of one hundred lakes that each represented different lake habitat types. Volunteers were recruited to survey the numbers of loons, including adults and young. The survey has been carried out the first week of July every year since 1993. Since the lakes were randomly selected, the data was collected in a statistically valid manner to identify state population trends. The data is available online on the DNR website. Interested citizens are welcome to offer their services if any lakes come open for the upcoming survey season.

Loon protection strategies have included advising boaters and canoeists to avoid approaching loons incubating eggs and for power boaters to avoid running over loons and their chicks, especially on Memorial Day weekend and July 4th. Those holidays are especially dangerous for loons because of the potential threat posed by uncaring or reckless boaters and canoeists.

Lakeshore owners, anglers, and boaters are advised to turn in any dead or dying loons they encounter so biologists can determine their cause of death. The data collected can be used to develop publicity strategies to help reduce human-caused loon mortality.

Volunteer Ken Perry collecting data for the Minnesota Loon Monitoring Program.

Protect Our Loons—Get the Lead Out of Your Fishing Tackle

Anglers are advised to use lead-free non-toxic small fishing jigs and sinkers to avoid poisoning loons. Loons can die from swallowing small lead jigs and sinkers that anglers lose while fishing. Loons routinely pick up small pebbles on lake bottoms to aid their gizzards in grinding up the fish they eat. Small jigs or sinkers lost by anglers can be mistaken by loons and ingested. Loons may also ingest lead jigs or sinkers that fish have previously swallowed. Loons may also go directly after fishing lures and swallow them. Just one sinker or jig can kill a loon.

Stones recovered from the gizzard of a dead loon. It was poisoned by ingesting the lead fishing sinker shown to the right of the pebbles.

There are many non-toxic alternatives available, such as tungsten, steel, and bismuth. Tungsten is perhaps the most popular and high-performing alternative due to its greater density and sensitivity compared to lead. Tungsten jigs and weights not only help loons but are also very effective at catching fish. People should consider making a family project out of getting kids involved in converting tackle boxes to lead-free and loon-safe tackle boxes.

Minnesota Pollution Control Agency: Leading the Effort to Get Toxic Lead Jigs and Sinkers Out of Fishing Tackle

The Minnesota Pollution Control Agency (MPCA) has an aggressive campaign underway to encourage Minnesota's anglers to switch to non-toxic fishing tackle to protect Minnesota's loons, trumpeter swans, and other wildlife. For more information on Minnesota's Get the Lead Out effort, go to

These tungsten jigs are not poisonous to loons. Look for them at your local sporting goods store. Photo by Steven Yang, Minnesota Pollution Control Agency

their website www.pca.state.mn.us/leadout. This effort was initially funded with $1.27 million in remediation funds made available in 2018 from the fines assessed to BP resulting from the 2010 Deepwater Horizon oil spill. In 2023, the Minnesota legislature allocated another one million dollars to continue their educational effort to help protect our Minnesota loons and trumpeter swans.

Lakescaping for Wildlife and Water Quality Benefits Loons, Lakes, and Lakeshore Owners

At a Nongame Wildlife Program staff meeting in 1993, regional nongame wildlife specialist Jack Mooty expressed the concern that he saw too many people purchasing lakeshore properties and then destroying the shoreline habitat. *Landscaping for Wildlife* had been so successful that I decided to write a sequel about landscaping for wildlife on lakeshores. I knew I could provide the wildlife expertise for this publication, but I needed the expertise of a horticulturist and a landscape architect. I recruited limnologist Carolyn Dindorf and landscape architect Fred Rozumalski as co-authors for the book. They were a great team for merging the diverse concepts for the book. It required five years of writing and production.

I felt one of the most endangered habitats in Minnesota included naturally occurring lakeshores. This state of over fifteen thousand lakes offers abundant opportunities to enjoy the natural beauty of lakeshores. However, people who buy lakeshore lots often don't recognize the biological diversity and ecological significance that natural lakeshores possess, but they love lake country and the outdoor traditions associated with those lakes. Then they destroy their natural lakeshore.

There is a terrible stereotype of what many Minnesotans think the perfect lakeshore lot should look like when developed. People want manicured bluegrass lawns treated heavily with fertilizer and pesticides. They want a sand blanket along the shore for a swimming area, and they want huge riprap boulders along the remainder of the shoreline. On Sunday mornings, when the neighbors are not watching, they tear out cattails, sedges, bulrushes, and other native emergent aquatic plant life because they consider them weeds. They create a biological desert for native lakeshore fish, wildlife, and plants.

Those landowners have good intentions. They do not wish to damage the environment. They are just trying to keep up with their neighbors' expectations for having a neat lawn or they manage the lakeshore like their parents or grandparents did. They create a labor-intensive yard—just like the one they left behind in the city. Their bluegrass monoculture then invites Canada geese to their yards, it creates loafing areas for mallard ducks that prefer open shorelines, and they mow so close to the water's edge that the owners become upset when their mower tires collapse into muskrat burrows. Then they call the DNR to complain about the Canada geese and muskrats.

That vision destroys habitat for pollinators, dragonflies, native wildflowers, lakeshore birdlife, spawning beds for fish, and shoreline space for muskrat burrows. It increases shoreline erosion and runoff of lawn pollutants, fertilizers, and pet waste into the lake.

As an alternative, people could provide habitat for hundreds of native plants, butterflies, dragonflies, damselflies, songbirds, ducks, grebes, and loons along their lakeshore. This is an especially important opportunity for hands-on efforts for conservation of loons on Minnesota's northern lakes.

The lakescaping concept involves creation of a natural buffer zone that extends perhaps fifty feet out into the lake and fifty feet onto the land. The goal is to preserve or restore as much of the native vegetation in that buffer zone as possible while still providing reasonable lake access and recreational opportunities for the family. For example, a one hundred foot shoreline might include protection or restoration on seventy-five feet of the natural shoreline and twenty-five feet of access for a boat dock and/or a swimming area. If vegetative restoration is necessary, local origin native plants should be used.

A well-planned buffer zone helps protect the landowner's lakeshore from shoreline erosion and helps filter out contaminants or pollutants from the shoreline property, whereas riprap rocks on a shoreline do not protect the lake from lawn chemicals or pet droppings coming from the landowner's shoreline property. A shoreline with native wildflowers will attract butterflies, bees, dragonflies, and damselflies and help filter out pollutants from the shoreline lawn. And consider that dragonflies eat mosquitoes. Aquatic vegetation along the shoreline becomes habitat for dozens of aquatic invertebrates and nesting habitat for fish, loons, and red-necked grebes. This is important for creating emergent vegetative zones along the lakeshore that protect nesting loons from wave action created by boaters, and it provides concealment from potential loon predators.

Lakescaping restoration site, before.

Lakescaping restoration site, after.

Lakescaping for Wildlife and Water Quality was published in 1998. The book became a popular reference for Minnesota's lakeshore owners and lake associations and was even popular in other states. There were no other comparable reference books on this topic.

The book became a popular reference for Minnesota lake associations, the DNR Section of Fisheries, and Minnesota Master Gardeners. The book sold over 27,000 copies. The content of *Lakescaping for Wildlife and Water Quality* has since been uploaded onto the DNR website under the title *Restore Your Shore*. It includes a sortable database for landowners to select plants from among six hundred native plants by county, soil type, and plant characteristics. The DNR website also has a separate category in its search engine called "native plant nurseries" where people can find nurseries with local-origin native plants.

In 1997, I submitted a proposal to the Legislative-Citizens Commission on Minnesota Resources (LCCMR) to implement our lakescaping concept. It

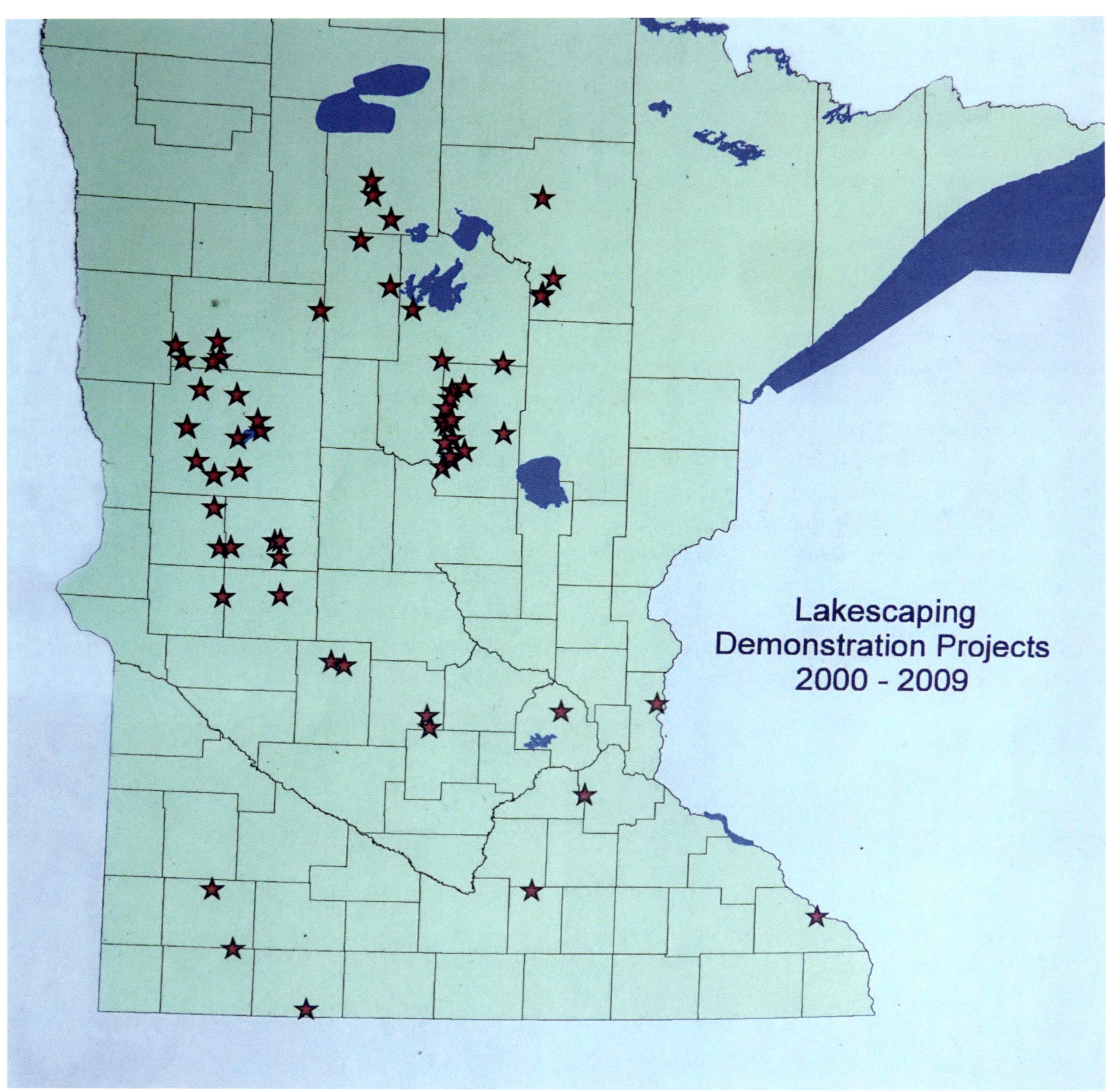

A map of lakescaping demonstration sites planned and installed with local origin native plants from 2000 to 2009 as part of the *Lakescaping for Wildlife* LCCMR project with funding from the Environment and Natural Resources Trust Fund.

would give people hands-on experience for creating ecologically appropriate shoreline plantings and teach them how to manage those plantings. Those practices help create shoreland habitat that could provide sheltering cover for loon nesting sites and foraging habitat for loons, grebes, and other waterbirds. The LCCMR approved $1,043,000 over an eleven-year period from 1998-2009. Funding came from the Environment and Natural Resources Trust Fund which was derived from state lottery proceeds.

A total of sixty-seven lakescaping demonstration sites were designed, planned, and planted on private lands. One of the most rewarding revelations among lakeshore owners was the increased use of their lakeshores by butterflies and bees because of local origin native plants, which included species like milkweed. As part of the LCCMR initiative, I organized forty-three targeted workshops for 1,482 participants including lakeshore owners, nursery managers, DNR staff, realtors, and officials from local units of government.

One of the most innovative developments from this project was the effort to obtain local origin native plants from DNR nongame and fisheries staff from across the state. Many native plants were previously unavailable commercially. In 2009 and 2010 a total of ninety-two native plant species, seeds, and propagules were collected. I contracted with the Ramsey County Corrections unit in St. Paul so the inmates could raise the plants for distribution to homeowners who were restoring their shorelines. Germination techniques necessary for many plants had been unknown, so those techniques were developed by Sean Uslabar of the Ramsey County Corrections staff. A DVD was developed for nursery owners and managers so they could collect seeds and raise them for sale to extend the long-term impact of the lakescaping initiative.

Nest Platforms Can Also Help Loons

One hazard for loons is that on lakes where there are no small islands for nesting sites, they are forced to nest on lakeshores where their nests are subject to predation by raccoons, otters, and other predators. In *Woodworking for Wildlife*, I published designs for loon nesting platforms that help reduce predation on shoreline loon nests. The 2009 edition of *Woodworking for Wildlife* includes information on how to build three different loon nesting rafts, which help protect nesting loons from predators.

I was assisted in this effort by loon enthusiasts Lyle Laske and Steve Maanum of the Big Mantrap Lake Association. They developed a highly successful approach to managing loon nesting platforms. I also included detailed information in *Woodworking for Wildlife* that explained where to place nesting rafts on a lake with respect to the presence of emergent vegetation, protection from prevailing winds, and protection from disruptive boating traffic.

Big Mantrap Lake loon nesting pontoon-the ultimate loon nesting platform. Notice that western painted turtles have found the loon nesting platform to be an ideal basking site.

When the content of the *Lakescaping for Wildlife and Water Quality* book is combined with the recommendations for building and placing loon nesting rafts in the *Woodworking for Wildlife* book, it provides lakeshore homeowners and lake associations with the best available information they need for protecting and managing loons.

Minnesota's Bookstore closed permanently during the pandemic era, and my books, including *Lakescaping for Wildlife and Water Quality* and *Woodworking for Wildlife*, are no longer available for retail sale. However, used copies are still available online via www.Amazon.com, www.ebay.com, www.abebooks.com and www.alibris.com. *Lakescaping for Wildlife and Water Quality* is now available online at the DNR website under the title *Restore Your Shore*.

Educating children about the importance of helping loons has been another outreach effort thanks to the efforts of Jan Welsh, the Nongame Wildlife Program Project WILD coordinator. Loons to Loan education trunks have been made available to teachers since 1984. The trunks included a mounted loon, examples of a preserved loon wing, loon wing bones, loon feet, and other educational materials that explain the uniqueness of loons and the importance of loon conservation.

Feature programs have been funded through Minnesota Public Television to educate Minnesotans with Venture North educational programs. Slide programs and Powerpoint programs have been developed and delivered by DNR nongame biologists about helping loons for the past forty-plus years. There have been additional habitat benefits provided by acquisition and donation of lakeshore property and islands to the Nongame Wildlife Program: Trout Lake WMA, Sugar Lake SNA, Carmen Borgerding WMA, Big Sugarbush Lake WMA, Pokegama Lake WMA, Whitefish Lake Galbraith easement, Big Turtle Lake Island AMA, and Bear Island WMA in Deer Lake.

We promoted conservation of Minnesota's loons by publishing posters encouraging people to donate to the Nongame Wildlife Checkoff on their state income tax and property tax forms in 1981, 1985, 1990, 1995, and 2001. That included publication and distribution of about a quarter million loon posters throughout Minnesota.

The Nongame Wildlife Program focus on loons changed dramatically on Earth Day in 2010 when the Deepwater Horizon oil spill occurred. About five million gallons of oil were spilled into the Gulf of Mexico and nearly two-million gallons of the dispersant Corexit was injected at the severed wellhead and applied to oil slicks floating on the Gulf waters. Corexit did not help break down the toxic effects of the oil. It prevented the oil spill from being detected by flights over the Gulf to assess the extent of the damage. Unfortunately, there were still loons from Minnesota that were wintering in the Gulf at the time of the spill.

Minnesota Senator Amy Klobuchar called a meeting of state conservationists to assess the extent of the damage from the oil spill on Minnesota wildlife. We decided the common loon and American white pelican were the species most likely impacted. I was asked to prepare a work plan for the Legislative-Citizens' Commission for Minnesota Resources (LCCMR) for use of Environment and Natural Resources Trust Fund dollars (state lottery proceeds) for a detailed research and survey plan to evaluate the impact of the oil spill on loons and pelicans.

The proposal included participation by the DNR Nongame Wildlife Program, North Dakota State University, University of Connecticut, Audubon Minnesota, and Wisconsin DNR. I submitted the workplan to the LCCMR for $250,000 in January of 2011. The proposal was temporarily scuttled by anti-science legislators. However, thanks to some remarkable legislative stealth maneuvering in the middle of the night, the funding was reinstated on July 18, 2011.

This project was renewed three times over the next six years for a total of $651,000.

One of the greatest revelations resulting from the research relating to the Deepwater Horizon oil spill was the discovery of the relationship between loons and deepwater ciscos. This cisco (*Coregonus artedi*), often referred to as tullibee, is a small variety of cisco about six to seven inches long that is an oily and extremely nutrient-rich member of the salmon/trout family. These oily fish contain about three times the number of calories as other minnows of comparable size, so they are important components of diets for walleyes, northern pike, lake trout, and muskies. Those fish may grow to trophy size in deep lakes with good cisco populations. The benefit of having good cisco populations is obvious both to fisheries biologists and avid anglers.

Thanks to DNR fisheries biologist Peter "Pete" Jacobson and research initiated by the U.S. Geological Survey research crew, we learned ciscos also play an important role in the life cycle of loons in northern Minnesota. Ciscos need cold, well-oxygenated water for survival in northern Minnesota lakes. These are lakes sometimes deeper than a hundred feet where the deeper coldwater zone, or hypolimnion layer, is maintained throughout the summer.

"Pete" Jacobson called me in 2015 to tell me that while doing cisco research in late summer they observed concentrations of loons gathered on those deepwater lakes. He suspected there was some kind of nutritional benefit derived by loons utilizing ciscos as a food source prior to migration. This was a wonderful example of the value of networking! It generated a big breakthrough in understanding loons. We set up a meeting in St. Paul on February 18, 2015, for Pete to give a presentation to our nongame staff and the U.S. Geological Survey research team to provide an overview of his research on coldwater cisco refuge lakes. Kevin Kenow followed up by collaborating with Pete on their research and by initiating geotagging work with loons on those cisco refuge lakes. We learned that loons gathered from lakes in the surrounding region on those cisco refuge lakes in late summer to feed on ciscos prior to migration. This oily, nutritious food source put them in good condition for migration.

The problem with this situation is that there are only about 171 deepwater cisco refuge lakes in Minnesota that offer this seasonal opportunity for loons to benefit from the cisco diet. Global warming threatens the long-term status of these lakes as the water temperature warms. The colder deep waters of these lakes are important cold-water reservoirs that sustain aquatic life for species like ciscos. The DNR is engaged in an aggressive program for protection and management of the cisco refuge lakes and protection of up to 75 percent of their adjacent surrounding forested lakeshore habitats. Legislative and conservation initiatives are underway for protecting those lakes and lakeshores with a $180,000 proposal to protect thirty thousand acres of those coldwater lakeshore habitats.

Loon molting into fall plumage with a cisco. Photo by Steve Houdek, USGS loon research team, 2015

With the completion of the LCCMR project, Jane Norris, Richard Baker, and I prepared a proposal for recovering damages to Minnesota's loon population caused by the BP oil spill. Recovery of those damages was derived through the federal Natural Resources Damage Assessment and Restoration Program (NRDAR). This fund was created to assess damage claims to any corporate entities that cause damage to natural resources from pollution caused by those industries. A total of seventy million dollars was available for remediation for birds lost by the BP oil spill through allocation of NRDAR funds by the U.S. Fish and Wildlife Service. The U.S. Fish and Wildlife Service received about four hundred proposals from northern states to pay for remediation actions for birds affected by the oil spill. They approved three proposals—and Minnesota was one of them. In October of 2018, they announced that Minnesota would receive about $7.7 million to cover remediation expenditures for restoration costs to benefit the recovery of loons.

A flock of loons fishing for ciscos on a deepwater cisco lake prior to migration.

Considering the investment of $651,000 from the Minnesota Environment and Natural Resources Trust Fund lottery proceeds, that $7.7 million allocation from the BP oil spill remediation funds was a potential return of about $11.80 for every dollar invested in the LCCMR loon research.

Meanwhile, I saw a TV news story about a loon researcher, Kevin Kenow, who was a biologist from the U.S. Geological Survey (USGS) in LaCrosse, Wisconsin. He and his field staff were planning to attach satellite transmitters and archival geolocator tags to loons in Wisconsin. Funded by the U.S. Environmental Protection Agency for the Great Lakes Restoration Initiative, they were going to document loon movement and foraging patterns to understand potential risk of exposure to Type-E botulism in the Great Lakes. I realized this could be an incredibly important tool for studying the behavior and migration of Minnesota's loons for the BP study. I found Kevin's contact information and called him. I asked if it would be possible to include Minnesota loons as part of this study. He called me back and said he and his crew could add that research to his USGS workplan.

After capturing a loon, the USGS loon research crew took it ashore for weighing, measuring, and banding.

Kevin Kenow, USGS research team leader, releases a loon outfitted with an implanted satellite transmitter.

The loon research required capturing loons at night. They were measured, weighed, banded, equipped with archival geolocator tags, and some were operated on to insert internal satellite transmitters. Blood, feather, and fat samples were taken to determine tissue contaminant levels and the sex of the birds.

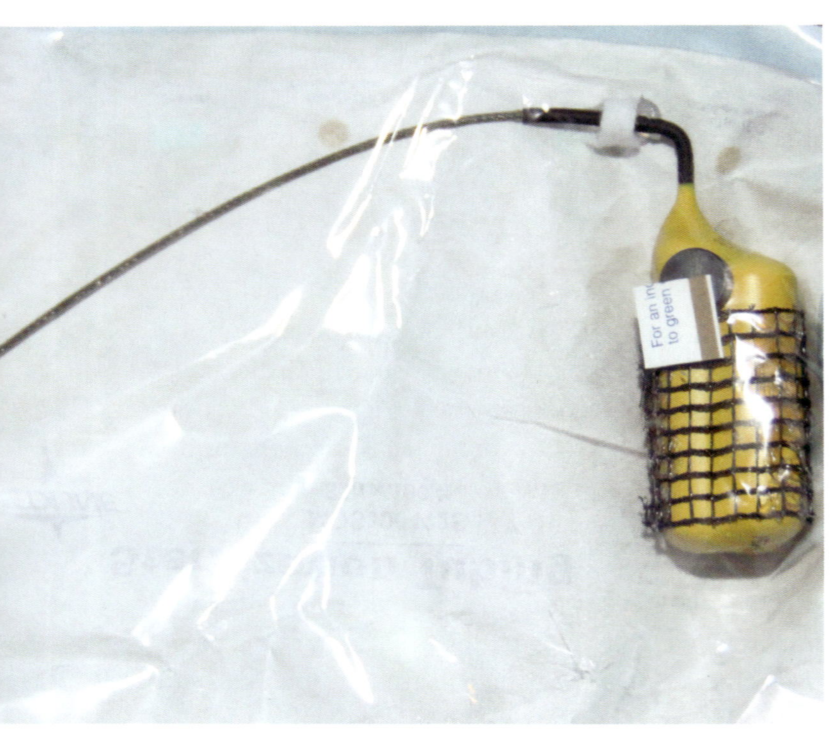

This is the satellite transmitter and the antenna which projects through the top of the loon's pelvic girdle.

The same loon after release showing the antenna that transmits its location to satellites that track its daily movements and migration patterns.

Fifteen adult loons and twenty-two juveniles were equipped with satellite transmitters. The batteries were expected to last about three years. A total of 119 loons were outfitted with geolocators, and sixty-one were subsequently recaptured or recovered to retrieve their data. DNR Nongame staffers Lori Naumann, Janine Kohn, Kevin Woizeschke, and I assisted with the nocturnal loon capture outings across central and northern Minnesota throughout the duration of the project.

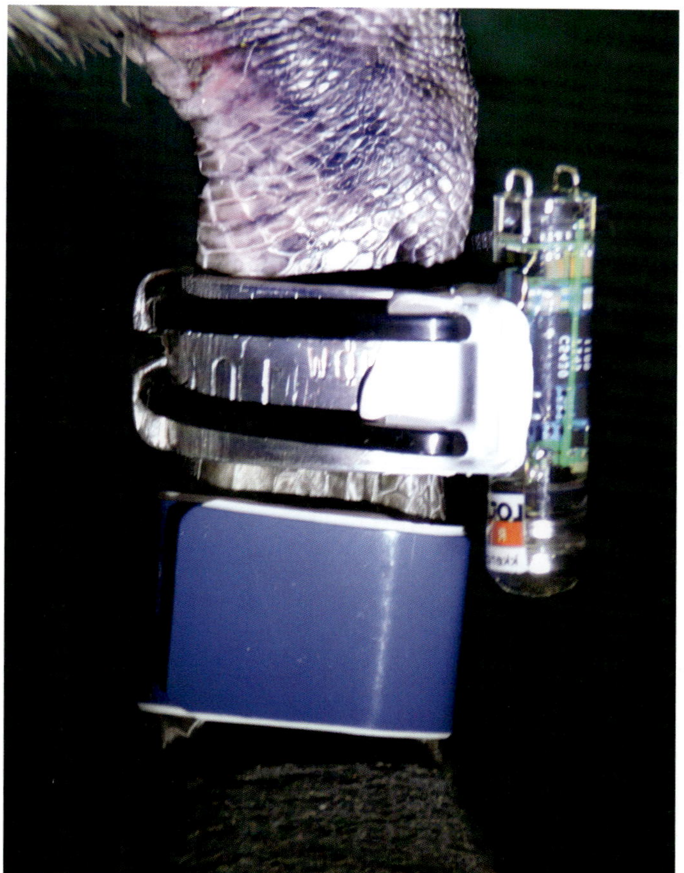

A geolocator attached to the leg of a loon. The geolocator above the band records the pressure of its surroundings, including the depths to which it dives for food and air pressure in flight when in migration.

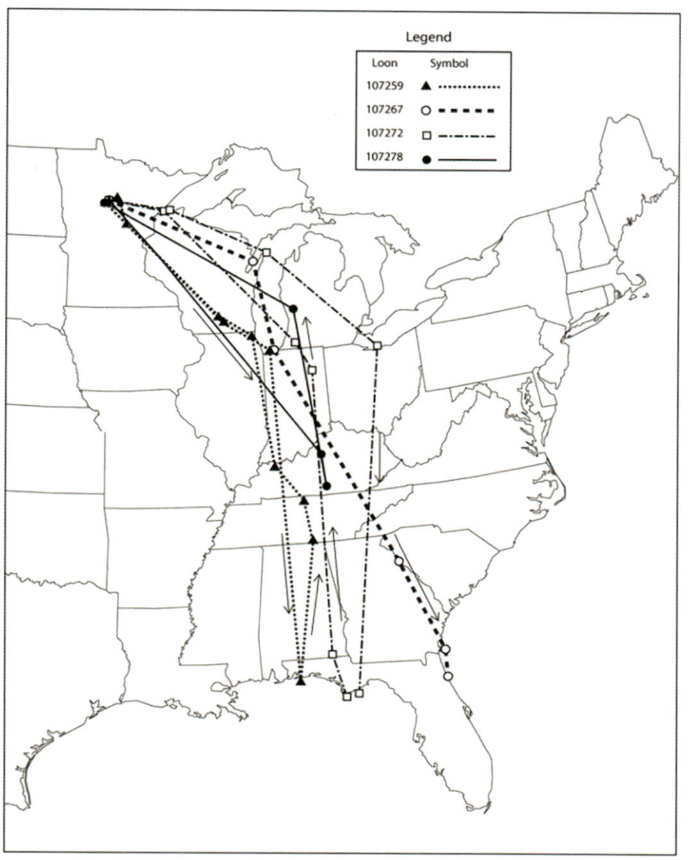

Movements of four common loons radiomarked on Mantrap Lake, MN, in July 2011. Source: Kevin Kenow, USGS. This data verified that Minnesota's loons wintered in areas potentially polluted by the Deepwater Horizon oil spill.

The USGS team did an extraordinary job on this project. They gathered new information about the migratory routes of adult and juvenile loons. On Minnesota's breeding lakes they learned that loons dive as deeply as sixty-five feet. Most adult loons migrated in fall to Lake Michigan and then south to the Gulf of Mexico. In Lake Michigan they fed on an exotic species, round gobies, at the lake bottom to depths of 197 feet. They also fed on the bottom of the Gulf of Mexico to depths from fifty to 164 feet. Satellite telemetry also documented loons wintering offshore in the Gulf of Mexico where BP oil pollutants settled. Author and naturalist Adele Porter reported on the loon telemetry research being done by the U.S. Geological Survey in the 2013 January to February issue of the DNR *Conservation Volunteer.*

Loon blood samples, unhatched eggs, feathers, and fatty tissues from loons found dead were also analyzed by Dr. Christopher Perkins at the University of Connecticut. I selected Dr. Perkins for this work because they were also doing contaminant analysis for other wildlife affected by the BP oil spill so the results would be comparable. Samples from Minnesota's loons were processed for polycyclic aromatic hydrocarbons (PAH) and dioctyl sodium sulfosuccinates, which are referred to as DOSS, a component of Corexit. PAH includes petroleum contaminants that cause carcinogenic, mutagenic, and teratogenic effects on living organisms. DOSS reportedly causes respiratory, nervous system, liver, kidney, and blood disorders. It can cause hormone disruption and has been designated by the Environmental Protection Agency for causing an Acute Health Hazard. Ironically, it is sold in drug stores for human use as a stool softener.

PAH contamination was confirmed in 28.6% of blood samples, 26.9% of fat samples, 14.3% of feather samples, and 17.9% of egg samples. DOSS contamination was confirmed in 14.6% of blood samples, 10.5% of fat samples, 8.6% of feather samples, and 1.8% of egg samples.

About five and a half million dollars of the settlement was for activities proposed from the DNR Nongame Wildlife Program, and $1.2 million was allocated for the Minnesota Pollution Control Agency (MPCA) to implement their Get the Lead Out program to reduce the loss of loons caused by lead poisoning in fishing tackle. Because of their previous experience and expertise in delivering this statewide program from 2000 through 2010, the MPCA was more experienced and able to deliver this program. They were selected to take care of that responsibility by the U.S. Fish and Wildlife Service.

When the Nongame Wildlife Program began in 1977, the federal breeding bird survey determined a baseline level for loons at an index of 1.05, and that baseline value increased through 2019 to 1.39. That is an increase of 34 percent over forty-two years. During that era, the original estimate for Minnesota's loon population was about 10,000, and the most recent current DNR estimate is about 12,000. A 34 percent increase would suggest the population would be approximately 13,000. Either way the population is estimated, it suggests a healthy and stable to slightly increasing number of loons in the state. No significant population trends or negative impacts have been detected because of the oil spill.

Of special significance for Minnesota has also been the creation of the National Loon Center in Crosslake. The National Loon Center's goal is to restore and protect loon breeding habitats, enhance responsible recreation, and serve as a national leader in advancing loon conservation and freshwater research and education. The National Loon Center has an exceptional staff and corps of volunteers who are developing educational and stewardship activities for loon enthusiasts across Minnesota and beyond.

Among recent accomplishments of the National Loon Center was creation of a new initiative to collaborate with fishing tackle manufacturers to transition from production of toxic lead fishing jigs and sinkers to production of non-toxic fishing tackle that is lead-free and loon-friendly. Lindy Legendary Fishing Tackle, headquartered in Brainerd, Minnesota, was the first fishing tackle manufacturer to sign the National Loon Center's "Loons & Lakes Legacy Pledge" by initiating a new line of Lindy Lead-Free tackle in 144 variations. Lindy officials say they have developed a unique blend of non-toxic materials, including bismuth, that will look, feel, and fish like lead. The Lindy company will be completely lead-free by 2027.

The development is a true game changer in the fishing tackle industry, said Ron Kiffmeyer, Lindy sales manager. "We have made the commitment to go 100 percent lead-free because we can, and it is the right thing to do, period." John Myers, the outdoor writer for the Duluth News Tribune, reported that this new tackle was designed for Lindy by Minnesotan Jeff Zernov. He is a fishing innovator inducted into the Minnesota Fishing Museum Hall of Fame in 2004. He's developed a formula that makes tackle that behaves like lead tackle, with similar sizes, shapes, colors, and weights, but it is safe for humans and animals. The new jigs will cost only slightly more than lead.

Jon Mobeck, executive director of the Crosslake, Minnesota-based National Loon Center, praised Lindy for leading the way for the tackle industry and said he hopes more companies follow. "...we are thrilled to support Lindy's commitment to designing lead-free tackle that guides Minnesota's storied angling tradition toward a more responsible future," Mobeck said. "Removing lead from our lakes improves our valuable freshwater resource and protects loons from an unnecessary and lethal toxin."

A Future for Loons...

Our dedicated state and regional DNR Nongame Wildlife Program biologists are available to assist lakeshore owners and lake associations with loon conservation projects by contacting www.dnr.state.mn.us/eco/nongame. You are also encouraged to contact the National Loon Center at Crosslake for further information on their loon conservation projects and events.

Chapter 18

Peregrine Falcon—Fastest Bird in the World

Thankfully, the peregrine falcon survived the era of oologists, raptor shooters, and DDT poisoning. It can once again be seen hunting in our Minnesota skies.

What is so special about the peregrine falcon? Just about everything. The fastest bird in the world, it is an avian missile perfectly designed to strike birds in flight at speeds up to 241 miles per hour. The scientific name, *Falco peregrinus*, means wandering falcon. Among the most widely distributed birds in the world, peregrines are found on all continents except Antarctica. There are nineteen subspecies found around the globe.

The peregrine became an avian hunting companion for humans over four thousand years ago through the tradition of falconry. This tradition began in China and Persia. It spread westward where it was adopted by European royalty in the Middle Ages. Falconry traditions came to America in the early 1900s and continue to the present.

The hunting abilities of a peregrine falcon are impressive, and their aerial maneuvers are stunning. Their exceptional maneuverability in flight creates envy among many accomplished human pilots. As I participated in the banding efforts of peregrine falcon chicks over the past thirty years, I was constantly challenged

Peregrine falcon spreading its tail to slow its dive.

This peregrine was diving at me while we were banding its chicks in Minneapolis.

to photograph their flight maneuvers as the falcon parents circled overhead and dove at us to drive us from their aerie as their chicks were being banded. Following are photos I took over the years that demonstrate the beauty and aerial dynamics of peregrines in flight.

The recovery of the peregrine falcon is a classic case study of a legendary, almost mythical, bird. It nearly disappeared from America and elsewhere in the world. We lost it from our state but, remarkably, we brought it back to grace the skies of Minnesota. Most early records for nesting peregrines in Minnesota came from University of Minnesota Bell Museum director and ornithologist Dr. Walter Breckenridge and Dana and John Struthers of Minneapolis. Dana and John were brothers and avid falconers who located peregrine nests known as aeries on cliff sites. From 1939 to 1955, the Struthers brothers located fifteen aeries on cliffs along Lake Superior, in the Boundary Waters, along the Mississippi River in southeastern Minnesota, and near St. Croix Falls along the St. Croix River. There were no peregrines nesting on tall buildings in large cities, on bridges, or atop industrial smokestacks in that era.

There had historically been about three hundred pairs of peregrines nesting in the U.S. east of the Rocky Mountains through about 1940, including about forty pairs in Minnesota and Wisconsin. By 1962, peregrines were totally gone (extirpated) from Minnesota eastward to the Atlantic coast. A similar phenomenon had befallen them in western Europe. Citizen concern for the peregrine, other raptors, and songbirds was aroused by the publication of *Silent Spring* by Rachel Carson in 1962. Her book alerted people to the worldwide toxic dangers caused by the pesticide DDT.

A 1966 peregrine conference was convened by ornithologist Dr. Joe Hickey in Madison, Wisconsin to discuss the demise of peregrines. That conference accelerated the dialogue focusing on the impact of DDT on the decline of peregrines. The pesticide DDT, introduced to control agricultural and forest pests after WWII, was identified as causing impairment of calcium metabolism in bald eagles, ospreys, and other raptors including peregrines. This resulted in thinning of their eggshells. The thin-shelled eggs were crushed under the weight of the incubating parents. They were listed as an endangered species by the federal government in 1970. In 1972, the United States banned DDT.

Dr. Tom Cade, of Cornell University, and The Peregrine Fund developed methods to propagate peregrines in captivity through artificial insemination of peregrine falcons that were donated by falconers. The Peregrine Fund began pioneering efforts in 1974 to release captive-reared peregrines at historic peregrine aeries in the eastern states using a falconry practice called hacking.

Inspired by the success of those early falcon releases in 1976 and 1977, Dr. Bud Tordoff and University of Minnesota grad student Mark Fuller released eight peregrine falcons provided by Cornell on historic Wisconsin aeries along the Mississippi River. Most of the chicks were soon preyed upon by great horned owls. The survivors were recaptured and returned to Cornell. Restoration would have to wait a few years for new developments including new sources of funding and the availability of peregrine chicks from other sources.

In 1981, University of Minnesota professors Bud Tordoff and Pat Redig began discussing strategies for reintroducing peregrines in Minnesota. Pat and Bud were the perfect team for this process.

They had an infectious passion for peregrines that quickly spread among fellow raptor enthusiasts, including myself. Dr. Pat Redig was director of The Raptor Center at the University of Minnesota. He was an international expert on medical care of raptors, professor of avian physiology, medical director of the North American Falconers Association, and a member of the California Condor recovery team. He had conducted pioneering research on the toxic effects of lead ammunition on bald eagles, and he was a falconer. Dr. Harrison B. "Bud" Tordoff was director of the Bell Museum of Natural History at the University of Minnesota. He studied ornithology at Cornell University and received his master's and doctor's degrees at the University of Michigan. In the middle of his college education, he served in the U.S. Army Air Force from 1942 to 1945. While flying eighty-five fighter pilot missions in Europe he became an ace. He was also one of the few pilots in WWII who shot down a German Messerschmitt ME 262 jet with his propeller-driven P-51 Mustang.

U.S. Air Force fighter ace Bud Tordoff and his P-51 fighter plane that he named after the European hoopoe, a bird whose scientific name is *Upupa epops.*

That incident became a defining moment in his life. He spotted two Messerschmitt jets below him while returning from a fighter mission in Germany with his P-51. Exceeding speeds of 400 mph, he dove on the jets vertically from an altitude of about 8,000 feet. He embodied the very spirit of a peregrine stooping on its prey. He opened fire after pulling in behind one of the jets, rocking his plane up and down to spray a vertical line of bullets. He hit it with one bullet which caused a spark in one of the jet engines! He later said that experience as a fighter pilot was as close as a human could get to being a peregrine. That personal connection inspired him to help return the peregrine to Minnesota's skies.

I was supervisor of the DNR Nongame Wildlife Program in 1980 with a statewide budget of only $30,000 per year. In April of that year state senator Collin Peterson amended Minnesota's tax bill to create a Nongame Wildlife Checkoff on the state's tax forms so citizens could make voluntary donations to help Minnesota's nongame wildlife. Citizens began donating in 1981, and in 1982 checkoff donations became available to the Nongame Wildlife Program and exceeded $523,000! The peregrine falcon was a **High Priority** nongame wildlife species for me. When I realized the amount and potential impact of the checkoff donations, I called Pat and Bud and excitedly exclaimed, "We've got money! We can resume reintroducing peregrines with funds from the new Nongame Wildlife Checkoff!"

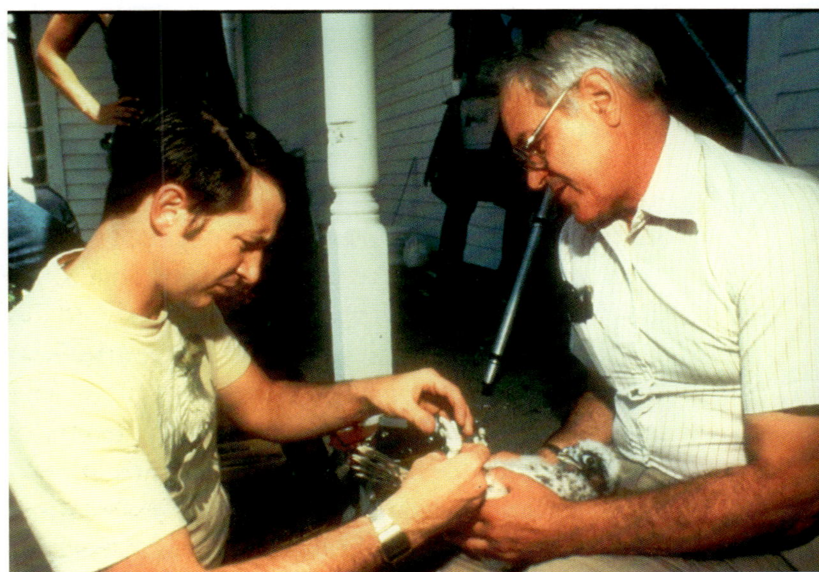

Drs. Pat Redig (left) and Bud Tordoff (right) banding a peregrine falcon chick.

We began planning the peregrine falcon restoration project in earnest. In addition to Bud, Pat, and myself, our original planning team included Geoff Barnard of The Nature Conservancy, regional endangered species coordinator of the U.S. Fish and Wildlife Service Jim Engel, Ed Lindquist of the Superior National Forest in the U.S. Forest Service, and Bob Anderson of the Raptor Resource Project. We also had support from the Minnesota Falconers Association along with over forty falconers-turned-falcon-breeders throughout the US and Canada. They would provide us with falcon chicks for release.

Additional project partners eagerly stepped forward: Minnesota DNR Division of Parks and Trails, Minnesota Department of Transportation, Winona Power and Light Co. (now Xcel Energy), Northwest Airlines, Great River Energy, Norwest Financial Center, St. Paul Dept. of Public Works, Big Game Club Special Projects Foundation, Farm Credit Leasing, Iron Range Resources and Rehabilitation, and Koll Management.

Our Minnesota goal for peregrine falcon restoration was to restore twenty breeding pairs—about half of the original population in the region. Falcon chicks would be purchased from falcon breeders and released by hacking in nest boxes atop cliffs, towers, and tall buildings in Minnesota. Hacking involved feeding the chicks remotely by attendants and then allowing them to fly free from their hack boxes.

Bud, Pat, and I faced one problem—the original peregrine falcon subspecies that had inhabited the eastern United States, including Minnesota, was totally gone. There was no potential breeding stock either in the wild or in captivity from which we could obtain the eastern birds for restoration. In the case of our river otter restoration efforts, we obtained river otters from northern Minnesota, so we reintroduced the same breeding stock that was native to the state. In this case that was not possible. There are nineteen subspecies of peregrine falcons in the world, and they have demonstrated incredible genetic adaptability to survive in many worldwide habitats. There were three subspecies of peregrine falcon native to North America, and additional subspecies could also become available from captive breeding sources.

We decided the best strategy was to obtain a mixture of available falcons from falconers who were breeding different subspecies, including the Peale's falcon (*Falco peregrinus pealei*) from the Pacific northwest, and Tundra falcons (*Falcon peregrinus tundrius*) from northern Canada, Northwest Territories, and Yukon, and peregrines from the Rocky Mountain regions of North America (*Falco peregrinus anatum*). We felt the peregrines would be genetically adaptable enough to survive and adapt to Minnesota's diverse habitats and prey species.

The restoration commenced in 1982 at a release tower on the savanna prairie of The Nature Conservancy's Weaver Dunes in southeastern Minnesota. The tower was near ten historic peregrine nesting cliffs along the Mississippi River. The first five chicks were obtained in 1982 from professor and falcon breeder Dr. Lynn Oliphant at the University of Saskatoon in Saskatchewan. In 1983, another ten chicks became available from Saskatchewan. Obtaining those ten chicks involved a harrowing experience.

Dr. Pat Redig and the author with their DNR plane in Saskatoon with cardboard boxes of peregrine chicks at their feet in 1983.

Peregrine chicks in cardboard boxes ready for their first flight—by airplane to Minnesota.

In 1983, I arranged for DNR conservation officer Tim Petersen to fly Pat Redig and me to Saskatoon again to pick up ten peregrine chicks. On our return we encountered an ominous blackish-purple thunderhead northwest of Bemidji. It was accompanied by heavy rain and lightning. We were forced to land on a rural grassy airstrip near Bagley and then we called the highway patrol. They sent a highway patrol officer to the airstrip to pick us, and the ten peregrine chicks worth $15,000, up in the driving rain. The officer drove us to the airport in Bemidji where we arrived just in time to catch the afternoon commuter flight to Minneapolis. An enthusiastic crowd of media and peregrine team members awaited us there.

The ten peregrines hacked at Weaver Dunes created quite a stir when project donors from The Nature Conservancy and The Raptor Center were out at the Weaver Dunes Prairie watching a newly fledged peregrine flying near the hack box tower on the prairie. The newly fledged peregrines needed to learn what flying creatures constituted appropriate prey. A juvenile peregrine dove at a monarch butterfly that was dipsy-doodling across the prairie. The hapless butterfly exploded into an orange cloud of butterfly scales!

On another occasion a great blue heron was flying across the Weaver Dunes prairie. A young peregrine stooped at it, struck the heron, and clung to its back with its talons, flapping madly to lift its prey. The heron kept a steady course with the peregrine flapping wildly but to no avail. It finally broke off the encounter. Hopefully, those peregrine chicks learned that the ideal prey was more the size of a blue-winged teal or rock pigeon.

Eleven more chicks were released at Weaver Dunes in 1984, along with five chicks at a new site sponsored by the U.S. Forest Service at Leveaux Mountain near Tofte. More chicks were released at Weaver Dunes and at Leveaux Mountain in 1985. Six birds were also hacked atop the Multifoods Building (City Center) in downtown Minneapolis that year. This latter site introduced peregrines to a safe urban location lacking predatory great horned owls, and it provided an abundance of rock pigeons, prime peregrine prey. Twenty-one peregrine chicks were hacked there in 1985 and 1986. More than eighty peregrines have subsequently fledged from there.

The author placing the first peregrine chick into the new hack box atop the Mayo clinic in Rochester in 1987.

From 1987 through 1989, four new release locations included the Mayo Clinic in Rochester, Rouchleau Mine near Virginia, Wolf Ridge Environmental Learning Center near Finland, and the Hill Annex Mine near Calumet. A total of eighty-seven falcons were released from these sites in subsequent years.

Much credit for the success of the peregrine's recovery goes to over forty falconers from the US and Canada who maintained breeding facilities for peregrines. They produced chicks from captive peregrines by artificial as well as natural insemination and sold them to our restoration effort. With the huge numbers produced by these falconers, Bud and Pat began collaborating with nine Midwestern states, Manitoba, and Ontario for allocating the release of the available falcon chicks. This evolved into a successful and well-coordinated regional restoration effort organized by Bud and Pat.

Bob Anderson, a major supplier of falcons for this project, had a green thumb for rearing peregrines. Once when I was visiting Bob in his home, I saw that his living room had been converted to a peregrine nursery. Peregrine chicks were pipping their eggs and hatching before my eyes. A bantam chicken was sitting on peregrine eggs on Bob's porch. Bob discovered that the hatching rate for peregrine eggs in an incubator was lower than for fertilized eggs placed under a bantam chicken. So, a chicken that would never fly would hatch peregrine chicks that would one day fly over two hundred miles per hour!

Brown-headed cowbirds also contributed to the success of our restoration project. Initially, dead laboratory quail were fed to the chicks. I was concerned that the mash fed to the quail might contain undesirable poultry feed hormones or chemicals. We needed a natural food that would not be contaminated with chemicals from laboratory quail food. It was time for me to "connect the dots."

Peregrine falcons have reoccupied historic aeries on cliffs along the North Shore.

Newly banded peregrine chicks from a cliff nest on the North Shore. Twenty-eight of the nests occupied by peregrines in the Midwest in 2024 were on cliffs.

I knew biologists involved with endangered Kirtland's warbler management in Michigan who had trapped brown-headed cowbirds that laid their eggs in warbler nests. I called them and asked what they did with the cowbirds. They said they euthanized and buried them. I asked if they could freeze the cowbirds and send them to me for use as peregrine food. Over the next couple years, I regularly received ice chests with hundreds of frozen cowbirds for the falcon chicks. Then Michigan began releasing peregrines, and they kept the cowbirds for feeding their own peregrine chicks.

By 1989, 202 falcon chicks had been released in Minnesota. The result has been a wonderful success! In 1987, the first wild-produced peregrine fledged from atop the Multifoods tower. By 1993, fifteen falcon pairs hatched thirty-three young in the wild. Our original goal was twenty pairs. We reached that goal in eleven years. The peregrine was removed from the federal endangered species list in 1999.

Whenever available, I joined Jackie Fallon, Lori Naumann, and their banding crew for the capture and banding of peregrine chicks in Minneapolis, St. Paul, and once on the North Shore. I photographed the peregrine banding process and the defense of peregrine adults as they flew past their aerie to protect their territory. It took steady nerves to focus my camera on a peregrine falcon diving directly at me at over fifty miles per hour. I used the images in our educational programs about peregrine restoration and promotion of the Nongame Wildlife Checkoff.

Dr. Bud Tordoff and Jackie Fallon banding a chick at the Norwest Bank in Minneapolis.

An unbanded tiercel (female) falcon atop the nest box at the Multifoods (City Center) building in downtown Minneapolis with the Metrodome visible in the background. This falcon began nesting in 2003, defended her territory through 2015 and produced forty-six young throughout her life. Photo by the author, June 21, 2005.

Bud Tordoff celebrating a happy moment for the return of peregrines to Minnesota.

From 2019 through 2024, an average of forty-eight successful breeding pairs of peregrines in Minnesota produced an average of 141 chicks per year. They nested on tall buildings, bridges, power plant smokestacks, and they reoccupied historic cliffs. Considering that there are probably some nesting pairs that have not been located, we have nearly tripled our original restoration goal.

Considering that the original cumulative peregrine population in Minnesota and Wisconsin was approximately forty breeding pairs, Minnesota's current peregrine population has equaled that historic regional total. A challenge for restoration is the high mortality rate typical for young peregrines. Whether raised in the wild or released, about 50 percent of the young are lost in the first year. About one in seven peregrines survives to adulthood. Capturing airborne prey at 150 to 200 miles per hour, there is no room for error. Once a peregrine survives its first year, it may live for four to six years. Among successful breeding peregrines, females can live twelve to fourteen years, and males can live sixteen to eighteen years. One peregrine, known as Meg, lived to the age of sixteen and reared forty-five young from 1988 through 2004.

An important part of this project has been long-term monitoring and banding of the newly established falcon population. Nesting sites were located, previously banded adults were identified from their leg bands, and all young in accessible nests were banded. Jackie Fallon took over this monumental task after the passing of Dr. Bud Tordoff in 2008. She has done an-exceptional job documenting the recovery of this species. This banding and survival data is archived on the online database that includes the online annual reports of the Midwest Peregrine Society. The task of annually visiting every accessible aerie in Minnesota was carried out initially by Pat Redig, Bud Tordoff, Jane Goggin, and Mark Martell. In recent years this was done by Jackie Fallon and in southeastern Minnesota by Amy Ries and the late Bob Anderson of the Raptor Resource Project. Jackie has done most of the banding in Minnesota since 2009.

DNR peregrine falcon, raptor, and bald eagle webcam specialist Lori Naumann assisting with capture of peregrine chicks atop the Norwest Financial Center in Bloomington, Minnesota.

The DNR Falcon Cam

The peregrine falcon is a high-profile species and exciting to watch in flight, but it is usually enjoyed at a distance. However, that changed in the spring of 2011 when Lori Naumann and I decided to use Nongame Wildlife Program checkoff funds to install a webcam focused inside a peregrine falcon nest box on the Bremer building in downtown St. Paul. The nest box is on the twenty-sixth floor of the twenty-seven-story Bremer building.

In 2011, the nest box was occupied by a nine-year old female named Jill. She hatched at Castle Rock on the North Shore in 2002. The male, Sota, was seventeen years old. He hatched atop the Mayo Clinic building nest box in 1994. For more information on the continuing recovery of peregrine falcons in Minnesota, check out the Midwest Peregrine Society website at https.//midwestperegrine.umn.edu. On that website you can access state reports by year to find the most recent statistics on peregrine recovery.

A female peregrine falcon, Jill, protecting her chicks in 2009. Photo courtesy of Lori Naumann via the DNR peregrine webcam and the Nongame Wildlife Program

Jill and Sota produced four eggs in 2011. Three of the eggs hatched, and all three chicks fledged. The pair produced three chicks in 2012. Jill and Sota were observed in St. Paul in January of 2013, but nineteen-year-old Sota was missing when nesting season arrived in April. A new male, Bach, had hatched from the Riverview Terrace nest box in Minneapolis. He bonded with Jill. Jill laid four eggs that did not hatch, but she was back with Bach in spring of 2014, laid four eggs and hatched three chicks. The chicks have been banded each year by Jackie Fallon and Lori Naumann. In 2022 none of the eggs hatched, but in 2023 two of four eggs hatched, and the two young fledged.

Minnesotans and peregrine enthusiasts beyond Minnesota can check the Minnesota DNR website and watch the falcons nesting, incubating eggs, hatching chicks, and raising their young courtesy of the

Nongame Wildlife Checkoff on their state income tax forms. The falcons provide a wonderful in-depth look at the day-to-day and year-to-year survival of the fastest bird in the world.

Lori continues to maintain the nest box atop the Bremer building and operate the falcon cam for the Nongame Wildlife Program. Thanks to Lori, the peregrine webcam has developed a huge following. The webcam allows incredible understanding of the daily lives and behavior of peregrines. It is exciting to see the chicks hatching and being cared for by their parents.

How Much Did it Cost to Bring Back Minnesota's Peregrine Falcons?

How much did this restoration project cost? The cost of reintroducing peregrines was estimated at $3,760 for each chick hacked. That totals $1,045,280. About $200,000 of that total was provided by Minnesota taxpayers who donated to the Nongame Wildlife Checkoff on their state tax forms. Additional matching donations came from generous donors to The Raptor Center, The Bell Museum of Natural History, and The Nature Conservancy. That expenditure does not include over ten years of in-kind salary, travel, field visits, propagation by falconers, and administrative costs covered by project leaders, team members, and project sponsors. That expense could easily include another two million dollars donated to the project. Bottom line—restoration costs totaled about three million dollars, nearly all from donations. It was a wonderful investment and a remarkable story of how peregrines were brought back to the skies of Minnesota.

Chapter 19

Trumpeter Swans: A Success Story in Minnesota—and Beyond

The sight and sounds of trumpeter swans have brought back a sense of wild avian beauty to Minnesota that we did not know had been missing. This is their story...

After my selection as Minnesota's Nongame Wildlife Program supervisor, I had the opportunity and authority to restore nongame wildlife species beyond the scope of any existing DNR wildlife programs focused on game species. Obvious choices were the bald eagle, peregrine falcon, and trumpeter swan. This is the story of how a restoration plan for trumpeter swans was transformed from vision to reality over the past forty-plus years. There were, however, significant limitations to my visions for recovery of those species. At first, I was the only person in my program... a supervisor in charge of no one. My total budget, about half of which included my salary, was only about $30,000 per year.

Three years later my fortunes changed. The Minnesota legislature passed the Nongame Wildlife Checkoff Law in 1980 after State Senator Collin Peterson noted that Colorado had enacted a voluntary tax checkoff law to use donations to help unhunted wildlife, referred to as nongame wildlife. His administrative assistant, Diane Vosick Barnard, quickly tracked down the wording for the Colorado legislation and provided Senator Peterson with the details he needed to introduce similar legislation in a middle of the night tax conference committee meeting on the last night of the 1980 legislative session.

Fortunately, Diane had previously worked for me in the Nongame Wildlife Program as a Young Adult

Conservation Corps employee. She understood how much Minnesota's nongame wildlife needed more funding and was an integral part of making it happen. Minnesota citizens donated more than $523,000 in the first year on the 1981 checkoff line of their tax forms. Restoration of the trumpeter swan was no longer just a vision—it became reality.

The trumpeter is the largest waterfowl species in the world, standing up to four feet tall, with a wingspread approaching eight feet and weighing up to thirty-five pounds. Adults have snow-white plumage with black legs and a black bill. Juveniles have pearly-gray plumage and pinkish bills in their first year. Their trumpeting calls are dramatic and resonant. They can be heard over half a mile away. The loud call is made by a loop of windpipe inside the breastbone that creates an extra-long trachea. The windpipe creates a trumpet nearly three feet long from lungs to bill. Trumpeter swans can live over twenty-five years.

Their large size, conspicuous white plumage, and thick down contributed to the historic demise of trumpeter swans. Subsistence use of swans by Native Americans occurred for thousands of years without threatening the species, but the influx of fur trappers and European settlers, equipped with firearms across North America, hastened their disappearance across Canada and the northern United States. Swans provided fresh meat and swansdown. Skins of trumpeter swans and tundra swans became a product in the fur trade. Swans were killed by hunters and trappers, skinned out, and the skins were dried like beaver pelts. They were purchased by fur buyers and shipped to Europe where they were cut up and sold for use as ladies' powder puffs.

One of the first reports of swan skins in the fur trade was in 1806. The Hudson's Bay Company in Canada reported swan skins in their sales to Europe. From 1853 through 1877, the Hudson's Bay Company purchased 17,671 swan skins for export to Europe. Most skins would have been from trumpeter swans. By 1877, swan populations were greatly reduced. The Hudson's Bay Company purchased only 122 swan skins that year. The long, white wing feathers of swans were also used as writing quills and as fine-pointed artistic pens. Famous naturalist and artist John James Audubon preferred using trumpeter swan quills for drawing the details of songbird feet and claws.

As trumpeter swans disappeared from Canadian wetlands in the 1800s, they were also disappearing in the northern United States. An important portion of their US breeding range was in Minnesota. Prior to settlement, the lake near Mankato, now known as Swan Lake, was called *Manha tanka otamenda* by the Sioux—meaning Lake-of-the-Many-Large-Birds. The first nesting record by European explorers for trumpeter swans in the continental United States was provided by Count G. E. Beltrami on Stephen H. Long's expedition to the Minnesota and Red River valleys. On July 13, 1823, they encountered adult swans and cygnets in Nicollet County, now known as Swan Lake, which they referred to as the Lake of Swans. The last records of nesting trumpeter swans in Minnesota occurred at Heron Lake in Jackson County in 1883 and at Everson Lake in Meeker County in 1884 or 1885. There were no nest records after 1885. Trumpeter swans had become extirpated in Minnesota, and naturalists feared the species would become extinct.

By 1932, only sixty-nine trumpeter swans survived in the continental United States, mainly in Red Rock Lakes in Montana. With protection finally provided, the continental US population slowly rose to 907 swans by 1968, and the entire North American population was estimated at 3,600 to 4,400. There was also an undiscovered trumpeter swan population in Alaska that was not documented until later years.

Unfortunately, trumpeter swans disappeared from the American landscape so early in our history that their memory was relegated mainly to museums, place names like Swan Lake, history books, literary references like *The Trumpeter Swan* monograph by biologist Winston Banko, and the children's book *The Trumpet of the Swan* by E. B. White. It appeared that the trumpeter swan had a past but no future.

Enter Hennepin Parks commissioner Fred E. King. He began efforts to reintroduce trumpeter swans in Minnesota by obtaining a pair of trumpeter swans from Red Rock Lakes National Wildlife Refuge in 1966. In subsequent years, Hennepin Parks received forty additional sub-adult swans from Red Rock Lakes NWR. Hennepin Parks' goal was to establish a free-flying flock of one hundred swans, including fifteen breeding pairs.

Hennepin Parks (now Three Rivers Parks) benefitted from the enthusiastic support and involvement of their natural resources staff and administrators, including Dave Weaver, Larry Gillette, Donna Compton, Tim Dyer, Judy Voigt-Englund, and Madeleine Linck. In 1968, Fred King created additional momentum for trumpeter swans by founding The Trumpeter Swan Society, an international organization dedicated to promoting the recovery of trumpeter swans throughout their original range in North America.

The first cygnet hatched in Hennepin Parks on June 21, 1969. The flock increased slowly through the 1980s. Some birds began migrating to Iowa, Missouri, Kansas, and Oklahoma, but there were survival problems. Swans died from hitting power lines or swallowing old lead shotgun pellets lying at the bottom of shallow marshes. Some swans were also shot by inexperienced hunters or vandals. By 1984, their flock had grown to ninety-one swans, of which thirty-five were free-flying. There were seven nesting pairs that year. They fledged twenty-four young.

In 1982, the first donations received by the DNR from the Nongame Wildlife Checkoff became available. My mind was swirling with the possibilities for helping Minnesota's beleaguered nongame wildlife populations, including trumpeter swans.

I began collaborating with University of Minnesota professor and ornithologist Dr. Jim Cooper to write a proposal to build on the progress of Hennepin Parks' swan restoration activities and expand those efforts throughout Minnesota. Among wildlife managers and waterfowl biologists contributing to development of the plan were Forrest Lee, Bob Jessen, Mike Zicus, John Scharf, Jim Leach, Lloyd Knudson, Roger Johnson, Art Hawkins, and Frank Bellrose. The plan was published on June 10, 1982. Next, we needed to implement the plan. As I had served as an officer in the U.S. Air Force in the early seventies, I realized this was comparable to developing and carrying out a complex multi-year military operation.

The swan plan included several components. First, DNR Section of Wildlife Chief Roger Holmes specified that trumpeter swans were being reintroduced to restore an integral part of our state's biological diversity as a protected waterfowl species and not for eventual designation as a game species. Roger specified that no DNR game and fish funds, duck stamp funds, or hunting license revenues were to be used for bringing back the swans. The only funds to be used were donations from Minnesota citizens to the Nongame Wildlife Checkoff on state tax forms. To subsequently designate the swan as a game species would be a betrayal of trust to citizens who donated money to help bring back this iconic nongame species.

Second, Roger specified that as trumpeter swans became established, areas occupied by the swans would not be closed to waterfowl hunting to protect the swans. It was up to hunters to learn to identify the protected swans and help protect them. The consequence of shooting a trumpeter swan ranged from fines and restitution charges from $1,000 to $3,000 to confiscation of the hunter's shotgun. Those fines generated huge media attention whenever swan shooters were caught. This helped promote protection of the species among hunters.

As I think back on this project, there was also a third essential component. I am a patient, stubborn, and optimistic conservationist of Norwegian origin. Most significant and worthwhile wildlife conservation initiatives are not achieved within a matter of years; they require decades of dedication and determination to succeed.

Challenges to Restoration

Some people were reluctant to endorse a wildlife restoration project for trumpeter swans and opposed the restoration. They had strong opinions even though they had no experience or knowledge about wild swans. A federal waterfowl biologist said that the trumpeter swan was a wilderness species and that Minnesota had no wilderness left, so the project should be abandoned. I recalled that Aldo Leopold had considered the sandhill crane a wilderness species. Now they occur in backyards and suburban wetlands. Waterfowl don't know what wilderness is, but they know what kind of habitat they need to survive, and they can thrive in suitable habitat where they are protected from shooting or the presence of toxic chemicals or lead. I ignored those negative opinions and depended on the resilience of the swans' survival instincts to figure things out.

A regional game manager stated that there was no good habitat for trumpeter swans in northwestern Minnesota. He had never worked with swans, but he didn't want swans released in his area. I think he just didn't want his game managers to waste their time restoring a species that couldn't be hunted. I waited until he retired, and then I did it anyway.

Another person wanted Roger Holmes to fire me from the DNR for proceeding with the restoration plan. She thought we should invest in an expensive and lengthy feasibility research project to decide if we should proceed with restoring the swans, even though there were no researchers I knew of who had ever carried out a successful trumpeter swan restoration project.

The DNR, U.S. Fish and Wildlife Service, and private conservation organizations had restored many thousands of acres of wetlands in Minnesota. Those wetlands would have originally supported trumpeter swan populations. I believed that the swans would adapt to the diversity and abundance of those wetland habitats because of their resilience as a native species. Roger Holmes stood by me in proceeding with the plan.

Overall, there was great public support and enthusiasm for swan restoration. This project was a reaffirmation to our citizens that native nongame wildlife species are important holistic components of our Minnesota wetland habitats. Swans didn't need to be a game species to qualify for restoration funding and management.

Finding the Perfect Swan Habitat

Considerable effort and many meetings were held to discuss how and where trumpeter swans should be released. We looked at prairie pothole wetlands in Ottertail County, Sherburne National Wildlife Refuge, and Itasca State Park. Our top choices became Becker County's Tamarac National Wildlife Refuge, wetlands in the Becker County region including federal Waterfowl Production Areas, DNR's Hubbel Pond Wildlife Refuge, DNR Wildlife Management Areas in the Becker County area, and White Earth Band lakes to the north. There were fewer threats of mortality there: fewer powerlines, softer bottoms of forested wetlands where any historic deposits of lead shotgun pellets would likely have sunk out of reach of the swans, and the presence of the U.S. Fish and Wildlife, DNR, and White Earth Reservation biologists who could assist with the releases, protection, and management of the swans. Perhaps symbolic for our future success was that the White Earth Reservation biologist was named Michael Swan.

Which Came First? The Eggs!

There was no playbook for this project because Minnesota was the first Midwestern state to try a major trumpeter swan restoration project. Before proceeding, we needed to identify techniques for collecting wild swan eggs, transporting them to incubators at the DNR Carlos Avery Game Farm near Forest Lake, hatching the cygnets, caring for the young after hatching, and releasing the swans in suitable habitat. I also had to obtain state and federal permits for implementing this plan. This included obtaining approval from the Mississippi Flyway Council to carry out the restoration project in Minnesota, approval from the Pacific Flyway Council to obtain the trumpeter swan eggs from Alaska, and approval from the Alaska Department of Game and Fish for collecting 150 trumpeter swan eggs for the restoration project over a three-year period.

Steve Kittelson was our ace biologist who worked out the details for this portion of the project. Trumpeter swan eggs require thirty-two to thirty-seven days of incubation. We needed to collect the eggs between three and four weeks of incubation so the developing embryos would be strong enough to endure the jostling involved with egg transport and minor variations in temperature. The eggs needed to be maintained at about one hundred degrees fahrenheit.

We obtained permits to collect eight trumpeter swan eggs from the LaCreek National Wildlife Refuge in South Dakota in June of 1982 so we could practice the necessary hatching and rearing techniques for rearing the swans. Five cygnets hatched. The rearing proceeded well. At the end of the summer, we transferred the cygnets to Hennepin Parks to augment their flock. In 1983, we requested trumpeter swan eggs at Red Rock Lakes National Wildlife Refuge in Montana, collected twelve eggs, and hatched eight cygnets.

The cygnets were raised at the Carlos Avery Wildlife Refuge. University of Minnesota graduate student Clay Jobes studied the aquatic plants utilized as food by the cygnets to aid us in eventual selection of release sites that had good food resources. Those cygnets were transferred to Hennepin Parks at the end of the summer. In 1984 and 1985, we began identifying sources of captive swans for our first major swan release in 1987. We obtained twenty-one juveniles from the Minnesota Zoo, Brookfield Zoo in Chicago, and Hennepin Parks.

Steve Kittelson supervised construction of two outdoor wintering pens and rearing ponds at the Carlos Avery Wildlife Refuge in the fall of 1984. Biologist Peggy Hines Peters was hired as a wildlife technician in 1985 to begin selecting release sites for swans in the Tamarac National Wildlife Refuge and surrounding wetlands of Becker County. We were ready for the next step in our adventure.

1986: North to Alaska

The author (left) and U.S. Fish and Wildlife Service pilot Rod King (right) collecting eggs in the Minto Flats west of Fairbanks.

We planned to begin collecting eggs on the Minto Flats wetlands west of Fairbanks, Alaska, in summer 1984. However, the U.S. Fish and Wildlife Service first wanted to design a study to determine the impact of egg collection on the swan population of the Minto Flats swans. They wanted to be confident that this project would not be detrimental to the healthy swan population there. Egg collection was delayed until 1985. However, snowfall in the winter of 1984-1985 was so great that spring runoff flooded many swan nests in the Minto Flats. We had to cancel the egg collection trip a week before we were scheduled to leave for Alaska. We finally began three years of egg collection trips in June of 1986.

I needed an assistant to help me with collecting the eggs, and I got lots of offers from potential volunteers. My choice was Dave Ahlgren, a wonderful volunteer for the Nongame Wildlife Program who had helped initiate our bluebird recovery efforts. A pilot for Northwest Airlines and former Air National Guard pilot, Dave was a good friend of Bill Wren, vice president for Northwest Airlines. Dave and Bill arranged travel to Alaska for us and for our trumpeter swan eggs first class on the return trip to Minnesota.

MN DNR volunteer Dave Ahlgren assisting with egg collection.

Suitcase for transporting eggs from Alaska to Minnesota. The darker eggs are from nests in marshes with higher concentrations of iron in the water.

Steve Kittelson adapted a suitcase design for transporting eggs that had been developed by the U.S. Fish and Wildlife Service for transporting endangered whooping crane eggs from the Northwest Territories to the Patuxent Wildlife Research Station in Maryland. Each suitcase contained Styrofoam liners with hand-carved cavities for holding twelve eggs. The cavities were interconnected with small channels to allow air circulation from a battery-powered fan in the end of the suitcase. Four old-fashioned, rubber hot-water bottles were laid over the eggs to provide a portable source of heat during transport from Alaska to Minnesota. The hot water was replaced every two hours from the coffeemaker in the first-class compartment of the airplane.

In preparation for our trip, U.S. Fish and Wildlife Service pilot Rodney King surveyed the Minto Flats for making the egg collections. This huge 1,400 square mile wetland complex is forty miles west of Fairbanks. It had a trumpeter swan population of more than a thousand swans. Rod mapped the location of the trumpeter swan nests from the air and selected which ones would allow access with his Cessna 185 airplane equipped with amphibious floats. Rod calculated the stage of incubation. We needed to collect the eggs within ten to fifteen days of hatching. He determined that the eggs should be collected between June 5 and 10. With great anticipation and excitement, Dave and I flew to Anchorage, Alaska, on June 7. We then traveled to Fairbanks where we would join Rod for the final leg of the trip to a log cabin in the Minto Flats normally used for research by their state fisheries biologists.

On June 10, we collected the eggs. The aerial view of this wilderness wetland was awesome! We saw bald eagles, black bears, moose cows with calves, and then, our first swan nest. The pair of snow-white swans glowed like pearls against deep blue waters. One swan was incubating on the nest mound while the mate swam nearby.

Odd Man Out

I had an unusual adventure soon after we began collecting eggs. We landed on a small lake and taxied to the swan nest. We collected the eggs and were ready for Rod to take off. However, while we were collecting the eggs, the wind died, and the water became glassy smooth. That was bad. As a plane with floats is taking off, there needs to be some chop on the water to break the surface tension that bonds the flat-bottomed floats to the water. Rod said that this lake was so small that in aeronautical terms, it was a three-person lake for his Cessna 185 plane to take off if there was a wind to create waves, but it was a two-person lake for a float plane attempting to take off on a glassy-smooth lake with no wind. He taxied to the nearby shore, got out, turned the plane around and began his take-off. Two-thirds of the way across the lake, his floats had not broken free of the water. He shut down the motor, and we thunked into the opposite shore. Rod got out, turned the plane around and fired up the engine again. Once again, the floats didn't break free from the water. He shut down the engine, and we thunked into the opposite shore.

Rod turned to us and said, "One of you will have to go." We decided that Rod would return to our cabin with Dave so he could begin boiling water for our hot water bottles to keep the eggs warm. I was left on a tiny island in the middle of the lake. Before Rod began to taxi away from my new island home, he threw me a sleeping bag from his window. He smiled as he said he thought he could find his way back. Rod returned about an hour later for my wetland rescue.

When Eggs Fly

Rod artfully landed on each lake and taxied near each nest. Wearing chest waders, I entered the shallow water and stepped onto the bog mat to approach the nest. Several times I went through the bog mat and went in over the top of my waders. I discovered that Alaska's lake water is really cold in June! Once we arrived at a nest, I collected and labeled each egg and candled it to ensure it was fertile. We left two live eggs in each nest and took the balance of the clutch, usually three to five eggs. Each time we filled our twelve-egg suitcase, we flew back to the log cabin where Dave Ahlgren was boiling water to fill the hot water bottles to keep the eggs warm.

During the long Alaskan day, we visited sixteen trumpeter swan nests and collected fifty eggs. We began at 10:15 a.m. and finished at 7:45 p.m. We returned to Fairbanks, connected for a flight back to Anchorage, and took a Northwest Airlines midnight flight back to Minneapolis. We had the nucleus of swan numbers that we needed to begin our restoration effort. Our success rate for hatching those eggs was forty-three out of fifty eggs each year.

Swan Rearing and Cygnet Psychology

DNR nongame wildlife specialist Steve Kittelson using a stethoscope to hear pipping cygnets before they hatched.

Once the eggs arrived in Minnesota, Steve Kittelson took over the hatching and rearing process. We used retired pheasant egg incubators at the DNR's Carlos Avery Game Farm at Forest Lake. The eggs were incubated at a temperature of one hundred degrees. The eggs needed to be turned regularly as the parent swans would do in the wild. Steve misted the eggs to keep the humidity at sixty percent relative humidity and weighed them daily to ensure they were undergoing a steady weight loss. Eggs lose weight as the yolk and white are transformed into cygnets.

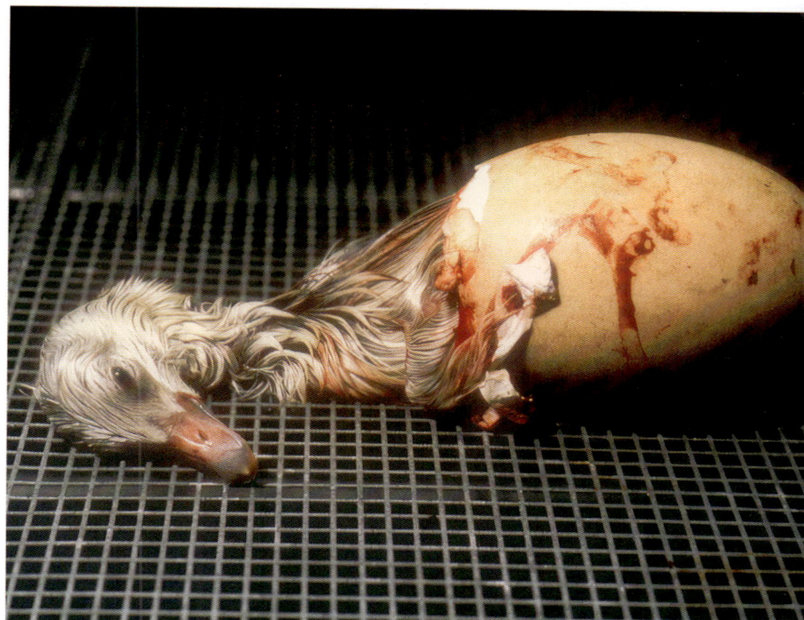

A newly hatched and exhausted cygnet. Notice the tiny "egg tooth" at the tip of its bill that it uses to break through the eggshell when it begins hatching.

As cygnets neared hatching, the eggs were placed close to each other so their peeping sounds would imprint on each other—and they would not accidentally imprint on people. After hatching, the cygnets were allowed a day in the incubator to fluff out and bond with each other. Then they were moved to indoor brooders for their first several weeks. Their diet was extremely critical at this point. If their mash contained too much protein, their wrist joints would develop a twisted wing deformity called angel-wings, and they would never be able to fly.

When the cygnets were moved outdoors, they were placed in a fenced enclosure in a shallow pond. The pen was covered above and on the sides to protect the cygnets from owls, eagles, raccoons, minks, and other predators. They were kept in this enclosure for their first summer until they were the size of a Canada goose. Their wing feathers were clipped to prevent them from flying, and they were placed in two separate fenced pens, each with an aerated pond that would keep water open during the winter.

When waterfowl biologists first began restoring Canada geese in the 1960s, they learned that when geese were all raised in one pen they were not interested in bonding and mating with each other after being released. It appeared to be an avian version of human brother and sister aversion! That is why we reared our swans in two different pens.

Murder by Mink

One of the most traumatic setbacks for our trumpeter swan restoration effort occurred in July of 1987 when a small female mink squeezed through a metal grid covering a drain tile that emptied from the floor of the cygnet brooder house into a nearby marsh. The grid was intended to prevent predators from entering our cygnet brooder house. It was adequate to exclude an average size or large mink from entering the brooder house, but this small mink got in at night and methodically went from one cygnet to another, killing all thirty-one cygnets in the brooder facility.

Low water conditions in the marsh had exposed the outlet of the drain tile in the marsh and the mink entered the dry tile which normally would have been filled with water. The brooder building had been used successfully for rearing cygnets for five years prior to this incident without problems. Mink are members of the weasel family and are utterly ruthless whenever they encounter captive birds which cannot escape. They typically kill all the birds encountered but do not eat them. We had previously predator-proofed the building and placed traps around the site, so this event was totally unexpected after taking so many precautions. The mink was later caught and dispatched.

After recovering from the shock of this loss, I immediately contacted local media representatives to inform them of this disaster. They needed to know what happened, how it happened, and how we had taken so many precautions to prevent this kind of disaster. Any delay in sharing this information could have been interpreted as covering up the loss of the cygnets and resulted in a loss of credibility with the media in keeping them informed about the swan restoration efforts.

A dozen cygnets derived from Alaskan eggs were being raised in another building, and they were safe. In addition, we were able to make up for some of this loss with twenty cygnets from captive breeding sources. The Minnesota Zoo provided twelve cygnets hatched at the zoo in 2007, the Brookfield Zoo in Chicago donated four cygnets, and four additional cygnets were donated by the Delta Waterfowl Research Station in Manitoba.

Rescuing Swans in Alaska While Dodging a Volcano

In 1992, Alaskan biologists informed us that there was an early freeze-up in the Minto Flats. Many flightless trumpeter swan cygnets would die because they were too young to fly, and the parent swans would migrate without them. We organized an emergency trip to Alaska in August to rescue up to twenty swan cygnets.

Steve Kittelson volunteered to make the trip to capture the swans with U.S. Fish and Wildlife Service pilot Rod King. It was a more harrowing experience than expected. One day was considered adequate to locate the swans, land a float plane on the remaining open water, capture the swans as Steve balanced on the plane's floats, and capture them with a salmon landing net.

However, shortly after Steve arrived in Alaska on August 17, a volcano called Mount Spurr erupted across the Cook Inlet from Anchorage. Seventeen inches of snow in Fairbanks on August 18 and fourteen inches of snow in Anchorage on August 19 prevented any rescue attempts. By August 20, the temperature had dropped to seventeen degrees and many wetlands were frozen over. The parent swans had left, and the cygnets were left behind to die. Steve and Rod used a float plane on August 22 to capture six cygnets by landing on the few lakes that still had open water, taxiing after them, and capturing them with landing nets while Steve was holding onto the float struts.

By August 23, the lakes were frozen over, and they switched to a helicopter to capture eleven more cygnets on the Minto Flats. The swans were herded by the helicopter toward shore. When the cygnets laid on the ice or were blown by the prop wash against shoreline vegetation, they were captured by Steve who grabbed them while reaching out from the helicopter skids. On August 24, a local trapper found another cygnet walking on a trail. He caught the swan and turned it over to the Alaska Game and Fish Department so the bird could be added to our group of rescued swans.

The eighteen cygnets arrived in Minnesota on Sept. 28 and 29. Funding and logistical support for the rescue operation was provided by the DNR Nongame Wildlife Fund, Dellwood Wildlife Foundation, H. B. Fuller Company, Northwest Airlines, and Alaska Airlines. Alaskan authorities subsequently shipped us four more cygnets in February of 1993. They had also been rescued during the freeze-up. These twenty-two swans were released at the Tamarac National Wildlife Refuge and surrounding areas in the spring of 1994, including Itasca State Park.

Increasing Odds for Swan Survival

Another important decision in the planning process was to decide at what age to release the swans. Not all released birds survive. We needed to increase their survival odds by releasing them at an age that would not place them at a survival disadvantage. We learned from our peregrine falcon restoration project that only one peregrine survives to become old enough to breed out of every seven to eight birds released. We hoped for better odds with the swans. We decided to hold them in captivity until twenty-three months of age because natural mortality is typically very high if released in their first year of life. Trumpeter swans normally select a mate in their third year and find a marsh where they establish their future nesting territory. They usually begin nesting in their fourth year. This gave the swans a year to become familiar with their release area before they reached breeding age. This strategy worked. About one swan in four survived to breeding age.

At last! Releasing the Swans in Northern Minnesota

After five years of planning, egg collection, development of rearing facilities, and site selection, we began releasing the swans in their new homes. The swans had their wings clipped when released so they could not fly away. New flight feathers would grow back in late summer. Some people asked if the swans were going to fly back to Alaska. No. Again, we were using swan psychology. Trumpeter swans imprint on the first place that they fly from. For them, Minnesota was their home where they would eventually nest, except for some wayward swans that pioneered to nearby wetlands in southwestern Ontario, southeastern Manitoba, eastern regions of the Dakotas, and northern Iowa. DNR regional nongame wildlife biologist Katie Haws oversaw swan coordination in northwest Minnesota.

The author releasing a trumpeter swan in Jim's Marsh on the Tamarac National Wildlife Refuge.

Peggy Hines was our intrepid DNR nongame biologist who selected outstanding lakes and wetlands for release of swans on the Tamarac National Wildlife Refuge and surrounding vicinity. Wildlife biologist Michael Swan of the White Earth Band selected lakes for swan releases on White Earth Tribal lands.

Releasing trumpeter swans at the Tamarac National Wildlife Refuge.

We released forty swans in the Detroit Lakes area in 1988. Transporting the swans in large dog kennels in a truck from Carlos Avery near Forest Lake to Detroit Lakes would have risked injuring the swans' legs during the bumpy ride, so I needed another option—but how could I transport flightless swans to Detroit Lakes? That's where my air force background became useful. I had served in the Military Airlift Command and was familiar with air force protocol. I had flown in C-130s and was familiar with the capacity and performance of C-130 transports.

Minnesota Air National Guard crew in 1988 with a trumpeter swan ready for release.

I needed a plane-a bigger plane! I called the Minnesota Air National Guard and posed my idea of flying one of their C-130 transport planes to northwest Minnesota as a training flight with a cargo of forty trumpeter swans. They loved the idea and thought it would be good publicity for them and for the Department of Natural Resources. This was a classic example of "connecting the dots" to achieve a project goal between two unrelated facts or issues.

On April 20, 1988, we planned our release of forty swans that were ready to be placed on wetlands in the Tamarac National Wildlife Refuge area. Recalling my University of Georgia graduate school journalism lessons in working with the media, an event becomes newsworthy if it is "first, biggest, or most." This release was all of those, so I contacted the news assignment desks of ABC, NBC, and CBS news in New York and pitched the swan release as the first and largest release of trumpeter swans in the history of the United States. ABC News agreed to send out their news crew to cover the story, including famous nature writer and reporter Roger Caras.

C-130 Minnesota Air National Guard plane ready for transporting our swans.

The Air National Guard had to get approval from the Pentagon for this epic flight since it would be covered on the national news by ABC's Roger Caras. I think that is the first time a Minnesota DNR project ever needed approval from the Pentagon. Accompanied by Roger Caras, we flew from the Twin Cities to nearby Fargo, North Dakota, in a C-130 transport plane courtesy of the Minnesota Air National Guard. A special highlight of this release is that we picked a lake on the White Earth Reservation where we had local children from the reservation help release the swans. The story aired on May 11, 1988. Roger estimated our story of the swans was seen by thirty to forty million people across the nation.

Roger Caras covering the release of forty Trumpeter Swans in 1988 for ABC-TV national news.

As the news story showed the final pair of swans swimming off in their new lake home to begin their life in the wild, Roger commented on national TV, "The magnificent trumpeter swans, gone from the lakes of Minnesota for over a century, have been summoned home… They are being restored with donations on state tax forms… the swans are gifts that Minnesotans have given themselves."

Protecting the Swans after Release

Once the swans were released, we needed to protect them so they could mature, select a mate, live long enough to reproduce, and create a new population of wild, free-flying trumpeter swans. We selected the best and most protected lakes and wetlands for releasing the swans, but once they flew free, they were subject to three hazards.

Power lines were a hazard in the vicinity of marshes where swans nested and migrated—especially in foggy weather when they couldn't see the wires. Such collisions either killed the birds or wounded them. Thankfully, there were few power lines in the vicinity of the large lakes and wetlands where we planned our swan releases.

The second threat was an insidious and long-term threat to swans, ducks, and geese—lead shotgun pellets. They do not degrade or rust away once they have been fired over a marsh and sink to the bottom of the marsh. They remain present and toxic on the bottom of lakes and marshes for many decades after being fired. Small lead fishing jigs or sinkers also poison swans in areas where they are lost by anglers. When swans tip downward to feed on roots and tubers of marsh vegetation, they also forage for small pebbles that help grind up their food, just like a chicken needs grit to grind up its food. A single lead shotgun pellet or fishing jig or sinker can kill a swan. Marshes with hard bottoms and a history of waterfowl hunting and shallow heavily fished sites can be dangerous to the survival of swans.

When a lead-poisoned swan was discovered in the early years of our project, it was transported to The Raptor Center at the University of Minnesota for treatment. In recent years, lead-poisoned swans were treated by the Wildlife Rehabilitation Center in Roseville, Minnesota. We sincerely appreciated the remarkable services that were provided by both The Raptor Center and the Wildlife Rehabilitation Center for their dedicated efforts to treat and rehabilitate injured and lead-poisoned swans. We sadly learned that even if they were treated for lead poisoning and survive, those swans were rarely able to reproduce as adults.

When we began the trumpeter swan restoration project, the trumpeter swan was a state threatened species. Shooting a swan was punishable by fines up to $3000 and confiscation of the hunter's shotgun. To avoid this problem, signs were posted at the public water accesses where swans were present, and billboards were posted along highways advising hunters not to shoot swans. Waterfowl hunters became some of our best advocates for protecting the swans. Some would yell across a marsh when they saw swans approaching to warn other hunters not to shoot. They called conservation officers if they saw hunters shooting at or killing swans. In cases where swans were wounded but not killed, they could be rehabilitated and donated to zoos or to the Iowa Department of Natural Resources for use as breeding birds in captivity for their trumpeter swan restoration project.

Continuing Swan Releases

We continued our swan releases through 1994. Cygnets hatched from Alaskan eggs were released in 1988, 1989, and 1990. Another 170 additional swans were donated from the Minnesota Zoo over the years through coordination with Minnesota Zoo senior bird curator Jimmy Pichner. Jimmy also provided invaluable coordination to locate additional juvenile swans for release that had been raised at the Brookfield Zoo, Delta Waterfowl Research Station, Dellwood Wildlife Foundation, Louisville Zoo, Topeka Zoo, Tulsa Zoo, and Watertown Zoo in South Dakota. The juvenile swans rescued in Alaska in 1992 were released in spring of 1994.

Later release sites included Itasca State Park in Itasca County and Black Lake near Hibbing. DNR Regional Nongame Wildlife Specialist Jack Mooty collaborated with Hibbing car dealer Don Hilligoss to have four trumpeter swans released at Black Lake near Hibbing. The release was successful, and the swans and their progeny eventually spread northward to the Boundary Waters Canoe Area Wilderness and southwestern Ontario.

We released 217 swans from 1987 through 1994. In 1988, we made our first release of swans in

Minnesota's trumpeter swan recovery effort has been a resounding success. This family nested in a backwater of the Rum River near Anoka in 2017. It was adjacent to the backyard of legendary teacher and conservationist Lyle Bradley.

southern Minnesota. In 1995, we began an extended effort to release more trumpeter swans in southern Minnesota. A total of 374 swans were released during this entire project in northern and southern Minnesota.

In 1988, two pairs of swans produced one cygnet. In 1992, a decade after completing our trumpeter swan restoration plan, twelve breeding pairs produced twenty-nine cygnets. By 1996, we reached our original population goal of thirty breeding pairs! We exceeded 100 breeding pairs in 2001. That total doubled in five years to 220 pairs. Since then, the population has reached critical mass in which the numbers appear to be doubling about every five years.

We estimated a statewide population of 1,450 swans in 2001, 2,400 in 2006, 6,070 in 2010, and 17,000 in 2015. The population was estimated to be 25,000 to 30,000 by 2020. Since 2000, trumpeter swans have been observed nesting in eighty of Minnesota's eighty-seven-counties. The most recent estimates, not verified by detailed surveys, have been approximately 50,000 swans!

Over the history of this effort, I calculated that there is an eleven to one ratio between the estimated total population of trumpeter swans and the number of breeding pairs in the state. We may now have over 4,500 breeding pairs of trumpeter swans in the state.

One of the most important aspects of this success is that the swans have provided an important source of birds for dispersal to adjacent states and provinces where the swans are pioneering into historical habitat where they have been missing for over a hundred years: northern Iowa, eastern South Dakota, and eastern North Dakota. Swans have also spread progressively north and northeast in forested lakes and wetlands of Minnesota to southeastern Manitoba and southwestern Ontario.

I initially believed that the swans would pioneer south and west to the prairie potholes of Ottertail County and adjacent pothole country in the eastern Dakotas. The natural resource agencies in South Dakota and North Dakota reported in 2023 that trumpeter swans are regularly nesting in the eastern regions of those states. However, they seem to have been slow to expand their nesting activities into the prairie pothole country of Ottertail County and southward. I suspect the harder bottoms of those shallow prairie pothole wetlands have likely retained spent lead shotgun pellets from over half a century of intense duck hunting pressure. That could have resulted in more lead poisoning among pioneering swans than in the boggy softer bottoms and deeper lakes and wetlands of forests north and east of the release areas in Becker County.

The family swam to within fifteen feet of me, came ashore, and fed on grass at my feet as if to show off their new family.

This pair of trumpeter swans was photographed by the author on June 4, 2008, in southeastern Manitoba where they are believed to have expanded their historic range from Minnesota to both southeastern Manitoba and southwestern Ontario.

I recently received an impressive sense of the enthusiasm and support that exists for trumpeter swans as a protected nongame species from Anthony Hertzel of the Minnesota Ornithologists' Union (MOU). MOU members have submitted 154,143 observations of trumpeter swans, including nesting records in eighty of the state's eighty-seven counties from 2000 through 2023.

Sheila Lawrence, the "Swan Lady of Monticello"

Sheila Lawrence with swans at Monticello.

In the first few years following swan releases, the swans spent considerable time wintering on the open waters of the Mississippi River. This was downstream from the power plant at Monticello where the river stayed open all winter. The swans were fed by swan enthusiast Sheila Lawrence who was totally dedicated to helping the swans. Whenever she saw an injured swan, she would wade into the river to rescue it. She saw to it that it got medical care from the Wildlife Rehabilitation Clinic in Roseville, Minnesota.

She kept the swans so well fed that they typically came through each winter in such good condition that I believe they likely had larger broods the following spring. That probably helped speed the recovery of the swan population. She kept daily records of all the marked swans present with data on leg bands, neck bands, and wing tags.

Sheila began feeding swans when they first showed up in 1988. The number of swans kept increasing annually, and eventually she was feeding 1,200 to 2,200 swans about 1,300 to 2,000 pounds of corn daily at a cost of about $20,000 each winter. The swan wintering season lasted from early December through April.

I spent many pleasant mornings at Jim and Sheila's home visiting with them. We discussed their latest swan revelations, the latest swan counts, the latest sightings of swan #9 and her cygnets, and I enjoyed their hospitality, including generous servings of coffee and cookies. Sheila passed away from cancer in 2011. Her husband Jim continued feeding the swans for a few more years, but the practice was discontinued. It was felt that the swans would adapt to the change by seeking more desirable wintering destinations in states to the south. At this stage of the project, I felt we were so much closer to achieving our vision for restoring a migratory population of trumpeter swans across Minnesota.

Rehabilitation for Sick and Injured Swans

In the early stages of restoring a rare species like trumpeter swans, every individual swan is important to help reestablish the population. Whenever swans became sick or injured during our restoration efforts, we benefited from the dedication and expertise of veterinarians at The Raptor Center of the University of Minnesota, the Wildlife Rehabilitation Center in Roseville, and veterinarian Debbie Eskedal at the Garrison Animal Hospital. They saved hundreds of injured swans so they could be returned to the wild. Most injuries were caused by collisions with power lines, lead poisoning caused by ingestion of lead shotgun pellets, lead fishing jigs and sinkers, illegal shooting, and injuries caused when swans became hooked or entangled by fishing lures and abandoned fishing line. Generous donations by citizens to both The University of Minnesota Raptor Center and the Wildlife Rehabilitation Center in St. Paul are gratefully appreciated for the rehabilitation efforts that helped in the restoration of the swans.

Development of New Trumpeter Swan Migratory Traditions

One question could not be answered in the early stages of trumpeter swan restoration. We did not know if, when, or where the swans would migrate to wintering areas in more southerly regions. With Sheila Lawrence's passing and after Jim Lawrence discontinued feeding the swans, it forced the swans to seek more southerly wintering destinations. There were sporadic records of trumpeters wintering in Missouri, Arkansas, and elsewhere, but details were often lacking on these sightings because they depended mainly on reports of neck-banded swans.

The most intriguing question regarding this issue is whether the migratory traditions of trumpeter swans ended when they became extirpated from Midwestern states and central Canada. Those traditions had developed over thousands of years. There was no documentation where trumpeter swans would have originally wintered. Because of a trumpeter swan's heavy coat of downy plumage, it is likely that they would not have migrated to warmer southern states like Mississippi or Louisiana. My hypothesis was that central states of the Mississippi Flyway would have been more logical wintering sites—like wetlands and backwaters along the Mississippi River and its tributaries in Indiana, Ohio, Missouri, and Arkansas.

Regardless of my hypothesis, there was a significant challenge for the establishment of new migratory traditions and wintering destinations among trumpeter swans. A pair of trumpeters migrate together with their cygnets to their wintering grounds, so cygnets learn the location for a wintering site from their parents. After returning to their natal marsh the following spring, the parents drive the young from the natal marsh. The yearlings become independent from their parents, but they continue to winter in the areas where they first wintered with their parents.

In the early years of the trumpeter swan project, there would have been no traditional knowledge of wintering sites among swans. Adult swans had to locate potential wintering locations by trial and error after migrating south to find suitable wetland areas with open water, protection, and adequate food. If they and their offspring survived to return to Minnesota in the spring, it marked the beginning of an entirely new learning process for selection of desirable wintering areas. It is likely that some historic wintering habitats have been drained or lost by urban development or agricultural drainage. It is also possible that new reservoirs, wetlands, lakes, or refuges have been created that are now suitable for wintering swans.

Added to this challenge was the irony that waterfowl hunters in southerly states had no knowledge of swan presence, swan identification, or understanding that those swans were federally protected. There were incidents where hunters, or just uninformed shooters who didn't care, shot entire families of trumpeter swans—sometimes even from their vehicles. That ended any potential for selection of lakes or wetlands that might have otherwise been acceptable wintering habitats.

Radiotelemetry research on trumpeter swans was initiated in 2019 by Drs. David Andersen, David Wolfson, and John Fieberg of the U.S. Geological Survey's Minnesota Cooperative Fish and Wildlife Research Unit and the University of Minnesota. They have been investigating the migratory pathways, nesting grounds, and wintering areas that have evolved since swans were restored in the Midwest.

They received a grant from the Legislative-Citizens' Commission on Minnesota Resources (LCCMR) for $300,000 to study the migration ecology and habitat use of trumpeter swans from Minnesota. The funding was derived from the Environment and Natural Resources Trust Fund, which comes from state lottery proceeds and The Trumpeter Swan Society. In 2019, they deployed GPS-GSM transmitters on Minnesota trumpeter swans throughout the course of the project. If a swan died, the transmitter was redeployed to another swan.

The project involved capture and monitoring of fifty-seven trumpeter swans from 2019 through 2023. Twenty-two of those swans remained in Minnesota throughout the years their movements were tracked. A total of thirty-four swans migrated beyond Minnesota's borders, including nineteen breeders, five paired swans, five singles, and one cygnet. The migratory patterns of the swans that developed beyond Minnesota are shown in Figure 18-20. Since most of these swans were monitored over a several year period, a total of 154 "swan-year" data sets were recorded with this telemetry effort. This project was completed on June 30, 2024.

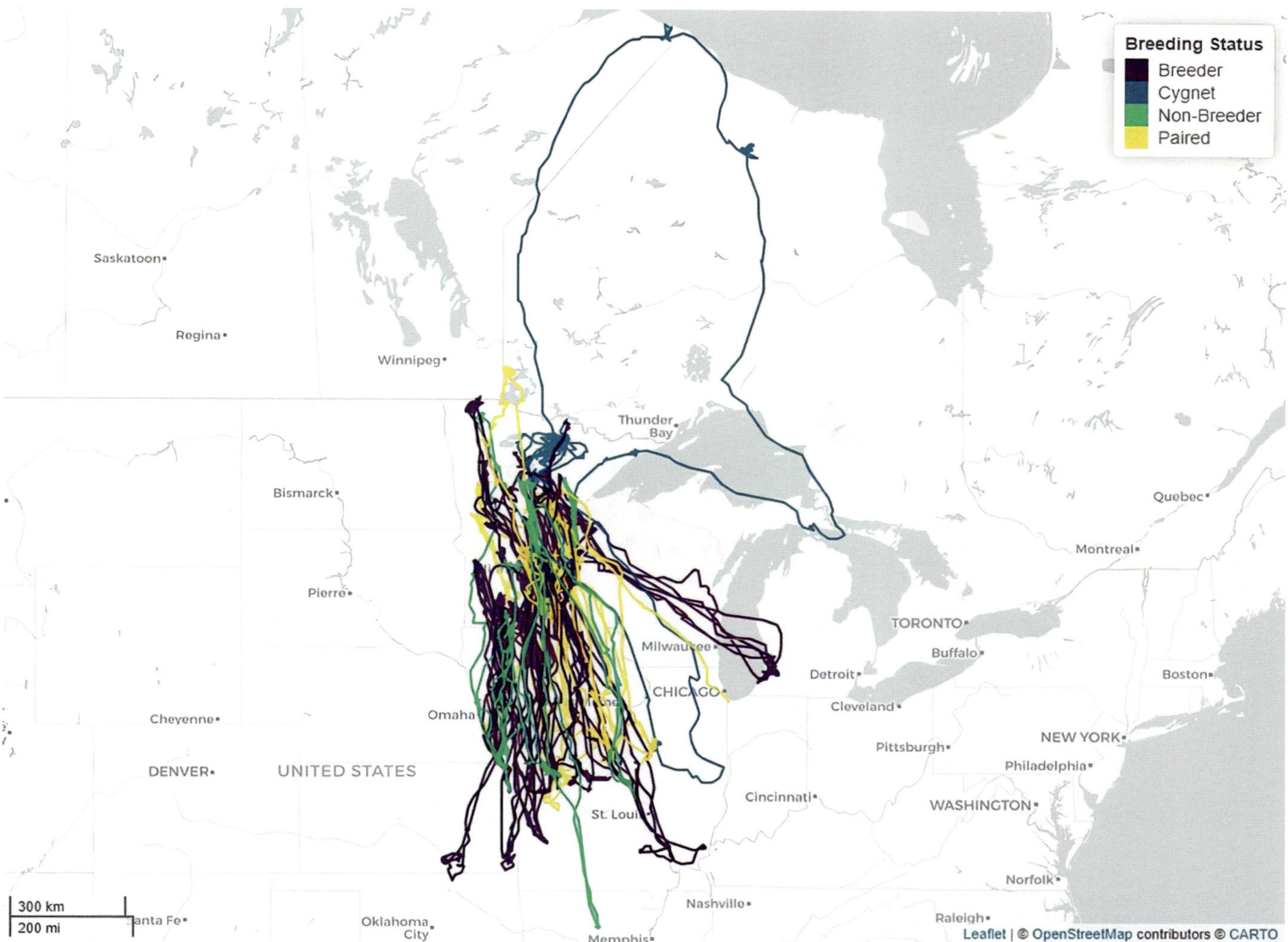

Swans migration destinations beyond Minnesota included Iowa, Wisconsin, Michigan, Illinois, Missouri, Arkansas, Nebraska, Kansas, Oklahoma, Ontario, and Manitoba. The migration destinations are color-coded. Data courtesy of Drs. David E. Andersen, David Wolfson, and John Fieberg supported by funding from the Environment and Natural Resources Trust Fund (LCCMR), and The Trumpeter Swan Society

I believe this study demonstrates the importance of viewing the recovery of the trumpeter swan as an event of regional, national, and international significance. In Minnesota, this was an ecologically-based effort to restore a lost and inspiring element back to the spectrum of our biological diversity, not to restore the trumpeter swan as a game bird.

The Trumpeter Swan Society (TTSS) is an international, non-profit conservation organization. It was founded in 1968 and dedicated to conservation, restoration, education, research, and habitat management for Trumpeter Swans across North America. They have a citizen science effort called "Trumpeter Watch" that invites citizens to report their sightings and photos of swan occurrences across the United States and Canada. For further information or to sign up for their newsletter at: www.trumpeterswansociety.org.

A Trumpeter Swan Trilogy

As I look back on Minnesota's trumpeter swan restoration effort, it represented the culmination of my wildlife conservation odyssey. I am grateful for the generosity of Minnesota's citizens who donated to the Nongame Wildlife Checkoff to make this dream a reality. And I am indebted to the dedicated Minnesota DNR commissioners, wildlife and nongame wildlife staff, DNR divisions of enforcement and state parks staff, U.S. Fish and Wildlife Service staff, Three Rivers Parks staff, Trumpeter Swan Society staff, and White Earth Band staff who all made the return of trumpeter swans possible.

I wish to close my tale of trumpeter swan restoration with a trilogy of three profound experiences that revealed powerful qualities of trumpeter behavior, parental bonds, and natural beauty that have enriched my life beyond my wildest expectations.

The Legacy of Supermom Swan #9

During our restoration project, one swan emerged as an incredible survivor and supermom that attempted to bring back the species on her own. Swan #9 was a pen (female). She was the offspring of two bonded trumpeter swans that were hatched and raised by their parents at the Minnesota

Supermom swan #9 at the age of twenty accompanied by her fifty-fifth cygnet at Monticello, December 21, 2009.

Zoo in Apple Valley under the management of bird curator Jimmy Pichner. The pair was donated by the Zoo to the Minnesota Department of Natural Resources for release in the spring of 1987. The cob (male) from this pair was the largest of all trumpeter swans ever released as part of this restoration program. It weighed thirty-five and a half pounds. In 1989, this pair nested for the first time at the Hubbel Pond Wildlife Refuge a few miles south of Tamarac National Wildlife Refuge. Five cygnets hatched, but only one survived. That cygnet, a pen, was subsequently captured, banded with U.S. Fish and Wildlife Service band #619-17822 and outfitted with an orange wing tag displaying #9.

In the fall of 1989, this pair of swans, accompanied by their surviving cygnet, # 9, migrated to the Mississippi River near Monticello where they wintered along the Mississippi River shoreline home of Jim and Sheila Lawrence. Sheila provided shelled corn daily for the wintering swans at this site for the next twenty-four years. She took meticulous records of all the marked swans in the wintering flock each year including leg bands, neck collar numbers, and patagial wing tags. She also recorded the number of cygnets accompanying all marked swans.

Number 9 returned to Monticello in 1990, 1991, and 1992 with no young as would be expected for a swan less than four years old. In her fourth year she was accompanied by a mate and five young. This was the first of twenty-one years that she wintered at Monticello accompanied by a total of fifty-seven cygnets through 2014. She produced seven cygnets each year in 1996 and 1997.

On December 21, 2009, I made a trip to Monticello to visit Jim and Sheila after she notified me that #9 had returned with another cygnet. Her mate was missing. I found her resting peacefully on Sheila and Jim's lawn with her cygnet at her side. I spent about an hour watching and photographing #9 and her cygnet. I was able to photograph her leg band (619-17822) but her wing tag was gone. She was twenty years old... but still an elegant and beautiful swan doing her part to help bring back this remarkable species. It was the last time I saw her. From 2010 through 2012, the number of young was not recorded because Sheila had contracted cancer and was not able to document #9's young. Sheila passed away in 2011. Her husband Jim took over feeding the swans, but he did not record the bands and productivity data from 2010 through 2012. In 2013, #9 returned to Monticello at the age of twenty-four with two more young—a lifetime total of fifty-seven cygnets! It is possible that #9 produced over sixty cygnets during her life. She returned one last time in 2014 at the age of twenty-five, but she was not accompanied by any cygnets.

After Sheila's passing, Jim continued feeding the swans for several years, but this was an expensive and taxing endeavor. And, it was probably not in the long-term interest of the swans to have them so concentrated in winter because of the potential for avian disease outbreaks. In the big picture of things, I believe those early years of supplemental feeding by Sheila and Jim likely brought the swans through the winter in better physical condition and contributed to the production of larger broods during those early stages of swan restoration.

A Parental Bond of Steel

The parental instincts of trumpeter swans are especially important for protecting their cygnets. The ever-vigilant parents typically swim with their young cygnets bracketed between them.

Trumpeter swans protect their cygnets by swimming with the young bracketed between them.

When I first began working on trumpeter swan restoration, I did not realize or appreciate the powerful parental bond that swan parents have for protecting and raising their cygnets. Trumpeter swans are the largest waterfowl species in the world. They have few natural predators. Male swans, called cobs, have a calloused, bony knob on the leading edge of the wrist joint on their wings. They use it to strike any predators or other swans that might challenge their territory. The effect of being struck by a swan's wing knob has been likened to being struck by a baseball bat.

The parents are incredibly protective and aggressive against any threats or predators that might endanger their cygnets. U.S. Fish and Wildlife Service pilot Rod King told me that a pilot friend watched a pair of trumpeter swans drive an Alaskan brown bear away from their nest. The swans would have weighed about thirty pounds, and the bear could have weighed over one thousand pounds. It was no contest.

Wisconsin DNR biologist Sumner Matteson was collecting trumpeter swan eggs in Alaska for their restoration project several years after our Minnesota egg collection trips. He had a swan attack their plane and knock off the radio antenna. The swan was unhurt. Wisconsin's swan restoration efforts are proceeding well, and Sumner Matteson estimates their population is now about thirteen thousand swans.

Minnesota DNR Conservation Officer Karl Hadrits discovered the power of this parental bond when responding to a report of trumpeter swans being shot during the fall waterfowl hunting season of 2006. At the Deerwood Ricebed Marsh in Aitkin County, waterfowl hunters reported a shooting incident through the Turn in Poachers hotline. Two young hunters shot at a family of swans passing overhead. Two swans had gone down. The two young hunters hastily left the wetland after the shooting. They were gone when DNR conservation officers Karl Hadrits and Tom Provost arrived.

They took a canoe onto the marsh and located the injured swan. It was a cygnet with a broken wing. They also found a second adult swan near the cygnet. When they approached the cygnet with a large landing net to capture it, the adult swan swam between them and the cygnet to prevent it from being captured. Karl was finally able to net the cygnet and lift it into the boat. The adult swan, obviously its parent, remained beside the boat. Karl assumed it was also injured, so he picked it up and placed it in the boat beside the cygnet.

Karl transported these swans to the Garrison Animal Hospital, where wildlife rehabilitation vet Debbie Eskedal examined the birds to determine the extent of their injuries. The cygnet was severely injured. It had a broken wing and internal injuries. Examination of the adult male swan revealed a startling revelation. It was not injured at all.

In an extraordinary act of parental defense, the cob had fearlessly challenged the two conservation officers to protect its cygnet. When that failed, the swan submitted to being picked up by Karl and being placed beside the cygnet in the canoe. Once at the Garrison Animal Hospital, the cob rested quietly beside the cygnet as it was examined.

After the swans were examined, Karl and Debbie decided that the best option was to return the cob to the Deerwood Ricebed so it could rejoin its family. Debbie continued caring for the injured cygnet, but its injuries were too severe. It died several days later.

DNR Conservation Officer Karl Hadrits with the healthy parent, a cob, that allowed itself to be picked up so it could stay with its wounded cygnet.
Photo by Susan Hadrits

The Ricebed Cygnet Gets Justice in Court

Conservation officer Hadrits obtained information about the identity of the two young hunters from other waterfowl hunters on the marsh who had witnessed the violation. Officer Hadrits contacted the teenagers, and they admitted to shooting the swan. They were issued tickets for shooting and killing a state-threatened trumpeter swan. When the swan died at the Garrison Animal Hospital, it was placed in a freezer to be used as evidence. I was contacted to testify as a witness for the state to verify that the swan that had been killed was a trumpeter swan and not a tundra swan. Karl Hadrits wife Susan had taken photos of both the adult trumpeter swan and the injured cygnet at the Garrison Animal Hospital. They were of vital importance for proving that the swan that had been killed was a trumpeter.

The mother of one teenage violator learned that if her son had shot a tundra swan, the fine could be about $300 whereas the fine for killing a threatened trumpeter swan could be as much as $3,000. She requested a court hearing so she could claim that her son had shot a tundra swan. During the intervening time, the freezer at Garrison broke. The contents thawed and decomposed, including the swan's carcass. One of the hospital volunteers disposed of the spoiled swan, not realizing it was being held for use as evidence in the court case.

The trumpeter swans in the photos were significantly larger than the largest tundra swans I had ever encountered in my career. I testified in court regarding the characteristics that proved the swan that had been shot was a trumpeter swan. The photo of the adult parent swan revealed the typical black skin extending from the bill and surrounding the front half of the eye. This is a definitive characteristic of trumpeter swans. On a tundra swan the skin extends from the bill to the eye as a narrow strip of black skin, and there is usually a yellow teardrop marking on the black skin in front of the eye. Those markings were not present on the swan in question.

There are also no records of wild tundra swans nesting and raising young in Minnesota, so finding an adult tundra swan protecting a cygnet was not logical. The cygnet weighed twenty-three pounds. In a scientific summary of the weights of 702 tundra swans, the largest one weighed just over nineteen and a half pounds. Finally, the front edge of the feathers on the top of the bill is pointed like a widow's peak on trumpeter swans and is rounded on tundra swans. In the photo taken by Susan Hadrits, the feathers on the front edge of the cygnet's forehead were clearly pointed.

After citing these distinguishing characteristics supporting the identity of the swan as a trumpeter, the judge ruled in favor of the DNR. The judge assessed a fine of $2,542 to the two illegal shooters. Word of such substantial fines spread rapidly among waterfowl hunters, and it became a significant deterrent in limiting the illegal killing of swans during subsequent fall waterfowl seasons. My extensive experience in waterfowl identification as well as my hunting- related law enforcement experience from Lac qui Parle helped in seeing this case through to a successful conclusion.

Thanks from a Swan

A visit from an old friend.

On January 10, 1997, I visited the banks of the Mississippi River near Monticello to observe the trumpeter swans at their favorite wintering site by the home of Jim and Sheila Lawrence. I sat on the rocks at water's edge with my camera in my lap. While watching several dozen swans in the middle of the river, one swan parted from the flock and began swimming toward me. I photographed the swan as it drew closer. It came within fifty feet, then forty feet, then twenty feet. Finally, it swam so close I had to turn my camera sideways to get the whole swan in the view-

Revealing his band number 619-17888.

finder. Then the swan stepped from the water, and I could see a leg band! I focused on the band and took a photo. It was swan #619-17888. Since I was sitting on the rocks, I was looking at eye level to the swan—only about six feet away. As the swan stood silently looking at me, I began to talk to the swan in a calm, low voice.

I was reminded of a late friend of mine, Dr. Walter Breckenridge, who once told me that when he would check the wood duck nest box in his backyard along the Mississippi River, he would begin talking to the duck as he ascended the ladder to check the nest. When he opened the door on the side of the nest box, he could reach in, gently lift the hen, and count the eggs. Then he lowered the duck onto the eggs and closed the box, still talking to the duck. Breck said that wood ducks can live a long time, and he was sure this hen knew his voice. He also said that a predator never talks to its prey before it kills it, so the duck knew he meant no harm.

Well, I decided to engage in small talk with the swan for about five minutes. Finally, the swan turned, entered the water, and rejoined its flock. Upon returning to the office, I looked up the swan's band number. I had collected that swan as an egg in the Minto Flats of Alaska on June 10, 1988. We reared that cygnet at the Carlos Avery Game Farm and released it on North Chippewa Lake on the Tamarac National Wildlife Refuge on May 23, 1990. The swan was approaching nine years of age. I can only surmise that the swan had stopped by to say "Hi, Dad, and Thanks."

My vision for Trumpeter Swans comes true in Minnesota.

Appendix A

Life Lessons for a Career in Natural Resource Conservation

Looking back on my forty-four-year wildlife conservation career in the Minnesota DNR and another six years of conservation activism since retirement, I wish to share fifty years of project management strategies I incorporated into my priorities, goals, and conservation initiatives. I synthesized those experiences into twenty life lessons that have contributed to successful conservation efforts. These lessons began evolving in 2003 when I started making annual presentations for the Honors Mentor Connection class of the Gifted Education Services program in Plymouth, Minnesota. The program was managed by Dr. Dorothy Welch. She invited me every year to give a presentation to talented and gifted high school seniors from thirteen-Intermediate District 287 high schools in the southern and southwestern regions of the Twin Cities.

Each year through 2018 I gave an oral presentation over that sixteen-year period to over three hundred seniors that resulted in the following Life Lessons. I felt they could be helpful for aspiring high school and college students hungry for tips on preparing for their careers, including natural resource students, wildlife managers, biologists, and conservationists as they proceed with their careers. The Life Lessons could also be helpful for many other careers not related to natural resource conservation. Dr. Welch deserves credit for encouraging me to summarize how I have approached my career and conservation projects. My goal in sharing these Life Lessons was not so much to relate what I have done over the course of my career but to share my insights on how these projects were accomplished.

Every year after my presentation, Dorothy asked all her students to write a paragraph about what they learned from my presentation. Over the years I received several hundred comments from those high school seniors about the impact of my comments on their future careers. Following are some of their responses that were an inspiration to me.

"Thank you for sharing your story about your son and his experience with college. Your advice and information was very helpful, especially 'don't settle for silver when you can go for the gold.' Thank you very much. I will definitely use it and I appreciate it very much."

There were a few especially useful nuggets of wisdom, "There can be nothing more profitable to a young naturalist than journeys to far away countries."

"The multiplier effect and catalyst effect are also extremely useful pieces of advice."

"The most important assets are indeed a cheerful attitude and respect for employees."

"Something you said really caught my attention. Work smarter, not longer, and use other people to expand your network. Your own example of learning journalism, photography, and taking speech was instrumental to your incredible achievements and success."

Lesson #1

Follow your passion, study what you love, and love what you do. That is where you will find success.

Picking a University & Your Major

When entering Iowa State, I selected engineering science because friends discouraged me from studying natural resources and wildlife conservation. They said those careers offered low pay and few jobs. Bad choice. Bad advice. I signed up for a major in engineering science, but I felt low motivation. After one quarter I changed my major to zoology with minors in botany and physics. There was a dramatic change in my perspective. After changing majors, my grade point and attitude improved dramatically.

Our son Craig also provided a lesson in selecting what university to attend. He enrolled in the University of Minnesota Talented Youth Mathematics Program in middle school. By the time he graduated from high school he had earned thirty college credits, including calculus, from the University of Minnesota. He also took a special math course in high school summer school at Michigan Tech. His professor there asked him about his choice for college. Craig said he was considering Iowa State, Harvey Mudd, and Caltech, but he seemed uncertain with his response. His professor asked where he would really like to go. Craig said he would really like to go to MIT, but he didn't know if he was good enough to go to MIT. His professor responded, "If you are not good enough to go to MIT, make them tell you that you are not good enough! Why settle for silver when you can go for the gold!"

Craig scored well in his college entrance tests in math. He applied to MIT and got accepted. He earned a B.S. and M.Eng. from MIT. He has worked for several major corporations providing IT expertise. Don't sell yourself short in considering your academic career. Look for the best faculty and academic program that matches your career aspirations. Go for the gold. Within the scope of your dream or reach schools, it is also a good strategy to apply to a balanced spectrum of safety and target schools that could help you achieve your career goals.

Lesson #2

Choosing a grad school. If you want to be the best, learn from the best: "Learn from the one who wrote the book!"

When considering my graduate school options, if I wanted to be the best, I felt I should study under the best. My main interest was in pursuing ecology related to wildlife conservation. Dr. Eugene P. Odum was the University of Georgia (UGA) professor who wrote the highly acclaimed college textbook *Fundamentals of Ecology*, and he created the Institute of Ecology at UGA. He was subsequently a recipient of the Crafoord Prize in 1987, the biologist's equivalent of the Nobel Prize. He personally invited me to attend UGA, and I eagerly accepted the opportunity. He was the idea man and inspiration on the cutting edge of the ecology movement in the 1970s.

There was another consideration that played into my decision on where to attend graduate school. I grew up in central Iowa and rarely traveled more than twenty-five miles from home. I got invitations for graduate study at the University of Wisconsin and at the University of Georgia. I desired to benefit from learning ecology from Dr. Odum, and I also felt it would be beneficial to go to UGA to expand my horizons beyond the Midwest. It was the right decision. In graduate school at UGA I focused on my trilogy of interests which included ecology, wildlife management, and communications. I graduated with a four-point grade record because I studied what I loved!

Lesson # 3

Cross-pollinate your grad school major.

My graduate studies initially included ecology, forestry, and wildlife management. Then I crossed over to the liberal arts campus at UGA and took courses in journalism, feature writing, and public relations. I also took a class under Dr. Archie Patterson in the School of Forest Resources in informational methods to enhance my skills for appearing on radio and TV to promote wildlife conservation. This hybrid mixture of skills and education gave me a competitive edge in a world where most wildlife-related job applicants are specialized only in a single major or skill set.

Lesson # 4

Develop personal skill sets that will enhance your career.

Photography Skills

After I casually mentioned that I would like to try 35 mm. photography while home on leave from the air force, my father bought me a used Argus Rangefinder 35 mm. camera as a birthday gift in 1972. I received it while I was stationed at Keesler Air Force Base in Biloxi, Mississippi. I won several awards at the air force base photo contest after photographing monarch butterflies in migration that fall in the Biloxi area. Many cameras later, I have won seven awards in national photography competitions and have used hundreds of my photos to illustrate my wildlife books, magazine articles, slide programs, newspaper stories and Powerpoint presentations about wildlife conservation.

Two photos I took of humpback whales offshore from the Pacific coast of Costa Rica in January, 1990, documented that region as a humpback whale migratory destination and calving area. Those two photos convinced Costa Rican president Oscar Arias to designate over twenty square miles of the Pacific Ocean as the Ballena Marine National Park to protect the whales. Those are the two most important photos I have ever taken. Good photos can convey powerful conservation messages. Sharpen your photography skills. Use good equipment. Learn from other skilled photographers, take classes to learn photography techniques, learn to give impactful presentations, and create inspiring conservation messages with your images.

Writing Skills

I began writing articles at the Department of Natural Resources for the Minnesota Volunteer magazine in 1976. Since then, I have written thirty-nine articles for the *Volunteer*, sixteen books, many magazine and newspaper articles, and hundreds of news releases about nongame wildlife conservation projects. I wrote four field guides for the wildlife of Costa Rica using my photographs. Writing is an essential skill for developing support and understanding for your program and for sharing your passion. Keep writing! It gets easier the more you write. Learn to ruthlessly edit your work. Find friends who are good at editing who can help you sharpen your writing skills. Avoid redundancy and meaningless words.

If you wish to write a book, identify a unique perspective that has not been covered by other authors and a topic that will enrich the lives of your readers. I realized there was a significant lack of Minnesota-based information for citizens who wanted to help pollinators or songbirds through landscaping or gardening. Most landscaping books were written for national audiences and included information about wildlife and plant species not found in Minnesota. Minnesota conservationists needed hands-on books with techniques and plans to enhance their private land specifically written for Minnesotans as well as information on building nest boxes and bird feeding techniques.

Public Speaking Skills

Learn to present in front of people in a clear, pleasant, and entertaining manner. Some people are more afraid of public speaking than they are of death. There are unfortunately some natural resource experts who are introverts who avoid public forums, presentations, and media contacts. This is sadly a missed opportunity to generate support for the wildlife conservation and natural resources that we care about. Supervisors and program managers need to look for those presentation skills in the people they are hiring.

For most presentations I use Powerpoint and utilize my images in those programs. Don't be afraid of your audience. Assume they are really interested in your topic and that they want to learn from you. Share what you know. Keep your presentation interesting, fast-moving and with a clear outline of your main topics. Don't leave an image up for several minutes. I don't leave an image on for more than two or three seconds. Minimize text on single images to ten or fewer words. Avoid meaningless words like *you know*, *uh*, and *like*. Ask friends to provide helpful critiques of your speaking skills to help you avoid such annoying speaking habits.

International Travels

Take advantage of international travel and study opportunities when you are young, single, and not limited by family and parenting obligations. Charles Darwin wrote: "...there can be nothing more profitable for a young naturalist than a journey to distant countries."

While in grad school, my wildlife professor, Dr. Jim Jenkins, stopped me in the hall one day and asked me "How would you like to go study in Costa Rica?" I said "Sure!" and then I went to look up where it was. It was a life-changing experience. Dr. Jenkins was an innovative and inspirational mentor during my graduate years. He was the co-inventor of the hypodermic dart gun for capturing wildlife and spent a year as a visiting professor teaching at the University of Praetoria in South Africa.

I applied for and was accepted for a two-month course in tropical agriculture and land use through the Organization for Tropical Studies (OTS) at the University of Costa Rica in February and March of 1969. I was also accepted for a second course in principles of tropical ecology in July and August of that year. I drove to Costa Rica with Dr. Jenkins in an old $250 pickup for the second OTS course. It was the beginning of a marvelous life-changing experience where I met my wife Ethelle Gonzalez Alvarez at the freshmen orientation dance at the University of Costa Rica in 1969. We have now been married for 56 years. My OTS coursework dramatically broadened and intensified my international perspective on ecology and wildlife conservation.

Serendipity

Learning to take advantage of "serendipity" is an acquired skill. In 1985, Ethelle and I were visiting her family in Costa Rica when we ran into our travel agent, Karen Johnson. She was escorting Minnesota Vikings football coach Bud Grant and some of his friends on a fishing trip. We shared a happy hour visit with Karen, Bud, and his friends at El Bramadero restaurant in Liberia. We had a wonderful time visiting with Bud and learning about his interests in wood ducks, a pair of ravens he hand-raised as a kid, and other wildlife. He never mentioned football.

Later I arranged to meet Bud at the Vikings practice facility in Winter Park with DNR cinematographer Larry Duke. There we produced television public service announcements by Bud to promote the Nongame Wildlife Checkoff. Bud also arranged for my friend and bluebird enthusiast John Thompson to place and manage bluebird nest boxes throughout the Viking's Winter Park training facility.

After returning to Minnesota, Karen called and asked if we would be interested in leading birdwatching tours to Costa Rica. We cautiously agreed, not knowing quite what to expect. We led our first birdwatching trip to Costa Rica in 1987. We have led international birding trips throughout Latin America from Guatemala and Cuba to Patagonia, New Zealand, Kenya and Tanzania, and thirty-two birding trips to Costa Rica. I have also written four wildlife field guides for Costa Rica with the University of Texas Press.

The comment by Charles Darwin could not have been more profound: "...there can be nothing more profitable for a young naturalist than a journey to distant countries." Our chance meeting with Karen Johnson and Bud Grant created the opportunity to meet exceptional people, biologists, and guides throughout Latin America. We experienced stunning scenery, tropical rainforests, and remarkable wildlife from resplendent quetzals to condors, harpy eagles, jaguars, anacondas, and southern right whales!

In 1990, Ethelle and I were leading a birding trip to Peru and visited the famous Inca ruins at Machu Picchu. Our guide was a young woman of Inca descent who shared her insight about the Inca culture. She said their culture had been built upon a lifestyle that embodied three words: **Love, Teach, Learn**. What a memorable lesson for leading a meaningful life.

Lesson #5

Find the mentors in your midst who will share their vision, perspective, and lifelong passion for nature.

Mentors don't just happen. They grow on you. You eventually realize they have qualities for the kind of person you want to become. I am fortunate to have encountered many memorable mentors during my life. They have inspired me with their personalities, their commitment and dedication to wildlife conservation, and their sincere friendships.

Roger Holmes, Dave Vesall and Joe Alexander at the DNR inspired me with their passion for helping wildlife, preserving habitat, and their legislative savvy for achieving success with the legislature. Roger taught me to be a good listener; he was good at editing my technical reports for the Section of Wildlife. We enjoyed many memorable duck, goose, and sharp-tailed grouse hunts from the Lac qui Parle Wildlife Management Area in Minnesota to the wetlands and aspen parklands of Saskatchewan. One of Roger's most memorable phrases when deciding on a conservation action was an emphatic "It's the right thing to do!"

Dr. Walter Breckenridge taught me that you can be a concerned and involved conservationist until you are a hundred years old. Art Hawkins shared his passion for waterfowl management, keeping good records of his observations and wood duck conservation. Art had the ultimate mentor. Art was a graduate student of Aldo Leopold in the 1930s. He passed on Aldo's passion for wildlife conservation throughout his life.

Dr. Bud Tordoff's passion for peregrines was infectious. His passion for making the restoration of peregrines a success was obvious through his extensive networking contacts with falconers. At Bud Tordoff's memorial service, a former graduate student said one thing he remembered about Bud is that he would often gather up his graduate students and have a coffee break with them. That is where they really got to know each other and became inspired by Bud. They discussed their research projects as well as their latest woodcock hunting forays. I knew some people at the DNR who would never go for a coffee break. They never got to know other DNR staff members or appreciate the value of connections made over those informal moments. Dr. Pat Redig similarly inspired me with his broad knowledge of raptors and ability to plan and execute research not only on peregrines but also on research linking lead poisoning in bald eagles to the use of lead ammunition for both waterfowl hunting and deer hunting.

Dr. Daniel H. Janzen, a tropical entomologist from the University of Pennsylvania, inspired me with his dedication, hard work, enthusiasm, ability to keep up with the latest scientific technology and his determination to preserve tropical dry forests in Costa Rica. He discovered many new insect species and even named one of them after our son Craig. He received the international Crafoord Prize in 1984 for his professional accomplishments. That is the biologist's equivalent of the Nobel Prize.

These mentors provided me with a gold standard throughout my career for building professional and personal friendships, continuing personal development, learning the value of networking, demonstrating my dedication to wildlife conservation and respectful treatment and supervision of my employees and conservation partners. I would like to think that some of their passion, knowledge, and dedication was passed on to me in my wildlife conservation career, and I hope I have passed some of that passion on to my own friends and colleagues. Now I challenge you to find your own mentors.

Lesson #6

In picking your job, don't follow the dollars. Follow your heart.

After completing my graduate education at the University of Georgia in 1970 and my air force service in 1973, I was hired by DeLeuw, Cather and Company in Atlanta, Georgia, to be an ecological consultant to plan a four-lane tollway corridor from Chattanooga, Tennessee to Tallahassee, Florida. My salary was $15,000 per year. Upon completing the six-month project, I was to be transferred to their home office in Chicago. I was then offered a job by the Minnesota Department of Natural Resources as assistant manager of the Lac qui Parle Wildlife Refuge at a salary of $10,000 per year. I accepted the job in a heartbeat. Becoming a wildlife manager was the dream job I had always wanted.

Don't be deceived by the amount of your paycheck. If you hope to experience sustained success in your career, you need to find a profession that you will find personally fulfilling every day of your career. The size of your paycheck will be a secondary consideration. Now,– fifty-two years later, I am convinced it was the right decision.

Lesson #7

Learn to Connect the Dots. Connect two apparently unrelated facts or ideas to solve a problem.

Connecting the dots is a unique skillset. This involves connecting two apparently unrelated topics and linking them to create a unique revelation for understanding or resolving a problem.

After taking on my new position as the DNR Nongame Wildlife Program supervisor in 1977, I read an article about a study in the *Journal of American Veterinary Medical Association* about a bald eagle that had died after consuming about seventy-five lead shotgun pellets at a national wildlife refuge in Maryland. The pellets had been ingested because the eagle had been feeding on dead geese that had been shot and not retrieved by hunters. This was the first article I had seen about a connection between waterfowl hunting with lead shotgun pellets and lead poisoning causing the death of federally listed bald eagles.

Those were the same conditions that existed at the Lac qui Parle Wildlife Refuge where I had worked for three years. I recalled the dying bald eagle I had picked up at the refuge in November of 1974. It had symptoms of lead poisoning that I had not recognized at the time. I initiated a research project to verify if Lac qui Parle's eagles were being poisoned by exposure to the lead shotgun pellets. The research verified they were being poisoned by lead ammunition used for goose hunting. This resulted in the use of lead ammo being banned for waterfowl hunting in Minnesota in 1991, and in 1997 it was banned for waterfowl hunting nationwide.

A second example of connecting the dots occurred when I was developing a strategy for research on American white pelicans to determine if they were adversely affected by the Deepwater Horizon oil spill. We needed to assess the extent of contamination in pelicans nesting at the Marsh Lake pelican nesting colony. We would be capturing nesting pelicans at the colony to obtain blood samples and testing unhatched pelican eggs for petroleum-related contaminants. I wanted another type of validation to tie contaminants in the pelicans to contaminants picked up in the Gulf of Mexico during the previous winter. I knew from my visits to pelican colonies for banding pelicans at Minnesota Lake and Lac qui Parle that the pelicans possessed bill knobs that they grew while on their wintering areas in the Gulf of Mexico. Both males and females grew bill knobs each year. Once nesting was completed, they usually shed the bill knobs in the vicinity of the nesting colony. I felt bill knobs grown in the Gulf of Mexico on their wintering grounds should reflect contaminants from the oil spill. We picked up shed bill knobs in the Marsh Lake colony and had them analyzed for BP-related petroleum contaminants by the staff at the University of Connecticut. My hunch worked. BP-related petroleum contaminants were found in the bill knobs. Bill knobs had never been used previously for determination of environmental contamination.

My third example of connecting the dots occurred as I was developing a research strategy for assessing the impact of the Deepwater Horizon oil spill on Minnesota's loons that would have still been wintering in the Gulf of Mexico when the spill occurred in April of 2010. I heard a TV news story about a researcher with the U.S. Geological Survey doing a study on loons in Wisconsin and Michigan with satellite transmitters to determine their migration patterns.

That sounded like the kind of information we needed for studying the potential impact of the oil spill on Minnesota's loons. I found the name of the loon researcher, Kevin Kenow, and I called him to learn if he might be interested in doing a comparable loon study in Minnesota. Kevin said that he could make his research team available for an in-depth, multi-year research study on the impact of the Deepwater Horizon oil spill on Minnesota's loons. I reassured him that I could write a work plan for the loon study and raise the funding necessary for the research through the Environment and Natural Resources Trust Fund.

It all worked out to generate a study from 2011 through 2017 that received $641,000 in funding from the Environment and Natural Resources Trust Fund which is derived from state lottery proceeds. The information generated by the study resulted in $7.7 million being allocated to the Minnesota DNR and the Minnesota Pollution Control Agency for funding made available from Natural Resource Damage and Remediation (NRDAR) funds derived from BP for fines from the damage caused by the oil spill. All this resulted from listening to a television news broadcast and making a phone call.

One additional example of connecting the dots occurred when I was planning for the transfer of forty trumpeter swans from the Twin Cities to the Detroit Lakes area for release in the Tamarac National Wildlife Refuge area. Transferring them by trucks would likely expose the swans to too much jarring effect on their legs and could lead to lasting injuries.

I needed to find a method that would provide a more stable means of transportation for the swans—like a plane. We needed not just a plane. We needed a bigger plane! I served as a captain in the Military Airlift Command in the U.S. Air Force from 1970 through 1973. I was in the 4th Mobile Communications Group and had also served as a loadmaster for a C-130 on deployment. A C-130 military transport plane would be the perfect plane for the mission. I had no current connections with the air force, but I still recalled how to work within the air force structure. I called the air national guard unit in Minneapolis. I explained my background experience with the air force and asked if they might be willing to arrange a training flight with forty trumpeter swans to Fargo, North Dakota. They responded that they would get back to me. They called back a couple days later and said, "It's a go!" Mission accomplished.

Lesson #8

Know your publics.

There is no general public. There are unique publics and conservation partners associated with different wildlife species and habitats. Identify potential conservation partners and network with them. Effective networking is a key to project success. Include people of diverse cultural and ethnic backgrounds among your partners and include youths whenever possible.

Howard Hill was a world-famous archer in the 1930s who shot a longbow with a draw weight of 110 pounds. He won 196 consecutive field archery tournaments. He was an accomplished bow hunter and pursued game from birds to elephants. One of his most memorable comments about bowhunting was when he said, "When you go hunting afield, you must know absolutely everything about your quarry… what it eats, where it lives, where it sleeps, and its daily movement patterns." He continued, "If you don't know all these things when you go afield, you are not hunting. You are just walking in the woods."

The same principle applies to knowing your publics for media promotion. If you do not know who they are, how to communicate with them, and how to motivate them to help achieve your program goals, you are "just walking in the woods."

Every restoration project I have been involved with required a different mix of publics for support, planning, funding, and implementation, including the movers and shakers who know how to make things happen. Success will come from working with those publics who are dedicated to helping the species or habitats you are trying to benefit. And be sure to provide sincere and enthusiastic credits to those partners when you share in those successes.

Lesson #9

Keep a healthy balance between your professional and personal life.

Sometimes we become so obsessed with our work that we throw too much effort into our professional life, and our home and family life suffers. Some program managers or supervisors are controlling micromanagers who think that they must do everything themselves. They will not delegate authority to accomplish their mission. They end up putting in sixty to eighty hours or more per week to get the job done. That pace cannot last. It is not sustainable. They come in on Friday nights and weekends to work; they feel that they cannot afford to let any aspect of their job go undone. They also expect people who work for them to put in similar long hours. Don't fall into that trap. They will burn you out, and you are at risk of the same burnout fate.

Family Life is Number One...

Whenever I hire someone, I tell them that their personal and family life is Number One and that their job is Number Two in priority. I tell them that within the scope of everyone's life, a day will come when there will be some major crisis relating to health, an accident or other problem affecting them, their spouse, their children, or their parents. They need to drop everything to deal with that problem. I ask them to let me know when that is happening and how we can help. We will cover things at work until their problem can be resolved. This gives people an incredible peace of mind so they can deal with their personal problems until they get their life back under control.

If you wish to make a difference, you must work smarter, not longer. Schedule your time and priorities to make your forty hours per week meaningful. Channel your efforts to positive outcomes. Try to avoid office distractions. However, take time out for coffee breaks to have informal time to get to know your peers and job partners. In this current world of working remotely, those coffee breaks have become obsolete. They can be scheduled with your staff at offsite coffee shops.

Lesson #10

Channel your energies, keep the big picture in mind, think big, and be patient.

My goal was to manage and restore Minnesota's protected wildlife to healthy and diverse levels. Channel your energies to fulfill your goals somewhat like an actor does to channel their personality to become their movie character. Jim Carrey is an example of an actor who "channeled" himself into the many characters he portrayed to give his best performances. Channeling in this case means managing your time, attention, and priorities to avoid distractions. When I was writing my book *Wild About Birds: the DNR Bird Feeding Guide,* I would set aside my other work every afternoon at one thirty, and I worked on the book until I left work for my carpool at four. That way I made steady progress without impairing my progress on other activities.

Don't Be Afraid to Think Big

Keep the big picture in mind, and don't be afraid to think big. What is your long-term vision for your professional goals? Don't let small problems, obsessions with minutia or distractions with social media let you lose sight of your overall goals. Big projects often have the best chance for funding and approval. They may also require years of effort to achieve the desired results. It helps to be patient, thorough, determined, creative, and stubborn when necessary.

Lesson #11

A problem is just an opportunity that needs to be repackaged. Attitude is everything!

I had another strategy for success throughout my professional life. When I was diagnosed with Guillain Barré syndrome in 1976, I realized that I could be paralyzed for a long time and that there was also a 5 to 10 per cent mortality rate. I decided on the first day of that diagnosis that I would get better. At the most severe point in my affliction, my physical therapy consisted of lifting fishing sinkers. I could still lift a pencil, so I wrote articles for the DNR *Minnesota Volunteer* magazine about the wildlife of Lac qui Parle Wildlife Refuge and drew wildlife sketches. After three months at North Memorial Medical Center, I learned to walk again using a walker, and I was able to return home. Throughout the entire recovery period I maintained a cheerful outlook, optimism, patience, and faith that I would recover. There were no days that I felt depressed or sad.

Attitude is everything! Your three most important assets are a positive attitude, optimism, and an ever-present smile. We will all face personal medical or emotional crises during our life for ourselves, our parents, and our children. We need to be an inspiration to those around us to find hope and optimism in those situations.

My Inspiration from "The Plucky Plover" in Kenya

I met Kenyan guide John Ngigi when Ethelle and I were leading a wildlife tour in Kenya in 2000. John related the story of leading a family on a wildlife safari in Amboseli National Park in southern Kenya in September of 1999. They were enjoying wildlife in the shadow of Mount Kilimanjaro. John stopped his van when he spotted a blacksmith plover on its nest. As his tourists viewed the nest, he explained the uniqueness of this distant relative of the American killdeer. With dapper black, gray, and white markings, it is easy to identify by sight and sound. The plover gets its distinctive name from its metallic, clanging call that sounds like a blacksmith hitting an anvil with a hammer.

Blacksmith plover in Kenya—the Plucky Plover.

Like other members of the plover family, the blacksmith plover nest consists of a shallow depression in the ground. The plover lays one to four speckled eggs that are pointed at one end. As everyone was watching the female plover, it stood up. It was incubating two eggs. There was a problem. The plover had made its nest on a game trail used by antelopes and even elephants. No sooner had John realized the plover's dilemma when he spotted a procession of fifteen elephants approaching the plover, single file, on the game trail. The procession was led by the matriarch of the herd, a large female.

There was no way to help the plover. As the matriarch approached, the plover stood up, mantled the nest with its wings and began its clanging call. When the elephant was about ten to twelve feet from the nest, the plover flushed from its nest toward the matriarch. It flew for a spot right between the eyes of the elephant. It pulled up at the last second to strike the elephant with its breast and slapped the elephant with its wings. It pivoted in flight and returned to its nest, mantling its eggs and calling vociferously.

The startled elephant stopped in its tracks and stared at the plover. The other fourteen elephants stopped when the female halted. Then the plucky plover launched another flight at the matriarch, striking it between the eyes with its breast and slapping it with its wings. The plover peeled off after striking the elephant and returned to its nest, mantling the eggs and calling loudly. A person who understands elephants knows when an elephant is really upset and likely to charge. It begins flapping its ears. The matriarch began flapping her ears!

It was a classic David and Goliath confrontation. A blacksmith plover weighs about a third of a pound. An adult female African elephant weighs over six thousand pounds. That is a weight advantage factor of about eighteen thousand to one. As the matriarch stood flapping her ears, the determined plover launched toward the elephant a third time, again striking it between the eyes and returning to its nest, mantling the eggs and calling loudly.

There must have been some unspoken understanding between these two determined mothers. Each one was defending their family. Slowly, the matriarch stepped off the trail, walked around the plucky plover and returned to the game trail a few feet farther on. All fourteen of the other elephants followed in her footsteps. After they passed, the blacksmith plover stopped calling, settled on her eggs, and resumed incubation.

Lesson #12

Keep a Four-H strategy to balance your conservation program.

I recognized the need for identifying, protecting, and managing four priorities within a comprehensive wildlife conservation program: **Habitats** of primary significance to nongame wildlife. There is also a need for protecting and managing poorly known nongame species considered in a **Holistic** category. They are important ecological components of natural communities. There is a third need to provide benefits to **High-Profile** wildlife species as well-known species that have been neglected and threatened with extirpation or continuing declines—those species that will generate citizen support and enthusiasm for your initiatives. Finally, there is a need for getting Minnesota citizens to become personally involved with Hands-On efforts to help wildlife by preserving or restoring habitat, landscaping for wildlife, building and maintaining nest boxes and doing simple projects like feeding birds. I later realized there was also a Fifth H needed in my conservation playbook—a **Historic Perspective**. Citizens need to know how Minnesota's wildlife populations were devastated during the pioneer settlement era and explore our options for restoring those populations.

Lesson #13

Stealth mode. Just do it! There are times when, without breaking any agency rules, you can still make good things happen outside of normal bureaucracy. This is an example:

Copper Roundtable

There was a DNR Section of Wildlife mandate prohibiting their employees from discussing the impact of lead ammunition poisoning on wildlife. Without breaking any DNR rules, on August 22, 2012, Lori Naumann and I arranged for a gathering of what became the first Copper Roundtable at Davanni's Pizza in Anoka. We were not in the Section of Wildlife. We were in the Division of Ecological and Water Resources, so the Section of Wildlife mandate did not include us. Attending were Dave Orrick of the St. Paul Pioneer Press, Doug Smith of the Star Tribune, Ryan Bronson of Federal Cartridge, Dr. Pat Redig, Irene Bueno Padillo and Michelle Willette of the U of MN Raptor Center, and Alex Gutierrez of the DNR Enforcement Division. Staff from the DNR Section of Wildlife were not allowed to attend.

Participants discussed what they knew about this issue and common ground where this topic could be dealt with in an objective and professional manner. Resulting news stories about the impact of lead ammunition causing lead poisoning of bald eagles and the importance of non-toxic ammunition alternatives were subsequently published in the *Star Tribune*, *St. Paul Pioneer Press*, *Duluth News-Tribune*, and the *Grand Forks Herald*. We helped get the cat out of the bag—exposing the dangers of continued use of lead ammunition on Minnesota's wildlife, including federally protected migratory birds.

Lesson #14

Use the Multiplier Effect to spread your conservation messages.

With the same amount of time and effort, you can spread your message to one, ten, one hundred, a thousand or hundreds of thousands of citizens. It is important for people involved in wildlife conservation to sharpen their skills in public speaking and connecting with the media to reach the public with conservation messages. There are still some wildlife biologists in leadership positions who avoid the media. Some program supervisors fail to recruit people who have demonstrated skills to promote wildlife conservation. A failure to connect with the media cripples our programs. We need to hire wildlife supervisors and managers who understand the importance of hiring staff with media competence.

Develop media savvy. Learn what is newsworthy—First, Biggest, Most. Learn to contact media personalities so they can run timely stories. Develop rapport with reporters. Feed stories to the media. Call your contacts when you have an idea. Call the news assignment desk when you don't know who to contact. Get employees involved who can talk to the media who are doing the hands-on conservation work. They are the ones who should be telling your stories, not assistant commissioners or a media rep from another division. Provide your staff with the coaching or training they may need for dealing successfully with the media.

Youth Educational Outreach

We also need more educational programs to reach youths with compelling messages on wildlife conservation. The Digital Photography Bridge to Nature program was an example of implementing the multiplier effect by teaching the teachers, not the students. Over three years, we presented 114 teacher workshops to 1,560 teachers. Each teacher participant provided digital bridge training sessions and photo safari experiences to an average of sixty students. This program is estimated to have reached about 93,600 Minnesota children.

Lesson #15

Your success is determined by the extent to which your employees are successful in fulfilling their goals.

Give your employees the authority, budget, and flexibility they need to be both fulfilled and challenged by their work. Then help them achieve their professional goals.

Roger Holmes taught me to manage my employees by exception. That meant I was responsible for making routine management decisions, but I was to consult with Roger just when I had questions or issues needing resolution. He taught me not to micromanage employees. Look for self-starters when you hire new employees.

Sadly, some supervisors intentionally prevent employees from experiencing any sense of achievement or success. They are intimidated by employees who are smarter than they are. They require endless meetings to ensure control over their minions, and they obsess over minutia. They require reporting on meaningless details that demoralize and destroy program morale, creativity and initiative, and they fail or refuse to acknowledge or reward employees for their achievements. Such employees are typically helpless to complain about their treatment, and their only recourse is to file grievances that hopefully will force the rogue supervisors to receive counseling or consequences from higher level personnel officers. It is important for persecuted employees to document their mistreatment in detail so it will stand up to scrutiny by higher level personnel officers.

Lesson #16

Always have a pet project.

Encourage your employees to take on "pet projects" that will be professionally stimulating and rewarding. By that, I mean that your employees can benefit from a pet project within the scope of their position description. There needs to be a tangible product at the end of such a project that makes them feel good about what they do—like publication of a research report, a new initiative (like the DNR Eaglecam), preservation of habitat, or facilitating a major donation. These projects will sustain inspiration for them over the years. They are a great outlet for creativity, they generate a positive image for your agency, and they will help your employees avoid burnout.

Among pet projects that have captivated my own passion over the years have been landscaping for wildlife in our backyard, building and managing nest boxes and feeders for birds, writing books including *Woodworking for Wildlife* and *Landscaping for Wildlife*, promoting the Pine-to-Prairie birding trails in Minnesota and Manitoba, implementing the Digital Photography Bridge to Nature program, and my involvement with restoration of peregrine falcons and trumpeter swans.

Lesson #17

Most important wildlife conservation and restoration efforts require not just years, but decades, to accomplish.

We live in a world of instant expectations. That does not work with the real world of wildlife conservation. Problems like poaching, illegal killing, habitat loss, wildlife disease issues, and pollution cause incremental losses of wildlife over decades. Recovering from those losses may require decades.

Successful wildlife conservation efforts require long-term commitments from private citizens, organizations, politicians, media, and local, state, and federal agencies to make those restoration efforts a reality. It requires people to be patient, persistent, and stubborn when necessary. An example of recent efforts that have been successful are the restoration of peregrine falcons and trumpeter swans in Minnesota. Current efforts underway include advocacy for hunters and anglers to discontinue using lead ammunition and fishing tackle to stop poisoning our state's loons, trumpeter swans, and bald eagles. Other educational and habitat initiatives are necessary to improve habitat management for wood turtles and protection of timber rattlesnakes.

Lesson #18

Read voraciously. ("A room without books is like a body without a soul." Marcus Tullius Cicero)

Reading is a hobby that begins in childhood and continues through adulthood. Reading can give you a creative and competitive advantage in your work if you keep up with a broad range of books, magazines, and conservation organizations. I still have an Iowa songbird foldout poster by Maynard Reece that I kept from the "Picture Magazine" in the *Des Moines Register*. It was published on March 12, 1950. I was just shy of four years old.

My library has grown to a collection of over a thousand books. Those books allow me the joy and inspiration of being a time traveler who can go back in time more than 160 years with books of exploration from Africa to the Amazon, and it allows me to be a geographic explorer in destinations ranging from the Galapagos Islands to Cuba, Patagonia, Africa, New Zealand, and Kuwait.

My books allow me to appreciate the art of masters like Luis Agassiz Fuertes, John James Audubon, and John Gould and the natural history, ecological, and historic writings of E. O. Wilson, E. Thompson Seton, William Beebe, H. H. Hudson, Eugene P. Odum, Adolph Murie, Alexander Skutch, Aldo Leopold, Rachel Carson, Theodore Roosevelt, and even James Bond who wrote *Birds of the West Indies.*

There are a couple books I would highly recommend. *A Different Kind of Country* by Raymond Dasmann (1968) captures the importance of diversity in our lifestyles, our cultures, our languages, and in preserving the diversity of our natural environments. The other inspirational book is *Tales of a Shaman's Apprentice* by Mark J. Plotkin (2015). It describes the revelations of making the effort to learn from what many people would consider primitive cultures about how they learned how to treat medical problems, like disease and injuries using tropical plants from South American rainforests.

Lesson #19

Some of life's greatest opportunities and revelations come wrapped in a blanket of pure serendipity.

When Dr. Jenkins at UGA asked me "How would you like to go study in Costa Rica?" I said "Sure," and then I went to get a map to find out where Costa Rica was. Grad studies in Costa Rica changed my life, and it was where I met my wife Ethelle.

In 2006, my brother Don told me that he had visited an old farmhouse near Colo, Iowa, where his friend John Handsaker was planning to live after being married. I followed up to visit the farmhouse of the late farmer and oologist Ralph Handsaker. He was John's grandfather. I wrote the book *Oology and Ralph's Talking Eggs* based on the data I gathered from exploring that incredible collection of over five thousand wild bird eggs from around the world in that old farmhouse.

Sometimes helping wildlife is a real fluke. Based on two humpback whale fluke photos I took while leading a birding tour off the Pacific coast Costa Rica on January 29, 1990, Costa Rican president and Nobel laureate Oscar Arias created Ballena Marine National Park to protect the wintering and calving grounds for humpback whales—21.2 square miles!

Whale photo showing Costa Rica in background to document their presence as a wintering species in Costa Rican waters.

This is my whale photo of a humpback whale fluke that convinced Costa Rican president Oscar Arias to designate over twenty square miles of the Pacific Ocean offshore from Punta Uvita as a national park.

Lesson #20

Become acquainted with existing laws protecting wildlife and endangered species.

Learn techniques for presenting testimony before legislative committees, for testifying objectively against people who have violated game laws, and for drafting legislation to improve laws for wildlife conservation. Learn when you need state or federal permits to carry out wildlife conservation projects. Become acquainted with local, state and federal conservation officers. Learn when to contact them regarding enforcement issues, problems, or the need for wildlife rescue. Learn presentation skills for testifying before state, and federal legislative committees and for providing testimony in court.

Closing Thoughts

"Always do right. It will gratify some people and astonish the rest."

–Mark Twain.

"May we leave many astonished people in our wake."

–Carrol L. Henderson

Appendix B

Carrol L. Henderson—Recognition

Minnesota Awards for Conservation

Minnesota Chapter of The Nature Conservancy. Stewardship Award. 1976.

Minnesota Environmental Education Board. Environmental Educator of the Year. 1987.

Minneapolis Jaycees. Dr. Robert Green Award. 1989.

Minnesota Chapter of The Wildlife Society. Minnesota Award. 1993.

Minnesota Ornithologists" Union. Thomas Sadler Roberts Memorial Award. 1994.

Audubon Chapter of Minneapolis. Conservationist of the Year. 1995.

Minnesota Ornithologists' Union' President's Award. 2012.

National Conservation Awards

National Chevron Conservation Award. One of the nation's top ten conservationists. 1990.

National Fish and Wildlife Foundation. Chuck Yeager Conservation Award. 1992.

United States Fish and Wildlife Service. Gary T. Myers Bird Conservation Award. Top bird conservationist in North America. 2012.

Garden Clubs of America. Frances K. Hutchinson Award. Top conservationist in America. 2016. Previous recipients have included Roger Tory Peterson, Rachel Carson,

Lady Bird Johnson, Sigurd Olson, and Walt Disney.

Izaak Walton League of America. National Conservation Award. In recognition of outstanding work in the field of conservation. 2022.

Carrol L. Henderson Nongame Bird Conservation Award. 2023. Nongame Wildlife Technical Section of the Mississippi Flyway Committee. This award was presented for the first time and named for Carrol L. Henderson in honor of his many years of service for conservation of our migratory nongame bird resources.

Books

Baicich, Paul J., Margaret A. Barker, and Carrol L. Henderson. 2015. *Feeding Wild Birds in America. Culture, Commerce, and Conservation.* Texas A &M University Press. College Station. 306 pp.

Henderson, Carrol L. 1987. *Landscaping for Wildlife.* MN Dept. of Natural Resources. 148 pp.

________________. 1990. *Earth Day: Past, Present, & Future.* MN Dept. of Natural Resources. 19 pp.

________________. 1991. *Woodworking for Wildlife.* MN Dept of Natural Resources. 112 pp.

________________. 1995a. *Wild About Birds: the DNR Bird Feeding Guide.* MN Dept. of Natural Resources. 278 pp.

________________. 1995b. *Galapagos Islands. Wonders of the World.* 1995. (Technical consultant and primary photographer. Raintree Steck-Vaughn. Austin, TX. 64 pp.

________________, Andrea Lambrecht, et al. 1997. (Senior author) *Traveler's Guide to Wildlife in Minnesota.* MN Dept. of Natural Resources. 326 pp.

________________, Carolyn Dinndorf and Fred Rozumalski. 1998. *Lakescaping for Wildlife and Water Quality.* MN Dept. of Natural Resources. 175 pp.

________________. 2001. Grackle Junction Case Study Workbook. Steps in Developing Wildlife Tourism in Your Community. MN DNR Workbook. 91 pp.

________________. 2002. *Field Guide to the Wildlife of Costa Rica.* 2002. Univ. of Texas Press. 522 pp.

________________, Adele Porter, and Jan Welsh. 2004. *One Bird Two Worlds. Neotropical Bird Curricu-*

lum Guide for Teachers. MN DNR Workbook.

_______________. 2007. *Oology and Ralph' Talking Eggs*. University of Texas Press. 177 pp.

_______________. 2008. Birds in Flight. The Art and Science of How Birds Fly. Voyageur's Press. 160 pp.

_______________. 2010a. *Birds of Costa Rica: a field guide*. University of Texas Press. 388 pp.

_______________. 2010b. Butterflies, Moths and Other Invertebrates of Costa Rica: a field guide. University of Texas Press. 173 pp.

_______________. 2010c. Mammals, Amphibians, and Reptiles of Costa Rica: a field guide. University of Texas Press. 214 pp.

Acknowledgements

The achievements in this book represent collaboration and cooperation over the past fifty years between the DNR nongame wildlife program staff and at least 200 of Minnesota's most passionate and dedicated wildlife conservationists. It also represents successful partnerships with at least 100 conservation organizations, private businesses, and county, state, and federal agencies involving our nongame conservation projects. That is the source of my inspiration to use the word "legacy" in the title of this book. This is the story of the legacy of how these conservationists have contributed to the conservation Minnesota's wildlife over the past fifty years. Walter Breckenridge, Bud Tordoff, Pat Redig, John Moyle, Roger Holmes, Joe Alexander, Dick Peterson, Dave Ahlgren, Dorene Scriven, Roger Strand, Evadene Swanson, Bill Stevens, Lyle Bradley, Art Hawkins, Mark Martell, Scott Mehus, Dan Frenzel, and Jim Mallman are just a few of the many conservation heroes who created a legacy of conservation successes that are referred to in the title of this book. They inspired us to follow their example and continue to protect, preserve, and restore many hundreds of Minnesota's nongame wildlife species that still need attention.

Information regarding the participation and contributions of these many organizations, agencies, and individuals are detailed in the chapters of this book. This is a huge credit to the successful long-term vision of the Minnesota Department of Natural Resources for broadening the perspective for benefiting and managing the ecological diversity of our native habitats across Minnesota. This is especially relevant now because all Minnesota citizens contribute to natural resource conservation through the 0.375 percent increase that was added to the Minnesota sales tax in 2009 in the Minnesota constitution. The additional funds were specified for the benefit of "outdoor heritage, clean water, parks and trails, and arts and cultural heritage." The clientele of the DNR has now expanded beyond the world of hunters, trappers, anglers, and state park visitors. It became more inclusive to consider the interests of all Minnesota citizens including birders, naturalists, nature photographers, butterfly and dragonfly enthusiasts and their children. One-third of the receipts from those sales tax revenues are deposited in the outdoor heritage fund which was renewed by Minnesota citizens in 2024 for the next 25 years. Those funds may be spent only to restore, protect, and enhance wetlands, prairies, forests, and habitat for Minnesota's fish, game, and wildlife.

I wish to gratefully acknowledge the generosity of the talented photographers who provided their photos for use in this book. Credits are shown in the order of their placement in the book: Curtis and Leona Henderson, Marshall Johnson, Brad Reece and the family of Maynard Reece, Dawn Bovenmyer, University of Georgia Marketing and Communications, Rob Rakow, Cindy Dorn, Milan Standard, Richard Baker, Dr. Ron Moen and lynx research crew, Lori Naumann, Anthony Housey of Camp Ripley Public Affairs, Dr. Mark Martell, Dick Peterson, Mike North, Maikel Cañizares, Jaime Edwards, Gaea Crozier, Tricia Markle, Krista Larson Dr. Annie Bracey, Steven Yang, Kevin Kenow, Steve Houdek, Dr. Bud Tordoff. Lori Naumann, Dr. David E. Anderson, David Wolfson, and John Fieberg. All other photos in this book have been taken by or provided by the author. U.S. Fish and Wildlife Service breeding bird survey results from 1967 to 2018 are portrayed for purple martins, western meadowlarks, and bobolinks in their respective chapters. Special appreciation is extended to my friends Val Cunningham and Allison Campbell Jensen for their detailed editorial reviews and to Tony (A.X.) Hertzel for the extraordinary job he did editing the "References" which will be cited on a future website. Thank you, Val, Allison, and Tony for providing your expertise to my writing efforts! Additional review input was provided by Dr. Ron Moen and Richard Baker for the lynx chapter, Dr. Juli Ponder for the bald eagle and golden eagle chapters, Jaime Edwards, Barb Perry, and Shawn Fritcher for the timber rattlesnake chapter, Jaime Edwards, Barb Perry, Gaea Crozier, Krista Larson, Dr. Ron Moen for the wood turtle chapter, Fred Strand, Dr. Annie Bracey and Dr. Alexis Grinde for the common tern chapter, Kevin Kenow for the common loon chapter, and Dr. David E. Andersen and Dr. David Wolfson for the trumpeter swan section.

About the Author

Carrol L. Henderson grew up on a family farm in central Iowa in the 1950s. He was intensely curious about the natural world, exploring the land surrounding the farm, looking for animals. Henderson once heard a wildlife planner, Ted Eubanks, describe "portal wildlife species." He explained that most avid wildlife conservationists recall a pivotal moment with a bird or animal encounter that served as a portal into a lifetime passion for wildlife. Henderson's pivotal moment occurred watching a family of House Wrens raising their chicks in a nest box on our family farm and an encounter with a family of newly hatched Killdeer chicks in our cornfield.

His passion for all nature matured; one lesson in sixth grade remained with him throughout his life—memorizing this conservation pledge: "I give my pledge as an American to save and faithfully defend from waste the natural resources of my country—its soil and minerals, its forest, waters, and wildlife."

Henderson found his calling in 1974 when he was hired to be assistant manager for the Lac Qui Parle Wildlife Refuge in western Minnesota. In 1977 he applied to a new position in the Minnesota DNR Section of Wildlife—the Nongame Wildlife Program supervisor position. He applied, was hired, and spent the rest of his career in nongame wildlife conservation.